Green, Inc. shows that economic growth does not have to be at the expense of environmental protection. For the poor, growth is essential, to eliminate the threats to health and environmental security that poverty presents. As for the more affluent, they may be unwilling to sacrifice their living standards, even for a cleaner environment.

The question is rather: how can the environmental impact of growth be minimized? Here, as Frances Cairncross demonstrates, the role of business is crucial. New technologies and well-designed policies have to work hand in hand; and the interests of governments, of companies and of environmentalists lie in making a cleaner environment an opportunity for profitability. All of them will find this a stimulating survey and an invaluable practical guide.

Frances Cairncross is a senior editor of *The Economist* magazine and author of *Costing the Earth* (1991).

D1100584

Green, Inc.

GUIDE TO BUSINESS AND
THE ENVIRONMENT

Frances Cairncross

EARTHSCAN

Earthscan Publications Ltd, London

First published in the UK 1995 by
Earthscan Publications Limited

Copyright © Frances Cairncross, 1995

All rights reserved

A catalogue record for this book is available from the British Library

ISBN 1 85383 250 2

Typeset by JS Typesetting, Wellingborough, Northants
Printed and bound by Clays Ltd, St Ives plc
Cover design by Andrew Corbett

For a full list of publications please contact:

Earthscan Publications Limited
120 Pentonville Road
London N1 9JN
Tel: 0171 278 0433
Fax: 0171 278 1142

Earthscan is an editorially independent subsidiary of
Kogan Page Limited and publishes in association with
WWF-UK and the International Institute for
Environment and Development

Contents

PART III
POLICIES IN ACTION

PART IV
THE ROLE OF INDUSTRY

PART V
THE INTERNATIONAL ENVIRONMENT

Introduction

This book began life as a compilation of the pieces I wrote for *The Economist* during my five years as environment editor, between 1989 and 1994. As I edited and updated, it gradually started to turn into something different: an essay on the main environmental issues of the period.

The five years saw an extraordinary amount of activity: the emergence of global warming as a serious worry, the successful completion of several environmental treaties, rows about trade and the environment, the discovery of the severity of pollution in the Soviet empire, the greening of the World Bank and the emergence of a widespread view that industry could make money by pursuing responsible environmental policies. The following pages touch on all of these issues. But they are not a guide in a conventional sense. Unlike most environmental journalists, I have a background in economics. As a result, I have concentrated mainly on those aspects of environmental issues that have economic implications. Readers who want to understand exactly how CFCs are thought to affect the ozone layer or what acid rain does to soil should look elsewhere.

Three points make up the main themes of the book. One is the extent to which it is possible to combine economic growth with environmental protection. Environmentalists often resent growth – not surprisingly, since it so often causes environmental damage. Such resentment shows up in, for example, their criticisms of development aid and their hostility to large companies. But growth is inevitable and, in many countries, essential. The proper question therefore is how its environmental impact can be minimized. A second point is the need for a sense of proportion. The most serious environmental problems arise not in the rich world but in the poor; they are not global warming or the hole in the ozone layer, but more mundane and murderous threats such as dirty water, severe air pollution and the sort of deforestation and soil erosion that turns useful land into desert in a generation or two. Such horrors are often the result not of wealth but of poverty, or of breakneck industrialization. In the rich world, some environmental 'answers' risk creating larger difficulties than the problems they were supposed to solve.

The third theme is the key role for industry in finding solutions. Technological innovation holds out the main hope of environmental improvement. People will rarely change their behavior or accept a reduction in living standards for the sake of the environment. Instead, new technologies will have to be devised that reduce the environmental impact of human activity. The best stimulus for such advances will be well-designed policies, which create incentives for companies to develop new products and processes. Governments, companies and environmentalists have a common interest in making a cleaner environment an opportunity for profitability.

The market alone will not necessarily deliver a cleaner environment. Without government intervention, polluters will usually pass on to the rest of society the costs of the environmental damage they do. If polluters are to pay those costs themselves, government will need to step in – just as it steps in to prevent crime or to provide street-lighting. Where government cannot, or will not, set and enforce environmental policies, the prospects for the environment are poor.

Inevitably, these themes are similar to those in *Costing the Earth*, which I wrote in the fall of 1990, although hardly any of the examples used in this book are the same. But the tone is different. I have been increasingly aware that environmentalism attracts many who prefer to beat the drum than to pause and think. The worst offenders are not environmental lobbyists themselves, whose proper role is to protest and object, but the management gurus and politicians who seek to oversell green ideas, sometimes for decidedly ungreen reasons. In the US, a powerful backlash against environmentalism is now underway in the Republican-dominated Congress.

I have also realized just how difficult it is to convert good ideas into sound policies. Environmental degradation generally occurs because a powerful lobby is getting something for nothing. The forces against change are mighty, especially in the developing countries where the threat to the environment is greatest.

Yet the five years after 1990 saw some real advances. The Earth Summit at Rio de Janeiro in 1992 exposed a whole generation of statesmen and schoolchildren to environmental ideas. The treaties that were signed will be hard to implement, but they will provide governments with a forum in which to continue to talk about the environment. The new laws passed in many countries in the early 1990s will continue to influence domestic environmental policies for the rest of the decade. Governments have made commitments and set themselves targets which they may miss, but will find hard to abandon.

Several people have read and commented on parts of this book, including Scott Barrett, Brian Barry, Tom Burke, Richard Mcrory, Carrie Meyer and David Pearce. Their advice was useful and comforting. Natalie Greenberg enormously improved the style. Hamish McRae, my husband, has worked his way through the whole, and made wonderfully helpful suggestions and improvements. I owe them all a special debt.

Many people have helped me over the years to understand environmental problems. Environmentalists are a generous lot, on the whole, and environmental economists combine the best of two often-maligned callings. Among those who have been most helpful are Scott Barrett, Tony Brenton, Tom Burke, David Cope, Dan Dudek, John Elkington, Dan Esty, David Fisk, Bob Hahn, Nigel Haigh, Nick Hartley, Dieter Helm, Gordon Hughes, Brad Hurley, Dale Jorgenstern, Anil Markandya, John Martin, Marek Mayer, Ron McLean, Richard Mcrory, Richard Morgenstern, Derek Osborn,

David Owen, Miguel Pestana, Paul Portney, David Pearce, Kate Probst, Robert Repetto, Richard Sandbrook, Rob Stavins, Andrew Steer, Tessa Tennant and Jeremy Warford. This book is for them and all who have given me so many hours of help and friendship, with gratitude.

Part I

BASIC ISSUES

Chapter 1

Economic Growth and the Environment

Is it possible to have both economic growth and a cleaner environment? That is the single most important environmental issue for policy-makers. Economic growth will take place, much though many environmentalists might wish it would not. Even if people were content with their present living standards, the inevitable rise in the world's population would make growth essential, simply to keep existing living standards. So for the millions of people who still live in terrible poverty, growth is the hope, the only hope, of a better life. Besides, most governments believe that their people want to become richer. Many also believe that, if a choice has to be made, their people would rather be wealthier than protect the environment.

Environmentalists have often been seen as the enemies of economic growth, a perception they have sometimes encouraged. They are right to draw attention to the ways in which growth can be short-lived or self-defeating, as when it carries costs that offset its imagined benefits. Such costs are especially important in developing countries. There the environment is often more fragile, and has more impact on the quality of life, than is the case in richer countries. Much of what passes for economic growth is therefore at the expense of lasting damage to the environment. If that damage actually makes many people worse off, then the accompanying growth is illusory.

But merely to oppose growth will achieve little. Instead a wiser strategy for environmentalists is to look for ways in which growth and environmental improvement support each other, and to study ways to protect the environment at minimal economic cost. The experience of the rich world suggests that, as countries prosper, they come to want higher environmental standards. Those standards are more likely to be achievable without much loss of growth if governments look for policies that work with the grain of the market, and draw on the innovative energy of industry. Given the right incentives, many companies will find that cleaning the environment offers them new opportunities and new markets, not merely higher costs.

Environmentalists need to distinguish between the kind of environmental damage that is destructive and irreversible, and the kind that is superficial and reversible. They need to learn how economic forces operate, as well as how to fight political campaigns. They have damaged their cause by their long history of overstating their case. For years, some of them have expected the environment – or scarcity of natural resources – to set a limit to growth; many more have fretted about the harm growth does to the natural world. The first view has so far proved wrong: neither natural-resource scarcity nor environmental pollution has yet proved a serious check to growth, although both have offset some of the apparent gains from growth. The second view has been only partly right: while growth has sometimes brought environmental destruction in its wake, it also brings with it the best hope of improvement.

Compromise is especially important in the case of developing countries, where the trade-off between growth and greenery often seems particularly stark. Not only are their people the poorest; their numbers are growing the fastest. Their governments are unlikely to welcome policy proposals that appear to deprive them of the chance to improve living standards.

ARE THERE REAL ENVIRONMENTAL LIMITS TO GROWTH?

The idea of natural constraints on growth dates back to Thomas Malthus and David Ricardo, who first explored the idea that a scarcity of natural resources might place limits on human behavior. The resource that interested them was agricultural land, and the growth was in numbers of mouths that would have to be fed as population increased. Their predictions were confounded by technological change – by the arrival of the steamship, which opened up the colonies as a source of food. In fact, the combination of technology and market forces have so far confounded most of those predicting environmental catastrophe.

Malthusian ideas resurfaced during the first big upsurge of post-war environmentalism, in the late 1960s. Several influential publications argued that nature would limit growth in a fairly direct way: the world would simply run out of a number of essential raw materials, such as oil and coal. In 1972 the Club of Rome, a group of 70 eminent people who met to try to understand what it grandly called "the world problematique", produced with the help of a team at the Massachusetts Institute of Technology *The Limits to Growth*. This report, which sold 9 million copies, took every dismal trend and extrapolated it. Its conclusion was predictable: "If the present growth trends in world population, industrialization, pollution, food production, and resource depletion continue unchanged, the limits to growth on this planet will be reached some time within the next 100 years." Hard on the heels of such exponential gloom came *The Population Bomb* by Paul Ehrlich, predicting that a quarter of humankind would starve to death between 1973 and 1983.

In the subsequent decade, none of these gloomy predictions proved correct. A year after *The Limits to Growth* was published, the price of oil had quadrupled. Suddenly it was worth extracting oil from under the North Sea and Alaska's North Slope. Energy consumption in the rich world promptly stopped rising. The world's proven economic reserves of mercury, tin, zinc, copper and lead, which the Club thought would be gone by 1991, are now greater than they were in 1970. Since *The Population Bomb* appeared, the world's fertility rate has fallen by about one-third.

Yet the combination of rapid population growth and rising living standards means that natural resources are being used in larger quantities than ever before. In the final quarter of this century, population growth has decelerated everywhere but Africa, and there are signs of a slowdown in some African countries too. But global population will probably double from its present 5.3 billion, may treble and could conceivably quadruple before it levels out. As populations grow, people will live at ever-greater densities. Today only Bangladesh, South Korea, The Netherlands and the island of Java have population densities of more than 400 people per square kilometer.[1] By the middle of the next century, one-third of the world's people will probably live at such densities. The implications for the environment and agricultural production are beyond imagining.

The lesson of the years since the publication of *The Limits to Growth* is that exhaustible resources will not necessarily ever be exhausted. In the right circumstances, a powerful self-righting mechanism will protect some natural resources from over-use. That mechanism is the market.

Yet many environmental resources are undoubtedly at risk. Those in the most serious danger are not those that the Club of Rome was most worried about. They are resources which play no direct part in world commerce and are treated as free goods when, in reality, they serve the most basic economic function: enabling people to survive. Such resources include the ozone layer, the carbon cycle, Amazonia and fresh water. Some of these – such as the tropical forests – might appear to be renewable; although ironically some exhaustible resources may be more secure than some that are renewable. We will still be mining coal when the rhinos have become extinct.

THE MARKET'S ROLE IN DEALING WITH SCARCITY

The environmental resources least in danger of exhaustion are those that are privately owned and traded. As they start to become scarcer their price will rise. This is likely to encourage their owners to conserve the supply. However, where that happens, local shortages may still arise because individual countries or people are unable to pay for the resources that they need. Take two examples: energy and food.

The experience of the rich countries in the aftermath of the oil shocks of the mid-1970s suggests that not only is energy efficiency highly sensitive to sudden increases in price, but that price rises will also encourage new discoveries of fossil fuels. Far from running out, known reserves of fossil fuels have risen much faster than consumption in the past forty years. The world's reserves of oil and natural gas stood at 30 billion tons of oil equivalent (btoe) in 1950; today, they are more than 250btoe, even though the world has consumed 100btoe in the intervening forty years.[2]

But even if the world as a whole has enough, individual countries may face serious energy shortages. For example, many Asian countries simply do not have enough indigenous energy to meet their demands, especially for oil and gas. So Asian countries will increasingly import oil from the Middle East – and may sometimes be tempted to pay for oil by exporting military equipment. In the former Soviet Union, industrial chaos has seriously reduced its output of fossil fuels, and an absence of hard currency is making it extremely difficult for the ex-communist countries to import supplies. As a result, many of them are likely to continue to use their nuclear reactors in spite of pressure from the West to shut them down.

The case of global food supplies is similar. Global shortage is unlikely; regional crises highly probable. And overcoming shortage may bring harmful side-effects, environmental, political or economic.

For most of the two hundred years since Malthus worried about mass starvation, world food output has risen faster than population.

A striking instance is India: its population grew on average by 2.1 per cent between 1950 and 1990; its food output by 2.7 per cent. The country now exports food. The global average conceals some countries which have become increasingly hungry, such as Bangladesh, Nepal and more than half the countries of sub-Saharan Africa. But some estimates suggest that it would be technically possible to feed a world population of 11.4 billion with a diet that provided 6000 calories of "plant energy" (grain, seed and animal feed) a day. That is roughly twice the typical diet in South Asia today.[3]

In theory, then, there should be enough food: not just for today's population, but for one twice as large. Such calculations, however, rely on a considerable increase in yields in developing countries. These are theoretically possible: at the start of the 1980s cereal yield in the United States was 4.2 tons per hectare of harvested area, compared with 1.5 tons for fertile Kenya. For a growing number of countries, higher yields will be the only way to raise food output: the demand for land for housing and other activities will increasingly compete with farming. Technical advances, including advances in biotechnology, may well make it easier for even not very skillful farmers to produce more food from their land.

That is just as well. For the alternative to increasing yields is to take more land into cultivation. That may well mean destroying forests, and cultivating ever-steeper hillsides. Quite apart from the implications for wildlife habitats, such policies are frequently unsustainable. Marginal land is often marginal precisely because it has traditionally been considered too fragile for permanent cultivation.

The pressure of population on food supplies will rarely lead directly to famines. These are more often caused by some other disruption, such as a civil war, in a country where food supplies are already inadequate. But in those countries which cannot improve yields or afford to import food, a growing proportion of the population will either be permanently malnourished, or else try to emigrate.

While the working of the market may ensure that the world as a whole will not run out of energy or food, it gives no such protection to those environmental resources that are not privately owned, or that are for one reason or another treated as free. Two examples are the fish in the world's seas, and the supply of fresh water.

While a fish-farmer profits if the stock of fish increases, and the owner of a stretch of river has a strong incentive to limit the number of salmon or trout that are caught in it each year, those who fish at sea have an incentive to take as much as they can, rather than leave behind enough fish to ensure that the stock can replenish itself. The consequence has been persistent overfishing. The world's fishing fleet has grown, but throughout the 1980s, catches of the most valuable species, such as cod and haddock, were lower than they had been in the previous decade. From 1990 to 1994, the world marine catch appeared to have stopped increasing. This has serious implications: fish provides roughly a quarter of the protein eaten in many developing countries. If the yield of wild fish has reached (or passed) its maximum, any increase in the supply will have to come from aquaculture. That has so far proved an expensive way to mass-produce extra fish.

Fresh water, like the oceans' fish, is generally thought of as common property. Theoretically fresh water could be extracted and sold like oil; in fact, most countries believe it should be used freely by all. As a result, a growing number of countries are reaching the point where the availability of water will become a serious constraint to agricultural expansion and industrial development. For example, India is already using half the rain that runs off land into rivers and lakes, and half as much again from underground wells and springs. By the year 2025, India is likely to use 92 per cent of its available fresh water.[4]

In India, far and away the biggest demand for water is for irrigation, which consumes 360 times as much as Indian industry. Worldwide, irrigation uses 70 per cent of the world's fresh water, and the share is higher in poorer countries. The use of irrigation has been essential to the increase in food output over the past twenty years. Although only one-fifth of cropland is irrigated, a third of the world's food now comes from irrigated land.

On some estimates, about a third of all irrigation water is wasted:

channels are unlined, so water seeps away. It will be essential to find more frugal ways to irrigate in future, for two reasons. First, irrigation is increasingly doing irreparable damage to farmland. As water soaks into thin soils, it flushes salts and minerals to the surface. When it evaporates, these form a poisonous crust. Secondly, as industry and cities grow, they too need water. Governments in places as different as California, China and Egypt face politically awkward problems of diverting water from the country to cities, where it can be used more productively.

There is a third reason to take a new approach to the growing demand for water. Unlike some other natural resources – coal, oil, land – water moves by itself from one country to another. Of the world's river basins, 214 are multinational, and 13 are shared by five or more countries. Water is thus likely to be an increasing source of conflict. Already, rivers such as the Jordan, the Ganges, the Nile and the Rio Grande have been at the center of international disputes. As with energy and food, local shortages of water will increasingly be a source of political instability.

As supplies of fish and fresh water become scarcer, governments may find ways to treat both commodities more like oil and food crops so that the market mechanism can get to work. One way of so doing would be to bring them under private ownership and to allow the rights of ownership to be traded. (Indeed, as later chapters show, this is starting to happen, although only within countries, not between them.) The result would be to stimulate investment both in finding new sources of supply and in using existing supplies more efficiently. Without such policies, environmental resources in common ownership will always be at risk of over-use. Scarcity of such resources will become a constraint on economic growth.

HOW ENVIRONMENTAL DAMAGE CAN UNDERMINE ECONOMIC GROWTH

Pollution and scarcity of natural resources are rarely likely to be so serious that they offset economic growth completely. But they may still impose heavy economic costs on countries which do too little to protect their environments. Such costs are of three kinds: costs to human health; costs in lost economic productivity; and costs of a more intangible sort, such as loss of the pleasure people get from the existence of an unspoilt environment, whether it be the happiness of a good day's fly-fishing or the spiritual comfort of knowing that the humpbacked whale still swims in the oceans. Some are difficult to measure. But with others, the impact is readily perceptible.

For instance, when sooty air makes workers too ill to work, output suffers. When poisonous waste is discharged into rivers, fisheries are destroyed (and if they are not, the fish may become dangerous to eat). Towns may face a rising bill for the costs of abstracting water higher and higher upstream, to avoid pollution. When people draw too much water from a river (for example, for irrigation), the water table may sink and become contaminated with poisonous salts. The water table in Bangkok, a city with no waste-water treatment at all, has dropped at least 20 feet in recent years. A dramatic instance of the cost of environmental damage is the impact of a cholera epidemic on Peru in the early 1990s – the result, at least partly, of inadequate sewage treatment. In the first ten weeks of the epidemic, Peru lost revenues of $1 billion from agricultural exports and tourism: more than three times the amount the country had invested in water supply and sewage treatment in the entire 1980s.[5]

In most rich countries, a considerable loss of economic output is caused by traffic congestion. In Japan, congestion has led grocery companies to redesign their distribution systems. In the United States, several studies reckon that sitting in Los Angeles's notorious traffic jams costs Angelenos about $9 billion a year in lost output. According to 1991 estimates by the California Assembly Office of Research, the region's cars give rise to a further $4.7 billion of environmental damage. Trends in the early 1990s suggested that worse was to come: state officials reckoned that the region's average road speed of 35mph would drop to 19mph by 2010.

The environment itself can contribute to economic output; so degrading it may reduce its productivity. A vivid example is that of

Tunisia's Lake Ichkeul, which attracts many of North Africa's migrating waterfowl. In the 1980s the government began to dam the three rivers that feed it, to provide water for irrigation. One study of the exercise argued the case for suspending work on the dams in terms of economics, not waterfowl.[6] Examining the case of the irrigation scheme that had been in place longest, the study found that it was hopelessly unprofitable. It had cost far more to build than estimated, and the prices of farm inputs used by the farmers who cultivated the newly irrigated land had risen twice as fast as the prices for the crops expected to be grown there. Local farmers had also found it difficult to recruit local labor, and so irrigated a smaller area than originally expected.

Compare the poor prospects for future irrigation schemes around Lake Ichkeul with the certain earnings from livestock grazed on the lake's verges and from fish caught in it. Add in the revenues that might flow from developing tourism for bird-watchers. Add in the cost of having to build a sewage-treatment plant for the local town of Mateur, whose sewage was previously purified in the lake's reedbeds, and a piped water supply to replace dried up wells. The total makes it patently obvious that the economic value of the water is greater if it is left in the lake than if it is taken out.

WHY "DEVELOPMENT" IS A BETTER AIM THAN "GROWTH"

Economic growth as conventionally recorded may thus carry many environmental costs, some of them readily measurable and some of them not. As a result, it may overstate a country's true prosperity. Conventional measures often record the depletion of natural assets – the logging of a forest, for example – as growth, even though the commercial return on the timber should be balanced against the costs of increased soil erosion and the loss of firewood and fruit collected from the trees. A government that neglects the environment in the interests of what it believes to be economic growth may actually make many of its people worse off. It is thus important to aim for "development" – for improvements in the quality of life, even in ways that the market may not measure – rather than for growth.

This point was underlined in *Our Common Future*, published in 1987 by the World Commission on Environment and Development (usually known as the Brundtland Commission after Gro Harlem Brundtland, the Norwegian politician who chaired it). The report popularized the phrase "sustainable development" and argued for development which "meets the needs of the present generation without compromising the needs of future generations". The point was subsequently reinforced in a report that was every bit as influential as the Brundtland Report, although less popular with environmentalists: the *World Development Report* published by the World Bank in 1992. It argued, in persuasive detail, that economic development was more effective when it was combined with good environmental policies.

The *World Development Report* underlined a further point: the main sufferers from environmental degradation are often the poor. It argued:

> Unlike the rich, the poor cannot afford to protect themselves from contaminated water; in cities they are more likely to spend much of their time on the streets, breathing polluted air; in rural areas they are more likely to cook on open fires of wood or dung, inhaling dangerous fumes; their lands are most likely to suffer from soil erosion. The poor may also draw a large part of their livelihood from unmarketed environmental resources: common grazing lands, for example, or forests where food, fuel and building materials have traditionally been gathered. The loss of such resources may particularly harm the poorest.

Improving environmental quality may not make a country richer in the conventional sense – but it frequently improves the living standards of the poor.

This argument does not apply only to poor countries. In the United States, a growing theme of the environmental movement has been the links between pollution and poverty: for instance, the poorest states, and the poorest parts of town, are the places where new waste dumps are most likely to be located. The poor often suffer most from the side-effects of environmental degradation. A factory-owner whose plant is allowed to pollute a river, or a logger allowed to fell a forest, may have influential friends; those who lose as a result of their actions are the powerless.

WHEN RICHER MAY MEAN CLEANER

Environmentalists tend to emphasize the extent to which economic growth harms the environment. But the impact of economic growth on the environment is rarely in one direction. There are some ways in which growth – even conventionally measured growth – may foster environmental improvement. As countries grow richer, some kinds of pollution tend to decline. That will to some extent come about of its own accord: as people become richer, they come to spend a rising share of their incomes on services that cause little pollution, such as health care and eating out, rather than buying goods, such as cars, which cause a lot.

It is worth remembering that some of the most serious environmental damage is occurring in the developing countries. Sometimes it is a result of the desperate drive to grow wealthier, and sometimes a result of the even more desperate struggle to feed more mouths. Poor countries typically give low priority to environmental policies.

While developing countries include some of the most polluted places in the world, there are some kinds of environmental damage that rich countries perpetrate more often than poor ones. For instance, they produce far more rubbish and toxic waste. America generates much more waste per head than any other big industrial country (although the comparisons look worse because America defines waste more widely than most other countries do). Rich countries also use far more energy per head than poor ones, partly because they have many more cars. They therefore make a much larger contribution per head than the poor countries to the world's output of carbon dioxide, the main gas implicated in global warming – although the rich world's share is declining as the poor world's use of energy intensifies.

However, the experience of the OECD countries (including Mexico) suggests that, as countries grow richer, they spend more heavily on cleaning up. One of the first improvements that comes with wealth is a fall in the soot and dust in city air – not surprisingly, as dirty air is the kind of environmental damage from which the rich and influential find it hardest to protect themselves. Today, Londoners no longer choke on "pea-soup" fogs; Chicago's "big smoke" has cleared. The concentration of dust and soot in the air of Beijing and Shenyang is six or seven times as high as that in a typical West European or American city. Indeed, Shenyang, Xian and New Delhi have higher concentrations of suspended particulates (sooty airborne chemicals) than any other large cities in the world.

Other improvements come later. Lead emissions in the United States in 1989 were little more than one-tenth of their level of 1975. The use of pesticides in the United States dropped by 20 per cent in the decade to the mid-1980s. The concentration of sulphur dioxide in the air of Frankfurt and Tokyo was halved between the late 1970s and the late 1980s. And, while improvements in water quality have been slower and less widespread, some highly polluted stretches of water such as the Rhine and the Hudson are cleaner than they were in the late 1970s. Even some measures of natural habitat seem to improve with wealth. Between 1965 and 1989 the loss of forests and woodlands in the rich countries, which account for some 40 per cent of the world total, averaged only 0.1 per cent a year and has now stopped, while the loss in the rest of the world averaged 0.4 per cent a year and continues.

What has caused these improvements in the rich world's environment? Some are the result of changes in industrial structure that seem to come about inevitably as countries grow richer. Economies heavily dependent on the extraction and conversion of raw materials are bound to make a mess. Manufacturing in its early and primitive stages is highly polluting. As manufacturing has moved away from the rich world to the newly industrializing countries, it has taken its pollution with it. When countries prosper, a larger chunk of their economic activity takes the form of services: finance, entertainment, transport. These activities may pollute too, but rarely as much as basic industry. (Sweden's state telecommunications business runs the country's largest vehicle fleet, a fact gleefully pointed out by environmentalists when the company once claimed it did nothing more polluting than stringing up a few telephone wires.)

Other changes are the result of deliberate policies, which have often led to technological innovations that make possible a better environment. The declines in sulphur dioxide and lead in city air are two instances. Both have occurred in spite of a continued growth in economic activity. Another instance is the recovery of species such as the bald eagle in the United States, once almost exterminated by the pervasive use of DDT as a pesticide. New, more specific pesticides have allowed farm output to rise and threatened species to recover.

As poor countries grow richer, their citizens are also more likely to demand improvements in environmental quality. Hong Kong has built a plant to treat the poisonous industrial waste that was previously tipped into the city's sewers. Malaysia is trying harder to clamp down on deforestation. India has an elaborate program of ecolabelling. Tough environmental policies need effective government – sometimes lacking in developing countries. But, in theory at least, developing countries have the opportunity to skip a stage of environmental damage. The West's best technology, developed to meet rich-country standards, is far less polluting and more frugal in its resource demands than the technologies that existed when today's rich countries were becoming industrialized.

Indeed, one of the best things the rich countries can do for the environments of the poor is to maintain their own high standards. Most technological advances still take place in the OECD region. Poor countries are likely to be influenced by such advances, partly because the products they make will have to meet OECD standards if they are to be sold in OECD countries, but also because high standards will automatically become incorporated in the technologies that poor countries buy. To build a coal-fired power station with the low efficiency of a British pre-war model, or a car plant manufacturing vehicles as energy-intensive as America's 1950s gas-guzzlers would not just be perverse: it would be almost impossible. Greener technologies in the rich world will find their way, in time, to the poor.

Economic growth that does no environmental damage is an unattainable goal. The best governments can hope for is greener growth. That is more likely to take place if governments combine well-designed environmental policies with judicious use of the market. Badly designed policies can easily be a drag on economic growth, yet deliver little real improvement in environmental quality. The more environmental quality improves, the more important this point becomes.

Because each improvement in environmental quality is likely to be more expensive than the previous one, it is essential that governments choose environmental policies that achieve the maximum impact with the minimum burden on the economy. It is even more essential that governments avoid environmental measures whose benefits are less than their costs. In rich countries, the costs of environmental policies have risen rapidly. Their true costs are often largely concealed because they are imposed on companies or incorporated into regulations whose burden is difficult to detect. Some environmental standards now aim to reduce pollution beyond the point at which the value of extra clean-up exceeds the cost. The danger is that the public, wearied by paying too much for these programs, will lose interest in other, more important environmental problems.

Chapter 2

Environmental Priorities
and Values

Environmentalists often talk as though all green issues were equally important. But the poisonous air of some of China's big cities is clearly a pollution issue in a different league from, say, the accumulation of discarded packaging in the dumps of the West. Even within countries, some environmental issues deserve higher priority than others. Without a sense of hierarchy of environmental issues, governments can have no idea where first to spend taxpayers' money.

Setting priorities means finding some way to measure the costs of environmental damage. That idea makes many environmentalists, and many scientists, extremely squeamish. They doubt whether it is possible to put a specific cash value on any aspect of the environment. How, they ask, can conventional arithmetic deal with a policy whose consequences may be irreversible, such as the extinction of species? How can it allow for the intangible pleasure that the preservation of that species might give to people?

Such critics also point out that it is hard to talk sensibly about the benefits of a policy that may arise far into the future. Conventional tests of the return on investments are meaningless when applied to costs far in the future, particularly since those costs can be estimated only in the vaguest terms. Further, society has a moral duty to future generations that transcends economic arithmetic.

It is undoubtedly the case that, because environmental priorities involve governments in judgments about fundamental values, they are essentially moral and political decisions. But in the past, such judgments have frequently been made without a clear understanding of the implications. An attempt to balance the costs of taking action against the benefits of environmental protection will clarify what is at stake. The failure to attempt such a comparison has sometimes led environmentalists (and politicians) to press for measures whose cost clearly outweighs their benefit.

The Case for Reason

The rational way to set environmental priorities is to try to compare the costs of pollution and degradation with the costs of taking action to prevent them. Otherwise the list of threats will seem endless. Moreover, without an attempt at valuation it is impossible to know how much to spend on cleaning up environmental pollution. Environmentalists may argue, for example, that if water is dirty, then it should be made clean. But how clean? Clearly, the water in the Thames does not have to be clean enough for people to drink, and London air cannot reasonably be expected to be as pure as the air of mid-Wales. An economist would argue that water and air should be cleaned to the point where the environmental benefits of further clean-up operations are smaller than the costs they entail.

In the US, almost the only country where cost–benefit analysis is often required by law, the principle is in danger of being taken to extremes by the Republican-dominated Congress. That is as foolish as the alternative. In most countries, environmental legislation takes goals as given and then devises regulations or policies intended to meet them. Rarely do governments ask, at least

in a very coherent way, whether the costs of achieving environmental goals are likely to match the expected benefits, or whether
there are more cost-effective ways of achieving the same
environmental purposes.

There is no escaping the fact that the effects of environmental
damage are hard to fit into conventional economics. Some environmental values are certainly difficult to measure. But that is no reason
to abandon the attempt. Policy makers have many competing
demands on their budgets and administrative time: they trade costs
and benefits instinctively, even if not overtly. The job of economists
is to encourage people to think more clearly about the values that
are being taken into account and those that are being ignored. One
result may be to make decision-makers more aware of the environmental benefits of some decisions. Cleaning up a river may be worth
doing only if proper account is taken of the non-commercial ways
that people use it: for pleasure, say, and for recreational fishing.

Spending on environmental protection usually has to compete
against many other investments (or, as in the case of donations to
green lobbying groups or trips to national parks, with other sorts of
consumption). If companies are forced to spend heavily on – say –
cleaning up toxic waste, they are less likely to invest in developing
new products; if governments devote their road-building budget
to digging tunnels, in order to avoid desecrating beauty spots, there
may be less cash for bypasses around ancient city centers or for
public transport.

Governments make such decisions daily. If they do not establish
an explicit hierarchy of priorities, they must at least have an implicit
one. Top of any such hierarchy should surely be those
environmental problems that harm human health. Some environmentalists may believe that the health of the natural world should
come first. But governments need to accept that the kinds of
damage that impose the heaviest costs on humanity are the absence
of drinkable water and adequate sewerage, air pollution caused by
burning primitive fuels or coal, and soil erosion. Tackling these
environmental problems should be humanity's priority.

ENVIRONMENTAL DAMAGE TO HEALTH

In poor countries, the greatest threat to human health is dirty water, which each year kills 2 million children and makes many people ill. Providing clean water and sewerage is, said the 1992 World Development Report, the biggest single environmental priority. The second is tackling air pollution, especially the smoke and fumes from primitive fires of wood, charcoal and dung, which harm the lungs of millions of women and children as badly as cigarette smoking can do; and dust and soot in city air, often the product of burning coal and wood.

Many people in rich countries do not think of drinking water or sewerage as environmental issues. That is because long ago rich countries provided their citizens with clean water, and piped their sewage away (sometimes, admittedly, only as far as the nearest beach). People in rich countries rarely die from environmental pollution. When they do, however, governments find themselves under strong pressure to take action. The clamor for a treaty to phase out the use of CFCs was closely linked to worries about skin cancer. The pressure in the United States to spend a lot of money cleaning up toxic waste is driven by fears that carcinogens will seep into the water supply. And it is a fair bet that one of the main pressures on governments to regulate the use of road vehicles will be the growing evidence on the ways exhaust gases harm human health. One study by a London epidemiologist suggested that pollution from car exhausts may have contributed to the deaths of up to 160 Londoners in a few days of foggy weather in December 1991.[1]

In poor countries, the harm done to human health and economic output by pollution and damage to natural resources may be obvious. But once such obvious kinds of damage are cleaned up, it becomes increasingly difficult to establish a causal link between pollution and health. To do so may take many years: think how long it took to prove a connection between cigarettes and lung cancer. Some of the nitrates in Britain's water may have come not from the over-use of fertilizers in the 1970s and 1980s, but from the ploughing of grasslands after the Second World War.

Pollutants often come from one place and are thought to cause damage in another; or they may have an effect long after they appear in the atmosphere. The main arguments for reducing the sulphur in smoke from power stations have been the economic losses caused by acid rain, which has been blamed for the loss of fish and forests and for damage to buildings. Yet the link between output of sulphur dioxide and dead trees now looks less certain than it once did. An exhaustive study by the US National Acid Precipitation Assessment Program reported in 1991 that it could find 'no evidence of general or unusual decline of forests in the United States or Canada due to acid rain'.

It is particularly hard to trace whether small doses of substances affect human health. In the United States, Bruce Ames, a cancer specialist at the University of California in Berkeley, has argued forcefully against basing health regulations on the assumption that substances which cause tumors in rats and mice will do the same to human beings. But for the moment, there are few other ways to demonstrate a link.[2]

Because links between pollution and damage are often difficult to establish beyond a reasonable doubt, environmentalists have increasingly pressed governments to adopt the so-called precautionary principle: taking early action to limit the use of potentially dangerous pollutants. Even if there is not conclusive evidence of significant risk, such a course may be wise, especially if early, low-cost action is likely to prevent more expensive damage later, or if delay may have irreversible effects. In Britain the precautionary principle was used to justify an increase in taxes on leaded petrol before there was clear scientific evidence that atmospheric lead damaged health.

Even if pollution kills people, is that a good enough reason to prevent it? Not necessarily. It would, after all, be possible to stop almost all pedestrian road deaths by building huge bridges and forbidding people to cross roads any other way. But the cost and the intrusion into personal liberty would be unacceptable. In the same way, the chances of dying from some kinds of pollution are so small that a wise government should simply ignore them, when making environmental policy.

In rich countries, however, that is rarely what happens. Few governments try, even sporadically, to calculate the cost of saving a life when they introduce a new measure. A virtuous exception is the United States. The Office of Management and Budget, looking at the cost-effectiveness of a number of rules devised by the Environmental Protection Agency (EPA), has calculated that the answers range from $200,000 a life saved (for a drinking-water standard) to $5.7 trillion (roughly equal to America's GNP) for a rule on wood preservatives.[3]

When two economists at Resources for the Future, a Washington DC think-tank, analyzed a number of EPA regulations to estimate the implicit cost of a life saved, they also came up with huge figures. The average was $153 million (1989 dollars), but that figure was inflated by a court ruling in 1987 which specifically forbade the agency from considering the costs of measures to regulate air pollution until it had achieved an "acceptable risk" – which the agency has interpreted as a 1 in 10,000 cancer risk to somebody who has the maximum exposure to the pollutant. Strip out the effect of this ruling, and the average cost fell to $15 million a life saved.[4] That is still an immense sum: more than three times the implicit value of the risk of death from occupational injuries.

The fact that the EPA is willing to impose such high costs on the economy to save lives simply reflects to some extent the apparent irrationality of popular attitudes to risk. People are more willing to accept risks they freely impose upon themselves than risks over which they have no control. One study found that people will sometimes voluntarily take 1000 times more risk (by, for instance, ski-ing, hunting or smoking) than they will in ways over which they have no control.[5]

For governments, a difficult question is how far to acknowledge such apparent public irrationality and to build it into environmental regulations. After all, politicians might argue, if that is what voters want, why deny it? The trouble is, irrationality is terribly expensive. Michael Gough, another Resources for the Future economist, estimated that the whole panoply of EPA regulations might, at best, prevent 6400 of America's annual 485,000 cancer deaths. Yet environmental policies cost the United States roughly one-third as much as its entire expenditure on health care. Moreover, some measures that purport to save lives may inadvertently threaten them. Thus Britain has bowed to pressure from its European Union (EU) partners to stop incinerating sewage sludge at sea, where the fumes were well dispersed. More of the sludge will instead be incinerated on land, where the smoke is more likely to affect people.

In much of the developing world, and in the countries of Eastern Europe and the former Soviet Union, environmental threats to human health are still sufficiently serious to justify a place at the top of the list of environmental priorities. Such problems are not, however, the environmental issues that attract most public attention in the developed world. There, the worst environmental threats to human health have already been tackled. In rich countries, setting environmental priorities is made more difficult by the fact that damage is more often done to people's spiritual and emotional pleasure in the natural world than to health or the economy. Such damage is harder to measure, and therefore harder to weigh against economic activity.

Valuing Views

Difficult though it is to set a value on a human life, damage to health is at least an environmental threat which most people can agree should be tackled. It is much harder to get such agreement on damage to those aspects of the natural world which people treasure. Yet for rich countries, threats to the pleasures of nature tend to be especially important environmental issues. The trouble is, the value of such pleasures is particularly hard to establish in any objective way.

Economists are most comfortable when measuring people's preferences as revealed by their behavior in the market. But the environment is rarely bought or sold. So other ways must be found to put a value on environmental assets, or attach numbers to the damage done by environmental degradation. Some environmental assets can be valued by using indirect measures. For example, there are proxies for measuring some of the delight people take in the natural world. A house with a beautiful view generally costs more than a similar house without one, and the difference is a guide to the value home-owners place on a vista. A trip to a national park involves transport costs and, perhaps, an entrance fee. What people pay is some indication of how much they value the park.

But some people who never visit a natural park may still value its existence. They may simply be happy to know that they have the option to visit it some day. Or they may be content that to know that it will survive, well tended, for their children and grandchildren to visit. Or they may simply value the fact that the park exists. These "non-use" values will, indeed, often be much greater than the "use" value: consider Antarctica, for instance, or the snow leopard. Most people will never set eyes on either, but that does not mean they are of no value. The difficulty is to find out how much.

The technique used most frequently by economists is contingent valuation. They survey what people are willing to pay for a benefit, or what they would accept in compensation for its loss. Such calculations have been used, mainly in the United States, to estimate the benefits of some environmental policies in a way that can be compared with the cash costs of taking action. In the early 1990s, such calculations began to be applied elsewhere. In particular, Australia's Resource Assessment Commission used contingent valuation in 1991 to help the government decide whether to allow mining on the edge of Kakadu National Park (the stomping ground of Crocodile Dundee).

In that case, about 2000 people were interviewed in Australia at large, and a further 500 in the Northern Territory, where the mining would occur. Respondents were asked which of several specific amounts they would pay to protect the site. Half were given the environmentalists' assessment of the damage that mining would cause and half were given the mining industry's assessment.

The results indicated that, even if the impacts of mining were as small as the industry described them, Australians were willing to pay at least A$647 million (US$826 million) a year to prevent mining. That sum exceeded the value of minerals thought to be in Kakadu. Australians who were told the impact would be "major" said they would cheerfully have paid much more. But people in the Northern Territory, who expected to gain from jobs in the mines, were willing to pay considerably less.

The survey was attacked, predictably, by the mining industry and by other critics who complained that it put a value on a hectare of wilderness that was a hundred times that of land in downtown Melbourne. But land in public use is often differently valued from land in private use, which is why New York's Central Park or London's Hyde Park are not sold off for office development. A stronger criticism is that respondents were clustered at the far ends of the range of possible amounts, suggesting that most either replied, "I wouldn't give a cent for Kakadu" or, "I'd give anything I could to save the park."

In the end, the government rejected the mining proposal not because of the survey but because the area was considered sacred by the Jawoyn aborigines. The survey may have been more important as an indicator of public feeling than for assigning a cash value to Kakadu.

In the United States, however, legislation has tried to put more weight on contingent valuation. Under two acts, one in 1980 establishing the Superfund program and the Oil Pollution Act of 1990, the government is obliged to decide how to assess the damage caused by spills of hazardous waste and oil. A federal court ruling of 1989 instructed the government to take non-use values into account, and to make use of contingent valuation. In 1992 a panel chaired by two Nobel Prize winners, Kenneth Arrow and Robert Solow, cautiously ratified the use of contingent valuation as a way to discover non-use values.[6]

Because non-use values are almost always bound to be larger than use values, the effect of such legislation is to increase enormously the amount of possible damages for accidents such as that of the

Exxon Valdez, whose wreck caused a large oil spill in Prince William Sound in 1989. Indeed, a pilot survey for the State of Alaska suggested that the American public set such non-use values for Prince William Sound at about $3 billion – nearly three times the $1.15 billion out-of-court settlement that Exxon struck in February 1991, only to see it subsequently thrown out by the courts.

The basic problem with contingent valuation is that it does not use people's actions to discover how much they value something. It is thus fundamentally different even from the indirect ways in which economists use travel costs or house prices to discover how much people are willing to pay for goods and services which are not bought or sold, like a national park or a quiet street. The replies people give to a researcher's questions may differ from their behavior.

A study of contingent valuation by Peter Diamond and Jerry Hausman of the Massachusetts Institute of Technology set out some of the difficulties of using the technique. Respondents sometimes find the questions confusing, thinking in terms of a general amount they would spend on environmental good causes, rather than what they would give for a particular resource. And people lie. A sample of Norwegians was asked how much they would be willing to pay to join the country's most important environmental organization. The 101 people who replied with a figure above the actual membership fee were sent a brochure, and an invitation to join. Only six put a cheque in the post. Indeed, environmental charities generally collect far less in donations than people say they would give to protect the environment.[7]

It is surely a mistake to base a court decision on civil damages on such a foundation. But governments should not ignore the values people put on the continuing existence of natural beauty. The main use of contingent valuation surveys may be as a sort of public-opinion poll, testing how strongly people feel about an environmental issue. Indeed, that seems to have been precisely the way the Kakadu study was interpreted by the Australian government.

OTHER PEOPLE'S VALUES

Environmental values are not absolute. They tend to differ from one country to another, even among rich Western countries: Germans hunt birds but detest acid rain, which they believe threatens their forests; the British are passionate about birds but more tolerant of air pollution. Between countries at different stages of development, or from differing cultural traditions, the range of values is immense. People who emphasize the interdependence of humankind often ignore such troublesome divisions.

Such differences have profound economic and ethical implications. They were encapsulated in a memo sent by Lawrence Summers, chief economist of the World Bank, and leaked in *The Economist* in February 1992. "Just between you and me," Summers said, "shouldn't the World Bank be encouraging *more* migration of the dirty industries to the LDCs [less developed countries]?" He based this view on three arguments. First, the costs of pollution depend on earnings lost through death and injury. These earnings are lowest in the poorest countries. Therefore "I think the logic behind dumping a load of toxic waste in the lowest-wage country is impeccable and we should face up to that." Second, the costs of pollution rise disproportionately as it grows, so polluting the cleanest parts of the world may be less harmful than making the dirty parts filthier. Third, people value a clean environment more as their incomes rise. So if polluting industries move from rich countries to poor ones, the costs of pollution will decline.

The rage the memo aroused, both among environmentalists and in developing countries, was partly because of its flippant tone, and partly because it condoned the existence of differing environmental priorities. National environmental priorities do and should vary. The environment is not the only demand on a country's financial resources. When faced with a choice between cleaner air and less poverty, many poor countries will rightly opt for more pollution than a rich country would accept. If a developing country has a choice between investing in scrubbers on a power station to prevent acid rain and building hospitals, it will build hospitals first. And it will make no sense to force local industry to conform to American standards for dumping toxic waste.

But the differences in priorities, and the environmental standards that accompany them, create many tensions between rich and poor countries. For instance, they bedevil international environmental treaties. Are tropical forests a global resource, of special importance to all humanity for the range of species they harbor? Or are they a handy source of foreign exchange for the developing countries in which they are mainly found? At the Rio de Janeiro Summit in 1992 efforts by the rich countries to negotiate a world treaty on forests were stymied by the developing countries which saw it as an intrusion into their sovereign right to do what they wanted with their timber.

Such differences also affect trade and investment. The two big rounds of trade liberalization that culminated in the early 1990s, the North American Free Trade Area and the Uruguay Round of the GATT, both discussed how far countries should be allowed to impose differing environmental standards, if the result was to restrict trade. Multinational companies that invest in developing countries are affected by variations in standards too. They frequently find either that the law does not require them to meet standards as high as those set at home, or that it does, but is not enforced.

In time, environmental values may well converge – and converge upwards. Economic development will mean that developing countries will deal with the most pressing environmental threats to their citizens' health and wealth. As news becomes increasingly global and the larger green lobbying groups become multinational organizations, governments in many countries will be pressed to improve their environmental standards. They will also be influenced by scientists who, as one of the British diplomats involved in the climate-change treaty has observed in a penetrating book, "have increasingly taken to coming together in what can only be described as a highly political manner to produce agreed assessments of environmental problems".[8] Where environmental policies diverge, they may eventually reflect differences in the style and capacity of governments rather than large differences in environmental values.

A PRICE ON POSTERITY

Policies always have to balance the demands of future generations against the demands of those who are living today. The benefits of, say, investing today in the prevention of global warming will not be apparent for more than a century, because the costs of climate change will probably accrue very slowly. Indeed, William Cline, an American economist, has estimated that the costs of a doubling of atmospheric carbon dioxide in the second quarter of the next century will be about 1 per cent of American GDP. As carbon dioxide and other global-warming gases continue to build up, the cost will continue to rise: to 6–12 per cent in 250 years' time.[9] Compared with any reasonable rate of return, investing in the prevention of global warming makes no economic sense.

Benefits, too, may accrue over centuries: planting an oak tree today will give pleasure to people whose grandparents are not yet born. No rational investor would buy a share which earned no return until the end of the next century; why, then, should anybody invest in planting oak trees?

When making such choices, people and governments often show an altruistic desire to make life better for posterity – as they do when they invest in the education of children. People sometimes plant trees, for instance, for the sheer pleasure of beginning something that will live after them. But environmental quality is only one aspect of the package that future generations inherit. Should our ancestors not have built the railways or cities that we have inherited because of the environmental damage they did? We may often be wiser to make investments that earn high returns in the near future (monetary and non-monetary) rather than guess at the preferences and technologies of our great-grandchildren.

It is no easier to be fair to posterity than to apply more conventional tests to investments. When a government decides to build a road through a nice bit of habitat, it is inevitably removing a few environmental rights from future generations. But the decision to go ahead will be just as difficult if the government has to try to put prices on the land as part of a cost-benefit exercise, as if it has to worry about how much unspoilt habitat future generations will want.

When environmental decisions have to balance this generation's right to health and wealth against the unknown preferences of the unborn, the wisest course is usually to make the decision in the light of the known preferences of those living today. This is not an argument for ignoring species extinction or global warming. Some policies that slow global warming – such as the proper pricing of energy, which is still frequently subsidized or underpriced – would pass any of today's cost-benefit tests, and also benefit future generations. Those measures are worth taking. Others are not. Often, arguments put forward to justify action to slow global warming would be better used to justify other environmental policies, with faster results. For example, one of the main costs that global warming is thought likely to impose will be the loss of those species that cannot adapt fast enough to a changing climate. But species are already being lost at an accelerating pace. It would be wiser to spend to protect today's biological diversity than to use the prospect of distant extinctions as an argument for costly action to prevent climate change.

Chapter 3

Environmental Politics

Although this book is mainly concerned with economic aspects of the environment, political questions are inescapable. Many environmental questions are about sharing: among countries, within countries, between generations. The market cannot always be relied upon to produce the fairest, or even the most efficient, result. Governments therefore have to intervene to influence the way in which claims to the environment are met. Such intervention has made new demands on politicians. Environmental issues, being both global and extremely local, have proved difficult for them to handle. This chapter looks at the way environmentalism has intruded into politics, and how the machinery of politics has been adapted to cope with it.

Pitfalls for Politicians

"Environment" is a difficult concept to fit neatly into the existing pigeon-holes of political life. For some, the word instantly conjures up visions of green fields vanishing under concrete; for others, the Chernobyl disaster in Ukraine in 1986; for yet others, belching smoke from factories and cars. What unites these issues, and makes

32

them problematic for politicians, is the public passion they frequently arouse. Few other issues have such power to bring protesters to the streets, or letters swamping politicians' desks. This passion, which crosses the boundaries of political parties and social class, makes it hard for politicians to discuss policies in a rational way or to turn environmental debates to their advantage.

The environment draws into political activity many people who would never usually wield banners or write to their Member of Parliament or Congressman. In non-democratic countries, as in Eastern Europe under Communism, environmentalism can be profoundly threatening to government. The threat is greatest in countries where governments shield polluters, either by controlling the production of the most polluting industries (energy, minerals extraction, heavy industry) or by allocating to political friends the right to extract natural resources (such as timber). In such situations, environmentalism readily becomes a movement of the people – especially the poor – against the powerful. Even in democratic countries, with the safety valve of political response, environmental movements can still surprise governments (and companies) with their sudden vehemence.

In many countries, non-governmental organizations have learnt to foment and channel this popular emotion. One of the striking features of environmental politics is the role played by lobbying groups. Few other areas of political life have seen such a global burgeoning of campaigning bodies. Many are tiny and local. Some, however, are vast, such as Greenpeace with a worldwide income of about $150 million and membership of 3.8 million. In the early 1990s, bodies such as Greenpeace and Friends of the Earth were treated by some governments almost as though they were separate countries, with the power to negotiate and speak on behalf of a large electorate. A recurrent dilemma for politicians has been to know how far such environmental movements accurately reflect public opinion.

While on one hand governments have had to deal with the clamor of environmentalists, they have also had to tackle polluters. Those who cause environmental damage are often powerful citizens (electricity utilities, cattle ranchers, motorists) who must stop their self-serving behavior. Drivers think they have a right to use their cars; farmers think they are entitled to sufficient water supplies; fishermen to take what they can catch. None are happy about sacrificing such rights.

Worse, in the rich countries, polluters and their victims are sometimes the same people. Voters want to drive their cars, but also want their children to cycle to school; they want to buy products made by polluting processes, but not allow those processes to pollute; they want to have roads and jobs but also to protect the countryside. Few areas of politics so demonstrate the intransigent hypocrisy of voters. Voters do not want to be told that they are being illogical, especially by politicians: they simply want their own way. Both ways.

In picking their way through this minefield, politicians have often had to turn to scientists for help. When they do, two things become clear. First, scientific consensus is as rare and fragile in this as in any other field. Secondly, decisions must often be taken on the basis of the judgment of a relatively small number of scientists who specialize in an esoteric field. Is the ozone layer really being depleted by CFCs? Is overfishing responsible for the decline in fish stocks? Will the effects of global warming be so costly? In all these cases, politicians are pressed to intervene, but on the basis of advice from a group of scientists who may disagree – or, worse, find it difficult to accept dissent, even in their own ranks.

While all these pressures make environmental politics difficult, one aspect is heartening. Governments in rich countries have been surprisingly willing to take measures that benefit two groups of people whose votes they will never win: future generations, and foreigners. For example, British efforts to reduce acid rain will benefit not only the British, but Norwegians and Germans as yet unborn, although only today's British consumers of electricity will pay for the scrubbers for the Drax power station. Although it may be that voters simply do not understand the true costs of the measures which their government has agreed to take, it is also possible that voters may be motivated by altruism, a quality that economists find hard to incorporate into their models.

FROM PASSION TO POLICY

When one looks at the ebb and flow of environmental passions in the post-war years, a striking aspect is the extent to which periods of rapid economic growth tend to accentuate environmental concern. The late 1960s saw a phenomenal upsurge in public interest in green themes. Another upswing took place all around the world in the late 1980s. Green enthusiasm built up to a crescendo in 1992, the year of the United Nations Conference on Environment and Development (UNCED), or Earth Summit, in Rio de Janeiro. Since then, in the rich Western world at least, environmentalism has become a somewhat less potent political force. In the 1992 presidential campaign in the United States, George Bush made no promises to be an "environmental president", as he had done in 1988. Instead, he dubbed Al Gore, then Bill Clinton's vice-presidential candidate, who had written an emotional book about the environment, "Mr Ozone". By the mid-1990s, the excitement of Rio had faded.

In each period, environmentalism seems to have been stimulated by a period of extraordinary international economic growth. In 1950–70, gross world product more than doubled, and much of the growth took place in highly polluting industries, such as chemicals and energy production.[1] Wealth was a cause of pollution; it also gave people the security to campaign against pollution, even if the cost was a curb on the future increase in wealth.

When this bout of environmentalism subsided (though it survived in parts of northern Europe), it left behind a large number of institutions and laws which have been the framework of post-war environmental policy. Between 1970 and 1972, 14 environment ministries or agencies were set up in industrial countries.[2] A large amount of environmental legislation was passed: 14 pieces in Japan in 1970 alone, for example. In 1972, more than half the American states passed environmental laws. International conventions were passed to protect wetlands and stop the dumping of waste in the North Sea and north-east Atlantic. The first UNCED, in Stockholm in 1972, gave birth to the United Nations Environment Programme (UNEP).

Subsequent years saw plenty that was environmentally damaging: population continued to grow at a vertiginous rate, and nasty accidents occurred (a dioxin leak from Seveso in 1976, the *Amoco Cadiz* oil spill in 1978, the chemical disaster at Bhopal in 1984). But with the boom of the mid-1980s, the pace of environmental damage in the developed countries accelerated. Property development took place in areas that had previously been unspoilt, and the use of all forms of transport expanded. In the developing countries growth speeded the pace at which natural habitats were converted into farmland or building land. It brought spending power to countries that did not share new-found Western scruples about buying ivory or rhinoceros horn. Suddenly the nasty accidents got more space in newspaper front pages, culminating in the 1989 *Exxon Valdez* oil spill. Once sensitized by green lobbying organizations, people began to ascribe all sorts of disasters in the natural world to environmental causes. Americans blamed a drought on the greenhouse effect; the British blamed dying seals on waste dumped in the North Sea; the Germans thought acid rain caused their forests to wilt.

Once again, though, the economic recession of the mid-1990s seemed to cause a recession in environmental pressures. Every year MORI, a British firm of public-opinion pollsters, asks a sample of Members of Parliament about the subjects on which they receive most letters and representations from constituents. In 1992 more than 30 per cent replied "the environment or pollution". By 1994, that had fallen to just over 10 per cent. Governments began to slow down the pace of green legislation. In Germany, for instance, where the green movement had pushed through parliament an extraordinarily complex and expensive scheme for recycling packaging, other plans to force recycling of construction materials and electrical goods were quietly forgotten.

But like the environmental wave of the late 1960s and early 1970s, that of the late 1980s and early 1990s has left a mass of legislation which will be implemented during the rest of the decade. It has left new bureaucracies, such as the Environmental Agency of the

European Union, anxious to justify their existence by developing their powers. It has left a number of international treaties, which will force governments to continue to talk to each other about environmental issues. And it has left a whole generation of school children with an interest in green issues. In fact, the most pervasive effect of Rio may have been on the young. In almost every school in the rich world – and in many schools elsewhere on the planet – children did environmental projects. Since the young are tomorrow's voters, politicians will not be able to ignore the environment. Moreover, many of the environmental problems that caught the world's attention again at the end of the 1980s have not been solved in any lasting sense. All through the next century, there will be recurrent bouts of public alarm which will carry forward environmental legislation, especially in the countries that are now developing most quickly.

THE ORIGINS OF ENVIRONMENTALISM

At the heart of environmental politics are lobbying groups and other non-governmental organizations. With their huge membership – in Britain, some 5 million people belong to environmental groups, compared with perhaps 1 million members of the three main political parties – they have played something of the role that trade unions played in some European countries in the early post-war years. They have shaped the agendas of political parties, campaigned for changes with single-minded intensity, and effectively challenged the power of companies and other vested interests. Now such groups increasingly face a challenge. As long as environmental politics is essentially about protest, it is easy to muster public support. Lobbying groups then differ mainly in their willingness to compromise with government and business in the interests of pragmatism (at one end of the spectrum) and their idealism (at the other). Once government and companies turn the debate to the search for solutions, lobbying groups become exposed to the same pressures as politicians: caught between the desire of people for a healthier environment and their simultaneous reluctance to alter their way of life.

The roots of environmental lobbying groups are as diverse as the environmental issues they campaign on. Tom Burke, who once ran Friends of the Earth in Britain and subsequently became special adviser to the secretary of state for the environment, distinguishes three sets of antecedents in Britain: the nineteenth-century naturalists, such as William Morris, who wanted to preserve beautiful buildings, landscapes, birds and beasts; the protesters of the 1970s, who cared more about mobilizing public opinion than lobbying Whitehall; and the Utopian radicals, descended from a long line of dissenters, who believed in action, not argument.

All these elements are to be found, to some degree or another, in other countries. With striking frequency, the environment has provided a focus for protest in countries where political opposition is banned. Much of the opposition to Communism in the countries of Eastern Europe in the late 1980s, for example, clustered around environmental banners. In Hungary and Czechoslovakia and in the dissident republics of the Soviet Union, the environmental movement offered one of the few ways in which nationalism was allowed to express itself. So, for instance, some 5000 people marched against a planned chemical plant in Yerevan, Armenia, in February 1988; between 50,000 and 100,000 people linked hands on the seashore in September 1988 to call attention to the pollution of the Baltic Sea; 600,000 people in Lithuania signed a protest in October 1988 against a nuclear power plant. In that heady era, the ranks of Eastern Europe's green movement contained a curious amalgam of academics and political dissidents. Once conventional opposition parties were allowed, many of Eastern Europe's Green parties reverted to being pressure groups, rather than mainstream political organizations.

In the developed world, the concerns of environmental campaigners have clustered around three main themes: conservation; anti-nuclear protest; and worries about public health and pollution. In the United States and Britain, the oldest environmental organizations and those with the largest membership have typically been concerned with the **preservation of wildlife and the country-side**. In the United States bodies such as the Sierra Club, founded by John Muir, the Scots father of the National Parks, and the Wilderness Society grew out of the campaign, at the turn of the century, to persuade the federal government to protect rather than develop the finest tracts of the vast lands it owned in the western United States.

In Britain, the government owned no such tracts, and most land was developed centuries ago. An interest in rural conservation was fostered by Britain's early urbanization: the National Trust was founded in 1895 by Octavia Hill, who also did much to improve the housing of the urban poor. Making the countryside accessible to people from towns was the goal of the Ramblers Association, which grew from a mass trespass on Kinder Scout, in the Peak District, in 1932. In Britain, conservation has been the basis of two of the most effective environmental groups: the Council for the Preservation of Rural England and the most influential of all, the Royal Society for the Protection of Birds (RSPB).

Increasingly, the biggest preservation battles have been about not Yellowstone or Kinder Scout, but international issues, such as whaling, the ivory trade and the future of the Amazon region. Both at home and abroad, conservation bodies have found that it is not enough to campaign for the conservation of individual species or bits of land. The forces that drive extinction and destruction are too complex. The World Wide Fund for Nature, as it is now known in the UK, began life as the World Wildlife Fund, founded by Peter Scott, passionate bird lover and son of the Antarctic explorer. Its name change, in 1988, was intended to reflect this shift of emphasis.

Opposition to **nuclear power** has been a widespread theme of green politics. The anti-nuclear lobby has been the backbone of environmentalism in Japan and Germany. Greenpeace grew out of Canadian opposition to American testing of nuclear weapons at Amchitka, an island off the west coast of Alaska, in the late 1960s. Opinion polls in Britain (and elsewhere) frequently show that the disposal of nuclear waste is the public's greatest single environmental worry.

The third theme of green activity has been opposing **pollution**. This has been perhaps the most important theme pressed by Greenpeace and Friends of the Earth. Both grew from splits between traditional conservationists and the tougher new environmentalism of that period. Their most striking novelty has been their internationalism, and their hard-edged skill in campaigning. In the 1970s they started to campaign against acid rain. In the 1980s, when international issues were of prime importance in environmental politics, they used their affiliates in different countries to run global campaigns on issues such as deforestation and climate change.

All these non-governmental groups prospered in the late 1980s and early 1990s. Their numbers, membership and influence expanded rapidly. In Britain, membership of green lobbying groups rose from about 2 million in 1980 to 5 million by 1988. The growth was happening elsewhere: in the United States, membership of America's Wilderness Society shot from 40,000 at the start of the 1980s to 320,000 in 1989; and America's Worldwatch Institute, which once took one job applicant in 300, suddenly found it could pick one from 1000. By the mid-1990s, though, the public in some countries appeared to be suffering from "green fatigue". Membership declined and donations dwindled. For example, Wilderness Society membership faded to 275,000 by 1995; in the case of Greenpeace international membership fell by more than a quarter from its early 1990s peak to its 1994 level, while income fell by 13 per cent.

In the early 1990s, some of the older environmental groups came to realize that the specific issues on which they had campaigned in the past were too narrow. They became more willing to take part in political fights. For example, the spread of commercial tree-farming and the consequent loss of habitat for moorland birds, led the RSPB to challenge successfully the British government's tax breaks for commercial forestry.

In some countries, non-governmental groups have already become part of the established political process. Thus in The

Netherlands non-governmental groups have been involved in the negotiation of "covenants": voluntary agreements with various sectors of industry to aim for reductions in environmental pollution.

Making the step from protesting to policy-making has been difficult for many voluntary bodies. Greenpeace built its reputation on a number of eye-catching non-violent demonstrations – modeled on the Quaker tradition of "bearing witness".[3] As Greenpeace has become larger and richer, it has become more involved in developing solutions. In 1993, the group went to lobby British Treasury officials on issues of taxation and public spending. Indeed, the group must have been one of the first bodies ever to ask the Treasury to *raise* taxes – on cars and energy. Friends of the Earth has had to make a similar transformation: in 1990 it commissioned papers on ways to reform the Department of the Environment.

The transformation has caused tensions, most publicly in Greenpeace. With its large income and staff, it can no longer be as anarchically extreme in its protests as, say, the groups that opposed motorway building across Twyford Down in south-west England or through north-east London. Some Greenpeace supporters yearn for a return to the old campaigning days, such as the group of former employees who seized *Sirius*, a Greenpeace boat, and in 1994 announced they intended to use it against Norwegian whalers. Others argue that the old rubber-dinghy campaigning techniques are outdated, and that future campaigns need to use more marketing and communications skills.

While protesters have the luxury of choosing whether to suggest solutions or simply wave banners, political parties do not. Suspended between the two have been Green parties, which now exist in most industrial countries, but which have generally remained small. Only in western Germany, Switzerland and Belgium has support for Green parties been a significant force in mainstream politics. As Sara Parkin, a leading figure in Green politics in Britain, put it, "Almost without exception, the Green parties are squeamish about power – in their own organizations and in the world around them."[4] Their politics tends to be a mish-mash of eco-feminism, anti-nuclearism, and massive redistribution. Britain's Green party had a brief moment of glory in the 1989 elections to the European Parliament, when it captured 14.5 per cent of the vote (though no seats). But its determination not to choose a leader and its ramshackle finances meant that it got no further. In the 1994 European Parliament elections, it took a mere 3.2 per cent of the vote.

Rather than vote Green, most voters have preferred to urge their mainstream politicians to take more interest in green issues. The environment is an issue without any obvious political home. It became, at the end of the 1980s, a consensual issue, which no politician could afford to be "against". In America the most rabidly anti-environmental president for many years (Ronald Reagan, a Republican) was succeeded by another Republican, George Bush, who built part of his 1989 election campaign round a promise to clean up America. In Britain in 1988 Margaret Thatcher made a speech to the Royal Society about the danger of climate change; her successor, John Major, published one of the first national plans for sustainable development in 1994. But mainstream politicians have discovered that being green has brought fewer votes than they had hoped. Politicians have found that they can never do enough to satisfy the green lobby; and the green lobby has found that people periodically lose patience with protest.

THE MACHINERY OF GREENERY

The hydra-headed quality of environmentalism, which makes it hard for politicians to adopt as an issue, also makes it hard to integrate into the conventional machinery of government. After all, almost every policy, from agricultural to fiscal, has environmental implications. But governments have never found it easy to ensure (even when they have wanted to do so) that all policy decisions are taken in the light of environmental considerations.

After the 1972 Stockholm conference, most Western governments set up special environment ministries. Britain's Department of the Environment began life in the 1970–74 government of Edward

Heath. It was an amalgamation of the ministries of housing, local government, public buildings and works and transport. As a result, its secretaries of state have tended to devote most of their energies to rearranging the structure and financing of local government, rather than to worrying about environmental matters. Meanwhile, farming, transport and (until the early 1990s) energy have all had their own Whitehall department. Recycling is mainly a matter for the industry department. The Scottish and Welsh Offices have large powers over their own environments: the Scottish Office, in particular, is the main influence on forestry policy and has an important effect on fisheries policy. And the Treasury has the last word on issues of public spending and taxation which may sometimes be the most important environmental influences of all.

Some have argued for setting up a separate "green" ministry, such as exists in many other countries. But such ministers elsewhere typically control relatively small budgets. As it is the size of departmental budget that typically determines a minister's clout, the result is that environment ministers have to rely for their influence on personality alone. Some countries (The Netherlands, for instance) have experimented with a super-ministry, rolling together all environmental responsibilities. But the effect has been to transfer arguments from the cabinet to the departments.

One solution, pioneered by Mr Chris Patten, during his spell as environment secretary in Margaret Thatcher's government, was to set up a special cabinet committee, composed of ministers from all the departments whose activities impinge on the environment, chaired by the prime minister. The committee had the job of drawing up a white paper on the environment, "This Common Inheritance", published in September 1990. The white paper called for a minister in each department to be given responsibility for environmental policies and for departments to examine the environmental costs and benefits of important decisions.

Other countries choose different arrangements. One key organizational question is the relationship between politicians and the design of environmental policy on the one hand, and policymaking and enforcement on the other. The British environment department is headed by a politician and is a policy-making body; enforcement is in the hands of a number of separate bodies, of which the two most important are Her Majesty's Inspectorate of Pollution and the National Rivers Authority. Under the terms of a long-delayed plan, both are being combined into a single environmental agency together with the waste-regulation authorities. The aim is to encourage an integrated approach to pollution. In the United States, by contrast, the person who heads the Environmental Protection Agency does not have a seat in the cabinet and so has – in theory – greater political autonomy than the British environment secretary. Unlike environment ministries in other countries, the EPA is an enforcement agency, with (like Britain's HMIP) an army of officials to pursue polluters who break the law.

Environmentalists tend to assume that environmental policy should be made and enforced by a body that is as independent as possible from politicians. Enforcement of environmental regulations, like all kinds of law enforcement, is best sheltered from political influence. But the making of environmental policy is inevitably a political activity. The more it is left to an independent agency, the less power (and money) politicians are likely to allow that agency to have. Indeed, developing countries are full of environment departments and agencies devising all manner of adventurous policies, but without the cash, staff or political backing to enforce them. Meanwhile, the government decisions that have most effect on the environment – decisions about agricultural subsidies, road-building and industrial development – are taken by other, more powerful ministries.

International Environmental Issues

However elaborate their machinery of domestic environmental governance, few countries still see environmental policy as a purely domestic matter. The level at which environmental policy is made has been changing, most obviously in Europe. Britain's environmental policies have increasingly been made in Brussels, seat of the European Commission, not London. This is partly because some kinds of environmental pollution cross international borders. But the main reason the European Commission has demanded a say in environmental issues is that green policies influence competitiveness. Countries that impose tough standards on their producers want to ensure that neighboring countries do the same: otherwise, their producers will claim to be at a competitive disadvantage. And the environmental standards countries set for products can easily be used as an excuse to keep out imports. The European Union (EU) has, however, extended its say into some areas of the environment where it is hard to see the justification. The most obvious instance is the directive on the quality of bathing water, a subject that matters greatly to swimmers and surfers but hardly affects national competitiveness.

British environmental groups have been adept at lobbying in Brussels to raise environmental standards in Britain. Thus Friends of the Earth waged an astute campaign to persuade the European Commission to take a tough line with Britain's breach of rules on nitrates in drinking water. Britain in the 1980s was frequently pilloried by the green lobby for its reluctance to agree to ever-tougher environmental rules. British officials tended to reply tartly that Britain, at least, implemented the rules it had agreed to – unlike many other EU countries.

A fast-growing part of environmental policy is now made beyond Brussels, through international treaties.[5] Such treaties (dealt with more extensively in the final chapters of this book) are sometimes negotiated among a small number of countries (as with the convention that governs the Mediterranean, for example) and occasionally among all the members of the United Nations (as with the treaties on ozone depletion, climate change and biological diversity). They take governments into new territory, persuading them to take action for the benefit of other countries on the basis – sometimes – of uncertain scientific forecasts. The negotiation of such treaties, even more than international negotiations on trade or security matters, is characterized by highly public debates, great involvement of non-governmental groups, intense media interest and much public posturing.

As international environmental negotiations have proliferated, they have acquired institutions of their own. One of the main legacies of the 1972 Stockholm conference was the United Nations Environment Programme. UN agencies have to be shared out in a politically correct way; UNEP had the misfortune to be the UN agency sent to Africa. Being in Nairobi means that it is further from the UN's New York headquarters, in terms of airline timetables, than any of the UN's other children. In the 1980s its wily and energetic executive director, Mustapha Tolba, played a key role in pushing through the international treaties on hazardous waste and ozone depletion, although he was often criticized for poor administration. In the 1990s, which are likely at best to be a period of consolidation rather than the negotiation of new treaties, UNEP is finding it hard to retain its importance.

The Rio conference also created yet another UN body: the Commission on Sustainable Development, which is supposed to monitor environmental development issues. But Rio's main effect may have been on other UN institutions, especially the World Bank and the United Nations Development Programme. Both see the environment as a way to interest aid-weary public opinion in the North in the state of the poorer developing countries – and as an increasingly important aspect of development. The Bank in the early 1990s rapidly built up its environment directorate; UNDP's new head, James Speth, came from the World Resources Institute, an American environmental think-tank.

The challenge for these institutions, and for the secretariats of the environmental treaties signed in the late 1980s and early 1990s, is to find ways to make up for the absence of a world government that can tell polluters to clean up, as national governments do at home. Instead of doing what is most obviously in their national interest, countries have to be bribed – or bullied – into international co-operation. Environmental diplomacy will increasingly have to teach countries that some sacrifice of sovereignty is the price of a cleaner planet.

Part II

POLICY
MEASURES

Chapter 4

Regulation

Once governments have taken responsibility for environmental policy, there are various instruments they can use to influence what happens. The oldest remedies against environmental damage are through the courts. But since the nineteenth century, and the spread of industrialization, the machinery of common law has increasingly been supplemented, in two important ways. Governments have devised regulations; and, more recently, they have tried to develop various sorts of economic instruments. At the same time, there has been a growing awareness that the activities of governments can themselves be environmentally harmful. The market can fail, but government can also make mistakes.

The chapters in this part of the book look at these elements of government policy. They ignore one important aspect of policy: the increased use of intergovernmental treaties to try and protect the global environment. These are discussed in Part V. The theme that binds this section together is the difficulty of devising ways to intervene that combine the maximum environmental protection with the minimum harm to economic growth. Intervention invariably carries costs, and has unpredictable side-effects. The more governments can hold down those costs, the more they are

likely to persuade polluters to assume a different set of costs: those
of preventing pollution.

Most governments primarily use regulation to protect the
environment. They tell companies and other bodies what to do.
Sometimes, they tell them in great detail; sometimes, they merely
set out a goal. From the economist's perspective, such policies are
second best: regulation carries a variety of economic costs (discussed
below and in Chapter 5). Economists, therefore, devote much
energy to the search for alternative policies that minimize the costs
of intervention. Some have looked for ways to extend the concept
of property rights, so that individuals have a greater incentive to
care for the environment, and the courts can use the common law
to discourage damage. Others have concentrated on ways to use
economic incentives, such as green taxes, to encourage polluters
to reduce their pollution in the most cost-effective way.

Inevitably, though, economic efficiency is not the only factor
governments consider when devising environmental policies. People also have to be willing to support them. The policies that politicians often judge to be easiest to put in place are not necessarily
particularly efficient from an economic point of view. That is why
governments around the world so frequently prefer to stick to
regulation.

In looking at the impact of regulation, it is important to bear one
point in mind. While government intervention may carry costs, the
untrammelled market is unlikely to protect the environment. Paul
Portney, of Resources for the Future, sums up the dilemma:

> Regulation seldom goes exactly as planned when it is substituted for
> the forces of the market. It is often poorly conceived, time-consuming,
> arbitrary and manipulated for political purposes completely unrelated
> to its original intent. Thus the real comparison one must make in
> contemplating a regulatory intervention is that between an admittedly
> imperfect market and what will inevitably be imperfect regulation. Until
> it is recognized that this is the dilemma before us, we will be dissatisfied
> with either approach.[1]

HOW GOVERNMENTS REGULATE

The most basic question for environmental regulators is how to decide on the appropriate level of protection. The answer might seem obvious: surely a regulator ought to aim to get rid of pollution? Who, after all, wants to drink dirty water or breathe contaminated air? But the goal of zero pollution is rarely a wise one, for several reasons. First, a small amount of pollution may not be harmful. Smoke one cigarette in your life and you are unlikely to suffer as a result; smoke 40 a day for two decades, and you may die from it. Second, the goal posts may move: better measurement techniques may allow people to measure lower and lower concentrations of pollutants. Just because a pollutant can more readily be detected, it is not necessarily more dangerous.

But suppose a pollutant is dangerous, even in small amounts. Does that mean it should be banned? Again, not necessarily. People may quite reasonably want to trade off the risks from the pollutant against other kinds of risk, including that of being out of a job, or poor. The majority of the people of Cumbria in the north of England have not lobbied for the closure of the nuclear-waste facilities at Sellafield. They are prepared to accept the small risk of life-threatening contamination, in exchange for the prosperity that Sellafield brings to the region.

The level of protection is incorporated into regulation in a variety of ways. The two primary ones were summed up as long ago as 1912, in a report by Britain's Royal Commission on Sewage Disposal. "A chemical standard can be applied in any one of two ways," it pointed out: "either to the contaminating discharge by itself or to the stream which has received the discharge."[2] One way to set standards is to lay down, say, a minimum level for the amount of dissolved oxygen in water or a maximum for the amount of nitrous oxides in the air. An alternative is to decree that polluters can emit only a certain quantity of hazardous gases or liquids. Some of the debates in the European Union on environmental issues, especially over water-quality standards, have turned on which is the appropriate way to set standards. Britain has traditionally followed the first approach, measuring the level of pollutants in rivers and streams. Germany has preferred the second, insisting that firms invest in certain kinds of filtering equipment, regardless of their location. The second approach is much more common internationally, and, indeed, is followed by British legislation on air pollution.

One purported advantage of the emission-standards approach is that all manufacturers are treated equally and so none gains a cost advantage over others. For bureaucrats attempting to create a single market in Europe, that is an important consideration, as it is for German companies, whose government has been prodded by a militant Green movement for twenty years to raise environmental standards higher and higher. At least such a principle, enshrined in European Commission directives, ensures equal misery for European industry. Another claimed advantage of emission standards is that they are often easier to enforce. It may be simpler to measure the amount of pollutant at the moment it is discharged at a factory wastepipe than once it has spread out into the environment.

Frequently (but not inevitably), emissions standards are set by mandating a particular technology: all coal-fired power stations must fit scrubbers, for instance, or all landfills must have liners. Standards set in terms of "best available technology" can easily be monitored: it is simple to check whether that technology is being used. This advantage, again, has been important in the EU. Europe is not just a collection of nation-states; some of those nations are federations, with powerful regional governments. Standards set in Brussels may be more likely to be observed if they are set in terms of specific discharge permits and technologies than if they spell out appropriate pollution targets for different parts of the environment.

Finally, emissions standards are attractive to companies, especially those that make pollution-control equipment. If they can persuade governments to build into a regulation particular levels of discharge that their equipment can meet, or particular technologies, they can win market share as a result. For a country such as Germany, where companies are used to the idea of product standards, the environment simply becomes one more set of standards to build into plant and equipment.

Most economists, however, are more comfortable with the second way of setting standards: in terms of environmental quality. They argue that environmental standards should vary from place to place. The most vulnerable parts of the environment should have a lot of protection; those parts that matter less should not. It is clearly less important to keep pollutants out of a fast-moving river at a point only a few miles from the sea than from a sluggish river upstream from towns and villages that use it as their water supply. Similarly, the standard to which it would be sensible to clean up a piece of contaminated land ought to depend on whether it will be used as a playground for toddlers or as the base of a motorway junction. The assumption behind such arguments is that society will get more environmental protection for every pound or dollar spent if it sets the highest standards in the places that need them most.

THE CASE FOR INTEGRATION

One effect of concentrating on the state of the environment, rather than on the discharge of pollution, ought to be to make regulators ask what happens to pollutants removed from one part of the environment. Are they simply dumped in a different form? For example, Britain has agreed to stop dumping sewage sludge in the North Sea by 1998. Will beaches be cleaner as a result? Not if New York City's experience is anything to go by. In 1988 federal legislation banned the city from dumping sewage sludge at sea. The city therefore spent $2 billion it could ill afford to convert sewage into fertilizer. But most of the filth on beaches around New York comes not from sewage but from overloaded storm drains! In Britain, much of the sewage sludge will be incinerated. The ash will have to be disposed of on land – much nearer to human beings than if the sludge were dumped in the middle of the sea.

In fact, regulatory agencies and environmental legislation have usually been divided by the piece of the environment they are meant to control. The United States, for instance, passed a Clean Air Act in 1970 and a Clean Water Act in 1972. Britain has a National Rivers Authority, with responsibility for the cleanliness of rivers; it also has waste regulatory authorities, responsible for the way solid waste is disposed of; and Her Majesty's Inspectorate of Pollution, which monitors industrial pollution.

Some countries, by contrast, have tried to co-ordinate the business of pollution control. In 1969 Sweden set up a single permit process for discharges by large polluters to water, land and air, under a single Environmental Protection Act.[3] In Britain, where environmental regulation has long been highly fragmented, the Royal Commission on Environmental Pollution (an influential permanent and independent advisory body) suggested in a 1976 report that "the form and medium of disposal [of industrial pollutants] should be chosen to cause the least environmental damage overall."[4] This concept became known as "best practicable environmental option", or BPEO. But not until 1990 did Britain's Environmental Protection Act develop the commission's advice into the relatively untried concept of integrated pollution control. The pollution inspectorate was told to license 5000 of the most polluting processes, taking an integrated approach to all the pollution that a plant or process caused.

Such an approach, which the EU was considering adopting in 1995, not only makes much better sense than monitoring different kinds of pollution in separate ways; it ties in with the way the more environmentally sensitive companies are increasingly viewing the whole life-cycle of their products. It is, however, more complicated than older, cruder forms of regulation. To implement it, pollution inspectors have to learn a great deal about the way companies operate: how particular processes work; the way feedstocks are managed; and how materials are stored. To understand such detail, without developing a close relationship with the regulated company, has turned out to be extremely difficult.

NEXT, ENFORCE

Setting standards is the easiest part of environmental policy. Enforcing them is many times harder. One is typically done by politicians, often at a national (or, in the case of Europe, a supranational) level. The other is generally done by public servants, regionally or locally.

Often, politicians appear to have little understanding of the consequences of their decisions for the bodies that have to enforce them. In the United States, for example, the Toxic Substances Control Act calls for separate testing rules for each chemical. But new chemicals come on to the market at the rate of 1000 a year. Not surprisingly, only a tiny number has been tested for harmful effects.

More glaring examples of the gap between legislative intention and actual enforcement are to be found in Eastern and Western Europe. In Eastern Europe, many of the standards set by governments in communist days were at least as high as those in the West. For example, East European standards for air quality often set 24-hour top limits that were not only tougher than America's, but similar to the annual *average* concentrations implied in the standards of the EU. Water that met American standards for dissolved oxygen would have fallen into the second-lowest of four classifications typically used in Eastern Europe. Unsurprisingly, these ludicrously high standards were never enforced. A survey in Poland, in the first days after communism, looked at pollution fees paid by 1400 manufacturing enterprises. It found that, on average, these amounted to 0.6 per cent of costs.[5]

In the EU, there are notoriously wide differences in the extent to which member states comply with environmental directives agreed by the Council of Ministers. The British, who complain that they play by the rules, feel especially bitter about the failure of such countries as Italy and Greece to abide by environmental standards to which they have agreed. Where (as in the case of Italy, for instance) local governments have the task of enforcing environmental standards, it is particularly difficult for the Brussels Commission to do anything about non-compliance.

COSY OR DISTANT?

Countries vary considerably in the amount of discretion they give their regulators and the kind of relationship their regulators are expected to establish with potential polluters. Such differences are important: the more regulators collaborate with industry, the less regulation may impose unnecessary costs on an economy. But greater is the danger that polluters will not be forced to clean up.

At one extreme is the United States, where regulators tend to have an adversarial relationship with the bodies under their control. They apply legally enforceable standards in ways that allow little flexibility. If they deviate from the letter of the law, they risk law suits from indignant environmentalists. Such rigidity has drawbacks. It may make compliance more expensive. And it results in a great deal of litigation between regulator and polluter, which adds still more to the costs of cleaning up.

At the other extreme is Britain. Angus Smith, the man who laid the foundations of Britain's pollution inspectorate in the mid-nineteenth century, gave a classic description of the way a regulator might behave. "There are two modes of inspection," he said. "One is by a suspicious opponent, desirous of finding evil and ready to make the most of it. The other is that of a friendly adviser, who treats those whom he visits as gentlemen desirous of doing right." No prizes for guessing which approach Smith inculcated into British pollution inspectors! The tradition of negotiating ways to fulfill the spirit of the law has helped to hold down costs. But environmentalists suspect that sometimes it may have restrained clean-up operations as well. One of the aims of Britain's 1990 Environmental Protection Act was to encourage the government to drop its gentlemanly approach.

An insuperable difficulty with regulation – any kind of regulation

– is what economists call "regulatory capture". Regulators find it extremely hard to keep a proper distance from the companies they oversee. The more discretion they have, the more they are likely to ask for information from the company. That will give companies a great deal of power. Moreover, regulators, as public servants, are rarely well paid – especially when their pay is compared with the value to a company of getting a favorable decision. That makes them vulnerable to bribery in some countries, but to a more subtle kind of pressure in others, where they may hope to move eventually from the public to the private sector – to work for the very companies they have been regulating.

Regulators who snuggle up too close to companies may not push them hard enough to raise standards. But some regulators will succumb to an alternative temptation: of "gold-plating".[6] They may impose tougher standards than are strictly needed in order to increase their authority and (perhaps) the size of their budget. The temptation may be strongest for regulators allowed to recover their costs from the companies they regulate. As companies see it, some regulators simply get pleasure from bossing about better-paid businessmen.

Countries need to set the risks of such regulatory failures against the costs of a less flexible regime. The key problem is how far to allow regulators the freedom to balance the costs of cleaning up against the environmental benefits. The problem reveals what is, in the eyes of economists, the primary difficulty with regulation. If standards are applied rigidly across an entire industry, some companies will find it extremely expensive to comply, while others will find it relatively cheap.

In the United States, where regulators have little flexibility, legislators have typically dealt with this issue by imposing higher standards on new technologies and polluters than on old ones. The classic instance is that of the Clean Air Act. Under this act, standards for the sulphur dioxide output of coal-burning power stations were set in the early 1970s at a level deliberately chosen to protect the coal miners of the eastern United States.[7] The standard for high-sulphur coal was pitched at a level that would allow electricity utilities in the eastern states to invest in scrubbers to clean the sulphurous gases from their chimneys and yet continue to burn local coal.

But installing a scrubber was so expensive that the utilities found it cheaper to switch to low-sulphur coal mined in the west instead. Eastern-state miners lobbied Congress, and in 1977 the rules were changed: all coal burnt in new power plants was to be scrubbed, low-sulphur or not.

In most countries, flexibility in the application of regulations generally takes the place of legislated discrimination between old and new. In Britain, for instance, pollution inspectors would control air emissions by working out the "best practicable means" in consultation with the relevant industry. The Environmental Protection Act of 1990 introduced the concept of BATNEEC: "best available technique not entailing excess cost". The aim of the act was to insist that companies use the best technique available (and not just in Britain, but worldwide), while keeping in mind the trade-off between the cost of compliance and environmental benefit. That, however, has not been easy. Regulators have sometimes been dependent on companies to tell them what are the best means available; and inevitably have been dependent on them to some extent to work out which measures "entail excess cost".

Regulation, as Chapter 5 argues, often has shortcomings compared with the use of economic incentives to encourage polluters to clean up voluntarily. But those shortcomings are especially striking in the American regulatory system. It may be that, as European regulation grows tougher, the costs will increase. For the moment, the biggest savings to the economy from using economic incentives are to be made in the country where the regulatory process is most rigid.

Chapter 5

Taxes and Permits

Environmental policies cost countries a large and increasing amount of money. Most developed countries spend between 1 per cent and 2 per cent of their gross domestic product on environmental protection, and that proportion is likely to rise over the rest of the century. It is therefore important not just that environmental priorities are carefully chosen, but that policies are applied in the most cost-effective way possible. Otherwise, their impact on economic growth is more likely to be unacceptably high to the governments that have to enforce them.

As the previous chapter explained, regulation is by far the most common tool of environmental policy. Most economists agree, however, that regulation generally delivers less clean-up per penny than alternatives which create economic incentives to reduce pollution. That suggests a paradox, which this chapter explores: why have governments so rarely used the more efficient environmental-policy measures?

Economists do not believe that regulation works well as a policy tool, for the following reasons:

- Regulation encourages government to do what it does worst: second-guess companies about what is the best technology to achieve a particular goal.
- Regulation rarely attempts to balance costs and benefits. Indeed, the costs are often disguised: if water companies have to install expensive sewage-treatment equipment and so raise their rates, customers may blame the companies, not the government, for setting higher standards.
- If regulations are strictly enforced, they tend to load high costs on to some polluters, low costs on to others. A company that is installing new plant may find it relatively cheap to meet higher regulatory standards simply by changing the specifications for equipment. A company with a lot of old plant, making low profits and not investing, will find that stricter regulations drive it out of business. But in fact regulations are often tougher for new entrants to an industry than for existing firms. As a result, they may discourage investment in new equipment – even if it is cleaner than the old.
- Regulation tends to set a floor as well as a ceiling. No polluter has any incentive to discharge even less dirty waste into the local river, say, than the regulations allow; and no entrepreneur has an incentive to develop technology that reduces pollution even below the regulation minimum.
- Regulations work best when they are applied to a few large polluters. But as pollution increasingly comes from many small sources – cars, farms, dry-cleaners, rubbish bins – governments will have to turn to taxes and fees to encourage clean-up. What people do with their rubbish or their spent batteries is often as important a cause of pollution as what a steel mill does with its waste.

Given the drawbacks of regulation, why do governments persist with what Americans call "command and control"? Part of the answer, as the previous chapter argued, is that regulation is often more flexibly applied than economists realize. But regulation is also comforting: governments know what they are asking for, people know what they are getting, and companies know what they are supposed to deliver. Moreover, because regulation generally conceals the true costs of a policy, environmental standards can be set higher than they would be if their true costs were understood. That pleases environmentalists. But economic incentives have drawbacks too.

Using the Market

Broadly speaking, economic environmental instruments fall into two categories. Some, such as "green taxes" or fees, put a price on pollution that – in theory – reflects the cost it imposes on society. The extent to which pollution will then be reduced is often hard to predict. Other instruments, such as "marketable permits", discussed below, are based on an absolute quantity of pollution that is to be allowed, and then give or sell polluters rights to pollute up to that given limit. Polluters can trade these rights with each other if they wish. Tradable permits make it easy to predict the total amount of pollution, but extremely difficult to determine what the effective "tax" on polluters will be. While green taxes set a price and then allow quantity to fluctuate, tradable permits set quantity and then allow the price to find its own level.

These economic instruments, properly applied, can save money *and* deliver the same environmental quality as regulation. The savings arise primarily from the fact that companies decide whether to pay a tax (or buy a permit to pollute) or whether to invest in cleaning up. Those for whom cleaning up is most cost-effective will do so; and indeed may choose to go well beyond the standard set for all polluters. Those for whom cleaning up is not cost-effective will choose, instead, to pay the cost of continuing to pollute.

In the early 1980s, governments were rarely interested in taxing pollution.[1] Some levied environmental charges, but mainly as an adjunct to regulation rather than an alternative. Typically, such charges were a way to raise revenue to pay regulators. Moreover, they were almost always too low to have much of an effect on the behavior of people or companies. Of course, fees could always be increased, but governments hate doing that.

In the late 1980s, however, the use of economic measures to tackle pollution became more common. A survey by the OECD found that, between 1987 and early 1993, the number of economic instruments used by its member countries increased by between 25 per cent and 50 per cent, according to the country.[2] In Sweden, where they are most common, 20 separate instruments existed at the beginning of 1992, including a tax on nitrous oxides and another on batteries containing mercury or cadmium.

The most widespread application of an economic incentive for environmental ends has been the use of the tax system in eight OECD countries, including Britain, to give unleaded petrol a price advantage over the leaded sort. There are other examples. France, Norway and Sweden all tax sulphur. Several countries, notably Japan, Switzerland, The Netherlands and Germany, impose higher landing charges on noisier planes (a policy made easier by the fact that noisy planes tend to be old ones, flown principally by the airlines of the poorer countries). And many countries charge for water pollution, though frequently at a flat rate.

By far the most widely discussed economic instrument has been a carbon tax: a tax on the carbon content of fuels (intended to reduce the impact that carbon dioxide may have on global warming). Denmark, Finland, Norway, Sweden and The Netherlands have all introduced carbon taxes, although only Sweden has used the tax as a partial replacement for other energy taxes. Up to 1995, ministers of the European Union had several discussions of the carbon tax, but reached no decisions.

The OECD also recorded a strong growth in deposit-refund schemes. Countries have used deposits mainly to try to reduce packaging waste. Nine American states and several European countries impose deposits for drinks bottles and cans. A review of American schemes in 1990 by the General Accounting Office found that they reduced litter by 10–20 per cent by weight and 40–60 per cent by volume. Using deposit schemes for items with such low initial value is not cost-effective. Better are the deposit schemes applied in some countries to persuade people to return their old car at the end of its life, rather than dumping the hulk in the countryside; and to hand back lubricant oils, which amateur oil-changers often tip down the drain.

The rarest economic environmental instrument in use, according to the OECD survey, is the tradable permit. Outside the United States, there are only half a dozen instances. But in the United States, the OECD recorded eight such schemes, the largest of them set up by the 1990 Clean Air Act to allow trade in permits to emit sulphur dioxide.

The OECD's list does not include environmental subsidies. Yet many countries support environmental investments with government grants or cheap loans. Sometimes, the subsidy goes to municipalities (as in the case of the sewage-treatment program in the United States, 75 per cent of the cost of which comes from federal funds); sometimes the recipient is an individual, as in the case of Britain's grants to help low-income families insulate their homes. The OECD does not really like such subsidies, because they often go to polluters to help them to clean up, thus conflicting with the "polluter pays" principle.

GREEN TAXES

Environmental taxes offer one huge benefit to governments that are hungry for cash. They raise revenue. Regulations may achieve the same environmental goals, and may raise the costs faced by polluters in the same way taxes raise them – although polluters will be more conscious of the increase in costs when it takes the transparent form of a tax. But the rise in costs that regulation causes yields no revenue for the public purse.

Moreover, the revenue from green taxation is raised in ways that may well make the economy work better. Instead of discouraging behavior that makes an economy richer (such as hard work or saving) as most taxes do, environmental taxes are levied on behavior that makes an economy poorer (such as water pollution or waste creation). Just as an economy works better if its citizens are deterred by the tax system from smoking or drinking themselves to death, so it also works better if government does not have to spend money cleaning rivers and decontaminating land. In 1994 Denmark made this principle one of the keystones of a big tax-reform program: the government aimed to cut income tax over a period of five years, and to meet the cost partly by introducing a broad range of "green" taxes.

Where environmental taxes have been tried, they have generally proved effective. In Britain, for example, excise duties have been adjusted so that the price of leaded petrol has risen increasingly, relative to the price of unleaded. Partly as a result, lead emissions from the exhausts of British cars fell by 70 per cent in the decade to 1990. When Sweden introduced a charge of 4500 Ecus ($6000) per ton on nitrous oxide emissions from power stations in 1992, average emissions fell 35 per cent within two years. A Swedish tax on the sulphur content of diesel fuel resulted, within 18 months, in a ten-fold rise in the share of "clean" diesel in total diesel consumption.

Given their advantages, it is odd that environmental taxes have not been used more widely. Certainly in the late 1980s and early 1990s there was a notable increase in the frequency with which governments and their advisers talked about them. Governments (and academic economists) have been especially taken with the notion of a carbon tax. It offers a way to encourage a switch away from carbon-intensive fuels (basically coal) towards less carbon-rich fossil fuels (which means oil and natural gas) or even fuels that release no carbon dioxide when they are used (mainly nuclear fuels). To tax fossil fuels in proportion to their carbon content would be simple, at least compared with most other environmental taxes: it could be imposed at the mine gate or oil-well head. But few governments have actually introduced such a tax.

One reason for their lack of enthusiasm may be the difficulties governments encountered when they tried to raise energy taxes and present the increase in environmental terms. President Bill Clinton's attempts to introduce an energy tax foundered; the British government's plan to raise value-added tax on domestic fuel and light to 17.5 per cent in two successive bites was deeply unpopular (and withdrawn in November 1994). Environmentalists, keen on the idea of carbon taxes, did virtually nothing to support such policies, on the unreasonable grounds that their main aim was not environmental protection but revenue-raising. If environmental taxation is to succeed, environmentalists will have to learn to be less squeamish.

When Taxes Fail

Why have green taxes not been more widely used? There seem to be several reasons. Environmentalists often feel uneasy about supporting these taxes because they see them as a way of making money from dirt. More important, environmentalists – and politicians – are usually unwilling to see regulatory control removed when a green tax is introduced, and companies feel they are being charged twice: first they must meet a minimum regulatory standard, and then pay the taxes. As a result, it is hard for governments to set levies high enough to be effective.

The problem with all new taxes is that somebody has to pay them – and those who perceive themselves as hurt are usually better at complaining than those who will benefit. The key weakness of a carbon tax, in political terms, is that it would fall mainly on coal, and miners have been a highly effective lobby. At present, most governments tax oil heavily, natural gas more lightly, and coal hardly at all; indeed, several countries, including green Germany, subsidize coal-mining. The Clinton administration realized early on that a pure carbon tax would fall disproportionately on coal-producing regions and was therefore politically doomed. When the European Commission tried to invent a tax that would allow the EU to stabilize its output of carbon dioxide, it came to a similar conclusion.

A pure carbon tax would have fallen mainly on coal-burning countries (such as Germany and Britain) and benefited France, with its vast nuclear power industry. The Commission therefore proposed a mongrel tax which was half on the carbon content of fuels and half on the use of energy, thus destroying its internal logic.

Another problem has been the effect of environmental taxes on the poor. When they are levied on personal consumption, rather than on companies, they frequently tend to be regressive. This problem has especially bedevilled attempts in both Britain and the United States to raise taxes on energy. In Britain, the richest one-fifth of households use only 30 per cent more fuel than the poorest fifth. In the United States, too, energy makes a larger hole in the pockets of the poor than the rich: the poorest fifth of Americans spend 7.5 per cent of their budgets on energy, the richest fifth, 4.7 per cent.

Politicians have also worried about the effects of a new indirect tax on inflation and competitiveness. It was worries about competitiveness that led the European Commission to suggest exempting the most energy-intensive industries from its proposed carbon-cum-energy tax.

To such worries, there are ready answers. One way to avoid the inflationary impact of a new environmental tax is to announce it well in advance. That way, people and companies have a chance, when buying new equipment, to think ahead. That was exactly the policy followed by the British government when it increased value-added tax on domestic fuel and light. The drawback, it became clear, was that opponents of the tax had more time to fight it. The British government has also promised an indefinite increase in duties on road fuels, of 5 per cent a year in real terms. Such an increase, which will eventually make a substantial difference to the costs of motoring, gives people (and companies) ample warning of the need to invest in more energy-efficient vehicles.

The complaint that green taxes harm competitiveness also has an answer, which boils down to: compared with what? Opponents of green taxes rarely compare their effects with other ways of achieving the same goal. If environmental objectives are met by regulation, the costs to the economy will be higher, and the burden on individual industries at least as great as, if environmental taxation were used instead. And even if green taxes are not used as substitutes for regulation, and are intended mainly to raise revenue, their effects should be compared to other instruments for revenue-raising. If a budget deficit causes interest rates to rise, or if it is reduced by raising corporate taxes instead of taxes on energy, the impact on competitiveness may be greater. Moreover, if the budget deficit is reduced by cutting welfare benefits, the impact on the poor may be greater than if it is cut by increasing value-added tax on fuel and light. To look at environmental taxes in isolation is wrong.

Many of the politically controversial side-effects of green taxes can be partly offset by deftly using the revenue they yield. For example, the poor can be compensated to some extent by an increase in welfare benefits, or by grants to help them to insulate their homes. The effects on corporate competitiveness can be partly offset by using the tax revenues to reduce company taxes. The revenues may be used to subsidize the reduction of pollution. Thus the revenue from road pricing can be designated to build better public transport.

The British Treasury has always been hostile to the idea that revenues from a particular tax should be earmarked for a particular purpose. That hostility is based on a sound principle: the tax is never likely to yield precisely the correct amount to finance whatever project is linked to its revenue. But until ways are devised to recycle the revenue of green taxes, their use is unlikely to spread far.

One way around some of the criticisms of environmental taxes is to design a tax as a closed circuit: companies that produced more than a certain amount of pollution would pay a tax whose revenue would be recycled in a subsidy paid on a sliding scale to those who produced less than the benchmark. Such a tax-cum-subsidy would yield no revenue, but might be more politically acceptable than a straight tax.

Britain's transport ministry devised a scheme on these lines to increase the fuel efficiency of cars. Under its proposal, put to Brussels early in 1992, a single target would have been set for all

new cars produced in or imported into the European Community.
Manufacturers whose cars beat the target would have received
credits; those that did not would have to deposit credits with a
regulatory body. The credits could either have been bought from
the manufacturers of fuel-efficient cars, or earned on more frugal
vehicles from the manufacturer's own production line. The target
would have been progressively tightened over the years. The
scheme would have raised the price of large cars and cut the price
of smaller ones. It got nowhere. Why? Europe's biggest producer
of gas guzzlers is Germany. Germany was naturally unenthusiastic
about the plan.

MARKETABLE PERMITS

Permit-trading schemes have an intellectual elegance that academic
economists love, but they are even less common than green taxes.
They crop up more often in economic textbooks than on statute
books. They have been used mainly in the United States; outside
America, with one exception described later in this chapter, they
are virtually unknown.

In essence, a regulator sets a ceiling on the amount of pollution
allowed for a whole industry, and issues permits, or credits, to
individual firms for their share in that amount. If the permits are
auctioned off, the effect is like a tax: those who acquire permits pay
the regulator for the privilege. In the real world, permits are usually
"grandfathered" – an American expression implying that those
involved in the permitted activity are given enough permits to allow
them to continue to do what they have been doing. Polluters can
then buy or sell permits, so that those who can clean up cheaply do
so and then make money by selling spare permission to pollute to
those for whom cleaning up would be more expensive.

The key point about such schemes is that they allow governments
to set the precise amount of pollution that they are prepared to
allow: something they would do with regulation, but could not do

with a tax. If a tax is not set high enough to reduce pollution by as much as politicians want, then it has to be increased; a permit scheme, on the other hand, can (at least in theory) guarantee a ceiling on the amount of pollution that will occur. By lowering the number of permits over time, or buying them up and canceling them, government can reduce or even eliminate allowable pollution. Environmental groups can also, at least in theory, buy up permits and thus reduce the amount of pollution allowed.

Easily the most successful experiment with marketable permits (also known as tradable permits or pollution credits) was carried out in the United States. In 1985 the Environmental Protection Agency gave oil refineries two years in which to cut the lead content of petrol. Refineries received quotas for lead, which they could trade with each other. The effect was to let them phase in the cut in lead at their own pace. Half of all the refineries took part in trading.

The lead scheme worked because the amount of lead in petrol could easily be monitored with existing regulatory machinery; the number of firms involved was quite small; and the program ran for a limited time. A much more ambitious scheme was launched in America's 1990 Clean Air Act. It set a limit, which will be gradually reduced, on the amount of sulphur dioxide that can be emitted by power stations and other big polluters. The scheme grew out of the recommendations of Project 88, a highly influential review of market-based approaches to pollution, commissioned by two senators, a Democrat and a Republican, and delivered at the Republican presidential convention in August 1988.[3]

The sulphur dioxide trading scheme was designed with three key features. First, the act set a cap on the total emissions allowed. That, in the words of Dan Dudek of the Environmental Defense Fund, who helped to design the scheme, left a role for politicians: "that of passing out the pork". Instead of arguing about the level of emissions, they could argue about how emissions were shared out. Secondly, it had draconian penalties: essential, because the value of pollution permits is devalued if some participants cheat. Third, to ensure that some trading between firms took place, the government retained up to 5 per cent of the permits to auction off. That was intended to have two other effects: to stop established companies hoarding permits and so keeping out newcomers; and to provide a public reference price. If a utility demands a price rise to pay for scrubbers on its smokestacks, the regulator should be able to say, "The market price for polluting is much lower. Buy some permits and go on polluting instead."

Inevitably, the scheme has had teething troubles. American electricity utilities, the main targets, are highly regulated regional monopolies. They are not the best guinea pigs for a system designed on the assumption that they will behave like profit-maximizing companies. Moreover, the approach of state utility regulators has not always been helpful.

An earlier scheme to allow trading in air-pollution permits resulted in trades within individual firms, but hardly any between firms. The main reason was that America's litigious environment-alists objected to the idea that companies should have a right to pollute, let alone that they should be able to make money by selling the right to another firm. That attitude affected the way some American chief executives viewed the sulphur-trading scheme. The head of one chemical company, asked whether his firm would sell its sulphur dioxide permits, was adamant: "What would people say if we sold? That we had reduced our pollution simply in order to allow another company to pollute – and for a profit?"

A more promising use for marketable permits may be in the fishing industry. Several countries allocate to fishermen shares in a total fishery, and then encourage them to buy and sell their rights. If fishermen are simply given quotas, they have every incentive to cheat and catch fish that should be left in the sea to breed future stocks. If they can be persuaded to treat their share of the fishery as a farmer treats his land, then they may be encouraged to leave enough fish to breed at a sustainable rate.

In New Zealand, such a scheme has had mixed results. It has worked well with abalone beds, where fishermen have voluntarily stepped up security to stop poachers. But in one of the country's most valuable fisheries, for the orange roughy, there have been problems. After quotas had been allocated, scientists discovered that the breeding cycle of the fish was far slower than they had believed. The quotas had to be bought back by the government at huge expense and reduced.

To prevent such problems, the government of the Australian state of New South Wales came up with a different scheme in 1994. It created a system of dual rights. Fishermen will have a tradable right to a share of a fishery. The right will be registered, like a land title, and will determine matters such as the gear fishermen can use and the size of their boats. That right will last for ten years, renewable during the period. But the overall size of the catch will be set each year, and then shared out on the basis of the original rights. The idea is to build in flexibility, so that the total size of the catch can vary as conditions and scientific evidence change.

Some of the schemes proposed to limit the rate of growth of greenhouse gases rely on trading "carbon quotas" between countries. The richer countries agreed in the climate treaty signed in Rio to devise plans to restore to their 1990 levels the amount of global-warming carbon dioxide they produce. About half the OECD countries promised to reach this goal by 2000 or 2005. Reducing carbon dioxide emissions will be cheapest for countries that use energy uneconomically (like most of the former Communist countries). So other, more energy-efficient countries might meet part of their target by investing in energy-saving technologies in energy-inefficient countries. Norway has begun one project in Poland to substitute natural gas for coal (which gives off more carbon dioxide than gas for the same amount of energy) in residential heating, and another in Mexico to install energy-efficient lighting.

The most appropriate use for tradable quotas might be not between countries, but within them. The goal of stabilization is a fixed total, which might be allocated most efficiently by being divided up and shared out (or auctioned off). As most of the rich world's carbon dioxide comes from burning fossil fuels, the simplest method would be through rationing the amount of such fuels that could be burnt, but allowing companies to trade their ration. But even the suggestion of such a scheme makes most people shake their heads – a measure not of its impracticality, but of the improbability that countries will take their treaty commitment seriously.

THE LIMITS TO THE MARKET

Why have permit-trading schemes not been used more widely? Some of their shortcomings are obvious. The basic difficulty is persuading polluters (or fishermen) that they have a credible property right in the pollutant they are allowed to emit, or the fish they are allowed to catch. It requires a large political effort to make such rights as credible as the right to a piece of land or a share in a company.[4]

That credibility is undermined each time the underlying right is altered: for example, if the size of fish stocks changes, or a pollutant turns out to be more damaging than was thought. And it is undermined if there is widespread cheating, or if measurement proves difficult, as is often the case with discharges of gas or waste. Because correct measurement is essential to make an emissions-trading scheme work, the monitoring costs may be much higher than with ordinary regulation, which generally assumes that it is not cost-effective to prevent all cheating.

Measurement is easiest in a market where there is a relatively small number of large polluters. On the other hand, trading works best in a market with lots of smallish players. And the main sources of pollution are increasingly individuals and small businesses, rather than large corporations.

Trading schemes are most appropriate in situations where the impact of pollution is the same everywhere. In Britain, a plan to allow electricity utilities to increase the sulphur dioxide output of some plants if they made corresponding reductions elsewhere ran into protests from those living downwind of the plants that proposed to burn a highly sulphurous heavy oil. The impact of most pollutants varies from place to place; it is difficult to incorporate that fact into permit-trading schemes.

Finally, trading the right to pollute raises strong emotions. When the richer countries have offered to meet their goals for carbon dioxide cuts partly by paying for energy-saving measures in the developing world, the poorer countries have sometimes accused them of trying to buy their way out of their environmental responsibilities.

Given all the difficulties, should environmental economists abandon their enthusiasm for market-based incentives? Certainly not. There are obvious instances, especially in energy use, where market mechanisms will achieve more environmental improvement than regulation. But the first priority should be to look for ways of making regulation more efficient and market-friendly; and the second should be to stop governments pursuing policies that make neither environmental nor economic sense. Such policies are the subject of the next chapter.

Chapter 6

Natural-Resource Management and Subsidies

Green taxes and tradable permits are designed to remedy the environmental damage that takes place when markets fail to reflect the value of environmental assets and the costs of environmental damage. The solution is to increase government intervention: either to use the tax system to raise prices to reflect the true costs of pollution, or to establish property rights which can then be traded in the market. However, much environmental damage occurs because government, not the market, fails.

The role of governments in environmental management is difficult but inescapable. Governments have to reconcile the multiple demands on a country's most sensitive natural resources, such as fresh water, its forests and fisheries. Often, the ownership of such resources is vested mainly in the state. But the way governments allocate access to natural resources is frequently environmentally harmful. Sometimes, the state tries to manage the resources it owns, and does so badly. There are powerful arguments for separating the roles of owner and manager. However, even when governments allow the private sector to exploit state-owned resources – by selling logging or fishing rights, for instance – they may fail to set the conditions for access in a way that ensures efficient use of those resources.

Often, however, governments act in an even more harmful way. They actually subsidize the exploitation and consumption of natural resources. A whole range of policies, from farm-price support to protection for coal-mining, do environmental damage and (generally) make no economic sense. Scrapping them offers a two-fold bonus: a cleaner environment and a more efficient economy. Growth and greenery can actually go hand in hand, if politicians have the courage to confront the vested interests that subsidies create.

FORESTS

The vast majority of the earth's forests are state-owned. Their disappearance – one-fifth of the world's rain forests have vanished this century, and the pace is accelerating – is one of the most striking instances of governments' failure to protect the natural resources that they own.

In theory, the state should be a better owner of forests than a private individual or company, since its time horizon should be much longer than that of the private owner. But in practice, the forest may be managed by officials whose time horizon is as long as their expected tenure of their job, and who may therefore accept bribes to turn a blind eye to rapid deforestation.

Even when state officials are not corrupt, governments frequently set the fees for logging permits at levels too low to reflect the costs of replanting. A survey by the World Bank of such "stumpage" fees, as a share of replacement costs, found that they covered less than 5 per cent in Niger, Senegal and Sudan, and less than 15 per cent in Côte d'Ivoire and Kenya.[1] In the United States, too, the federal government has long sold rights to logging, grazing and mining in national parks for sums that not only fail to reflect the environmental cost of such activities but also often underestimate their commercial value.

Of course, higher fees for logging rights will not necessarily lead to better conservation, although they will provide governments with the cash to monitor logging practices properly. But it is also essential that loggers have concessions that run for long enough to give them an interest in future crops of trees, rather than simply in the first felling. In Borneo, for instance, concessions tend to run for 20 or 25 years, and to be handed out free to the government's political cronies, who subcontract them for one or two years to smaller operators. Their only incentive is to cut as fast as possible. One scheme, advocated by the Asian Development Bank, would give logging rights to whoever offered to post the highest guarantee bond. The bond, invested for the life of the scheme, would be forfeit if the logger failed to protect the forest. Another option is to award perpetual leases, for an annual rent, reviewed every five years and revoked if the holder misbehaved. Making the leases tradable would be an incentive to maintain the value of the concession.

It will be harder to protect forests if governments are simul-taneously encouraging deforestation in other ways. The danger with logging in rain-forest countries is that it opens land for farmers and settlers, especially if roads follow the loggers. Land law in many developing countries makes clearing the trees a condition of gaining title. In Brazil, the drift of settlers into the Amazon region has been fostered by government policies that subsidize the economic development of the north of the country, including (in the past) tax breaks for cattle ranching.

Private ownership of forests may sometimes give them more protection than the state does – especially if the state is loath to spend money on enforcing rules about logging and settlement. Private owners have an incentive to manage a forest to extract the largest possible yield – some of it, perhaps, non-financial – over a long period of time. If land rights depend on planting or maintaining trees, rather than chopping them down, they are one more incentive to preserve a forest.

Reconciling the goals of conservation and commercial exploit-ation is never easy. The New Zealand government adopted an inno-vative solution to the problem in its state forests. It sold off to commercial loggers the cutting rights to forests that were deemed to be of low environmental value. Meanwhile the remaining stretches of virgin rain forest are still state-owned, and managed primarily for their environmental value. Some developing countries have also tried to introduce "ecological zoning", setting aside the forests with the greatest environmental value for conservation. But when the British government proposed a similar division of forests, environmentalists complained that commercial forests would be closed to recreational use. Even in natural-resource management, environmentalists need to learn to set priorities.

FISHERIES

Similar problems of managing exploitation exist with fisheries. Since 1950 the world's fish catch has increased almost five-fold. But in 1989 it appeared to peak and then start to decline. If the catch were measured by value instead of by weight, the decline would be even more obvious: as the most valuable stocks are fished out, fishermen tend to catch other, less valuable species. The problem of overfishing is almost entirely the fault of government misman-agement: only 10 per cent or so of the world's catch is found in international waters. The rest is found within 200 nautical miles of some country's shore.

Just as governments rarely charge loggers much for removing wood from state forests, so they hardly ever charge fishermen for the right to catch the fish off their shores. The few governments that impose such charges generally set the price low: typically no more than 5 per cent of the value of the catch. If governments were to treat fisheries as communal resources, to which fishermen should be charged admission, the results would be dramatic. The fisheries of the Falkland Islands, whose management is handled with advice from academics from London's Imperial College, are exploited mostly by foreign fleets. When the islands introduced charges of up to 28 per cent of the value of the catch, the result was uproar from the foreign fishermen. But the increased fees also yielded vast revenues – enough to quadruple the islands' (admittedly small) GDP – and brought in a stream of revenue that could be used to pay for policing and management. Charges and policing together thus help to prevent overfishing.

Instead of charging fishermen for the right to catch, governments often subsidize them. State cash helps to pay for larger boats, longer nets and more sophisticated equipment. Yet at a guess, it would need only one-fifth of the world's fishing fleet to catch the maximum yield of fish that the oceans can sustain. If governments feel politically obliged to pay fishermen, they should create incentives to stop catching fish, not to encourage more capacity to chase a limited supply.

WATER

Countries generally regard water as a free good, which governments have a duty to supply. But water is frequently used wastefully, simply because it costs nothing. One result of this approach is that governments squander large amounts of taxpayers' money building new water-supply systems. Another consequence is environmental damage. Streams are diverted, rivers are run low, wetlands drained, dams built: all because governments find it politically easier to search for new water sources than to make users pay a price that reflects the true costs of supply.

By far the largest demand for water comes from irrigation, which uses 73 per cent of the world's fresh water. Even in rich countries, where industry is the largest single user of water, agriculture still uses 39 per cent. In poor countries, agriculture typically accounts for more than 90 per cent.[2] In most countries, farmers get water at prices that rarely reflect more than a fraction of the operating costs of water systems, let alone their capital costs or the environmental consequences of water withdrawal. In Arizona, for example, farmers pay less than 1 cent for a cubic metre of water, while the residents of Phoenix pay about 25 cents.[3]

In poor countries, public irrigation projects tend to be a huge burden on government budgets and aid programs (in the 1980s irrigation accounted for more than a quarter of World Bank loans for agriculture). Often other layers of subsidies promote the wasteful use of water. Crops are subsidized, for instance; so is the electricity used to drive pumps. In an increasing number of dry countries, the main use of water is to grow crops that are worth less than the water itself. One unpublished World Bank study of Cyprus argued that three-quarters of the island's crops were uneconomic and grown only because water was subsidized.

Even without such subsidies, farming is often the least productive use of water. In poor countries its use is even less productive than in rich countries: they typically use twice as much water per acre but achieve crop yields that are only one-third as high. If farmers had to bid directly against industries and cities for the water they use, they would frequently be outpriced.

The overuse of irrigation water has harmful environmental consequences, as well as economic costs. In 1986 the American Department of Agriculture said that more than a quarter of the country's 21 million irrigated acres was being watered by lowering the water table. Under parts of the north China plain, around Beijing and Tienjin, the water table is dropping by one to two metres a year. In the former Soviet Union the area covered by the Aral Sea dwindled by 40 per cent between 1960 and the late 1980s, mainly because of irrigation water drawn from the rivers feeding it.

For governments it is often politically difficult to remove subsidies from agriculture, especially when – as in many poor countries – the sector employs more than half the workforce. Instead, it is easier to build another dam (especially if foreigners will pay for it). So governments spend vast sums on developing new water supplies. Mexico proposes to pump water up over 1000 metres into the Valley of Mexico; China intends to divert 5 per cent of the flow of the Yangtze River to its dry northern provinces; Alaska's erstwhile governor, Walter Hickel, daydreamed of piping water from his state to California.

Often, the cost of such grandiose schemes is borne by foreigners, or by the central government. As a result, local water users get a bargain. In the American west, federally financed dams have in the past been a routine alternative to sensible allocation and pricing of existing water resources. In developing countries, most dams have been financed by foreign aid, and especially by the World Bank, the largest single financing agency for dams.

As cities grow, governments will increasingly be forced to reconsider their approach. At an international conference in Dublin in 1992, a large number of governments signed a declaration which said, in effect, that water was an economic good and should be treated as such. Once that fact is recognized, the opportunities for imaginative husbandry of water are greatly improved. The gap between the value of a gallon of water to a farmer and to a thirsty townsman is so enormous, and agriculture's use of water so large, that deals can be struck.

During the 1980s, a vibrant water market (complete with its own quarterly trade journal) sprang up in the western United States, with buyers snapping up farmers' water rights to provide water for cities. Los Angeles made a deal with the farmers of the Central Valley in California: by paying for improvements to reduce wastage from irrigation channels, the city acquired more water at less than half the cost of the cheapest alternative, while farmers got cash and no reduction in their quotas. Such deals work only when it is clear who owns the water. When water rights are state property, deals are harder to reach.

Some people argue that charging for water will not encourage more frugal use. They should examine what has happened in the United States. There, water consumption by manufacturing industry in 2000 is expected to be only one-third of what it was in 1977, mainly because of the increased costs of disposing of wastewater. And whenever farmers draw their water from privately owned tube wells, as they do in the Punjab, they irrigate notably more efficiently. If water is cheap, it will be wasted. Price it properly, and people will find more efficient ways to use it.

ENERGY

The production and distribution of energy are, in many countries, closely controlled by the state. The failure of governments to price energy properly means that consumption is higher and grows faster than ought to be the case. The problem of underpricing is worst in developing countries. But it exists in rich countries too. For example, many subsidize company cars in a variety of ways. Indeed, one Dutch study argued that company-owned cars produce five times as much pollution as privately owned vehicles, because they tend to be larger and driven further.[4]

The effects of undercharging are clearest in electricity generation. In the developing countries, according to World Bank estimates, average electricity tariffs are half those in industrialized countries. In India prices are about 40 per cent of the global average; in China, about half those of India. Whereas average tariffs in the OECD countries rose by 1.4 per cent a year in real terms between 1979 and 1988, they fell by 3.5 per cent a year in developing countries.

The reason electricity is cheap in many developing countries has nothing to do with efficient supply industries. On the contrary: building power stations typically takes longer than in the rich world; the average utility often employs more people (120 customers per employee is typical, compared with nearly 300 per employee in efficient South Korea); and losses during transmission, partly from theft, run at extraordinary levels – 22 per cent of electricity generated is lost in transmission in India, for example, compared with only 8 per cent in the United States. Underpricing reflects, instead, the prevalence of government subsidies. A great many third-world utilities are kept afloat by state hand-outs. Worried about the effect that increases in energy prices might have on inflation, third-world governments have perversely preferred to print the money and try to hold prices down instead.

Underpricing, inevitably, encourages consumption. The World Bank reckons that developing countries use 10–20 per cent more electricity than they would if consumers paid the true marginal cost of supply. Other energy products are often subsidized too. Developing countries frequently impose high taxes on petrol, but subsidize kerosene, diesel and fuel oil. The subsidy on kerosene might be justified on the grounds that it is the fuel the poor use to cook; the alternative might be greater deforestation. But in Brazil, which probably uses 5 per cent more petroleum products than it would if prices were not distorted, the kerosene subsidy goes mainly to the rich, because they buy the most fuel.

State support for bankrupt power generators has another noxious effect. It discourages the introduction of new technology, which is generally more efficient and therefore more environmentally benign than older installations. Most new technology saves capital. If a utility is not under pressure to cut its costs, it will not give much thought to whether, say, a new gas plant might be better than another expensive dam.

By the mid-1990s, many developing countries had begun to think seriously about raising electricity tariffs. Some were privatizing their energy industries, and giving them more freedom to raise prices. They did so not because of concern for the environment, but because they realized that there was no other way to finance the expansion of generating capacity that their economies clearly need. Much of the vast debts that developing countries ran up in the 1980s was money borrowed to increase the capacity to generate electricity, which was then sold at prices too low to service the debt. Before eager environmentalists clamor for third-world debt relief, they should consider whether some of the policies governments will have to adopt to pay off the debt may not be rather good for the environment.

FARM SUBSIDIES

No activity affects more of the earth's surface than farming. It shapes a third of the planet's land area, not counting Antarctica. And the proportion is rising. World food output per head has risen (by 4 per cent between the 1970s and 1980s) mainly as a result of increases in yields from land already in cultivation, but also because more land has been brought under the plough. Higher yields have been achieved by increased irrigation, better crop breeding, and a doubling in the use of pesticides and chemical fertilizers in the 1970s and 1980s.

All these activities may have damaging environmental impacts. For example, land clearing for agriculture is the largest single cause of deforestation; chemical fertilizers and pesticides may contaminate water supplies; more intensive farming and the abandonment of fallow periods tends to exacerbate soil erosion; and the spread of monoculture and use of high-yielding varieties of crops have been accompanied by the disappearance of old varieties of food plants which might have provided some insurance against pests or diseases in future. Soil erosion threatens the productivity of land in both rich and poor countries. The United States, where the most careful measurements have been done, discovered in 1982 that about one-fifth of its farmland was losing topsoil at a rate likely to diminish the soil's productivity. The country subsequently embarked upon a program to convert 11 per cent of its cropped land to meadow or forest. Topsoil in India and China is vanishing much faster than in America.

Government policies have frequently compounded the environmental damage that farming can cause. In the rich world, governments typically guarantee minimum prices for crops at levels above those the market would deliver. In the poor world, the mistake is often the reverse: governments suppress the prices farmers receive in order to ensure cheap food for the cities, while subsidizing pesticides and artificial fertilizers. Both policies, in different ways, have undesirable effects.

In the rich countries, subsidies for growing crops and price supports for farm output drive up the price of land. The annual value of these subsidies is immense: about $250 billion, or more than all World Bank lending in the 1980s.[5] To increase the output of crops per acre, a farmer's easiest option is to use more of the most readily available inputs: fertilizers and pesticides. Fertilizer use doubled in Denmark in 1960–85 and increased in The Netherlands by 150 per cent. The quantity of pesticides applied has risen, too: by 69 per cent in 1975–84 in Denmark, for example, with a rise of 115 per cent in the frequency of application in the three years from 1981.[6]

In the late 1980s and early 1990s some efforts were made to reduce farm subsidies. The most dramatic example was that of New Zealand, which scrapped most farm support in 1984. A study of the environmental effects, conducted in 1993, found that the end of fertilizer subsidies had been followed by a fall in fertilizer use (a fall compounded by the decline in world commodity prices, which cut farm incomes).[7] The removal of subsidies also stopped land-clearing and over-stocking, which in the past had been the principal causes of erosion. Farms began to diversify. The one kind of subsidy whose removal appeared to have been bad for the environment was the subsidy to manage soil erosion.

In less enlightened countries, and in the European Union, the trend has been to reduce rather than eliminate subsidies, and to introduce new payments to encourage farmers to treat their land in environmentally friendlier ways, or to leave it fallow. It sounds crazy, but such payments need to be higher than the existing incentives for farmers to grow food crops. Farmers, however, dislike being paid to do nothing. In several countries they have become interested in the possibility of using fuel produced from crop residues either as a replacement for petrol (as ethanol) or as fuel for power stations (as biomass). Such fuels produce far less carbon dioxide than coal or oil, and mop up carbon dioxide as they grow. They are therefore less likely to contribute to the greenhouse effect. But they are rarely competitive with fossil fuels unless subsidized – and growing them does no less environmental harm than other crops.

In poor countries, governments aggravate other sorts of damage. Subsidies for pesticides and artificial fertilizers encourage farmers to use greater quantities than is needed to get the highest economic crop yield. A study by the International Rice Research Institute of pesticide use by farmers in the Philippines found that, with pest-resistant varieties of rice, even moderate applications of pesticide frequently cost farmers more than they saved. Such waste puts farmers on a chemical treadmill: bugs and weeds become resistant to poisons, so next year's poisons must be more lethal. One cost is to human health. Every year some 10,000 people die from pesticide poisoning, almost all of them in the developing countries, and another 400,000 become seriously ill.[8] As for artificial fertilizers, their use worldwide increased by 40 per cent per unit of farmed land between the mid-1970s and late 1980s, mostly in the developing countries. Overuse of fertilizers may cause farmers to stop rotating crops or leaving their land fallow. That, in turn, may make soil erosion worse.

A result of the Uruguay Round of world trade negotiations is likely to be a reduction of 36 per cent in the average levels of farm subsidies paid by the rich countries in 1986–90. Some of the world's food production will move from Western Europe to regions where subsidies are lower or non-existent, such as the former Communist countries and parts of the developing world. Some environmentalists worry about this outcome. It will undoubtedly mean more pressure to convert natural habitat into farmland. But it will also have many desirable environmental effects. The intensity of farming in the rich world should decline, and the use of chemical inputs will diminish. Crops are more likely to be grown in the environments to which they are naturally suited. And more farmers in poor countries will have the money and the incentive to manage their land in ways that are sustainable in the long run. That is important. To feed an increasingly hungry world, farmers need every incentive to use their soil and water effectively and efficiently.

Keeping Government at Bay

Why do so many government policies aggravate environmental damage? A part of the problem is that governments are often reluctant to treat a natural resource as a scarce commodity, as a private owner would do, and to protect and price it accordingly. A play on the London stage in the early 1990s made fun of the idea of charging for access to the air; but unless governments are prepared to ration access to the natural resources whose allocation they control, those resources are bound to be overexploited. The simplest and best mechanism of allocation is usually the market.

Yet instead of admitting that the availability of – say – fish or fresh water is finite, governments frequently use public money in a vain attempt to expand the supply. Thus they build a dam to increase the supply of water, or subsidize the building of more sophisticated fishing vessels, or finance a new power station, or widen a road. The results burden taxpayers, encourage inefficiency and impoverish the environment. If governments are to be good curators of the environment, they need to pay more attention to influencing demand. That can best be done by the astute harnessing of market forces, and by avoiding all subsidies that underwrite environmental destruction.

Chapter 7

The Law and the Environment

When government is reluctant to act against polluters, environmentalists increasingly look to the courts. That is an ancient tradition. Long before governments began to pass laws to protect the environment, some protection from pollution was provided by the older framework of common law: legal principles developed through case law, rather than expressed in a code or statute. It was the common law, not legislators or administrators, that established the earliest rights of the victims of pollution. Now, the threat of being found liable for environmental damage is one of the most powerful influences on corporate policy. That liability is sometimes defined by legislation, but interpreted by the courts.

For economists, the shape of the legal framework is significant: the more individuals have legal rights to protection from environmental damage that can be enforced through the courts, the less the state needs to intervene directly to regulate pollution. A classic instance of the way private rights or obligations can be turned to the common good is that of the British lighthouse. Most people assume that lighthouses have always been provided by the state, on the grounds that it would be impossible to make those who benefit from a lighthouse pay for the service. In 1974 a paper by Ronald Coase, who subsequently won the Nobel Prize for economics, pointed out that at least ten lighthouses in seventeenth-century Britain were built by private enterprise because their keepers had a legally enforceable right to levy the cost from local ports. If the courts can create some sort of property right in an environmental asset, then individuals will have an incentive to protect it without any further government action.

There is a powerful modern equivalent of Coase's lighthouse. One of the quirks of English law are riparian rights over rivers and other inland waterways. The owner of a stretch of river bank has an ancient right to receive water of accustomed quality and quantity, and owns the fishing rights.[1] The owner can thus take a private action against anybody upstream who damages the water quality or the owner's rights to fish. The people with the greatest interest in the quality of river water are anglers. In 1948, the Anglers' Co-operative Association was formed to fight river pollution. With its backing, angling clubs, which have often acquired riparian rights, have sued for and won compensation from over 2000 upstream polluters. They have lost only one action, and won hundreds of thousands of pounds of damages.[2] This important right is not necessarily available to individuals in other European countries where the concept of private property is not always as extensive.

EXTENDING PRIVATE RIGHTS

Common law offers private individuals a way to obtain compensation for damage to their property, where that is patently caused by pollution. In recent years, environmentalists have looked for ways to extend their right to sue a polluter for damage, in part by persuading the courts that their interest in the environment is akin to the interest of an owner. They have won some interesting victories. In The Netherlands in the mid-1980s, for example, sea birds were damaged by an oil spill. An amenity group voluntarily cleaned up as many birds as it could, and then sued the owners of the oil tanker to compensate them for their expenses. The Dutch court awarded damages to the environmentalists, extending in a remarkable way the concept of private loss and private remedy.

In the United States, non-governmental groups can sue the federal government for failing to enforce its own rules. Therefore, legislation has sometimes deliberately allowed a right of public redress if current statutes appear not to be properly enforced. In Britain, although legislation has rarely given the public a specific right to prosecute the regulatory authorities if they are failing in their duty, the public has an unusually large amount of freedom to bring a private prosecution against a polluter who is breaking the criminal law. In such a situation, the individual who sues does not need to show that he or she has suffered damage. In Britain, Greenpeace sued Albright & Wilson, a chemicals and household goods group, for breaking the terms of its discharge license and polluting the sea. The freedom to bring a private prosecution for a breach of criminal law is extremely rare in continental Europe, where it is usually only the public prosecutor who can take to court a polluter who breaks the terms of a license to discharge pollutants.

Suppose the regulatory authority has not failed to enforce the terms of a license, but has given out a license improperly, or otherwise acted perversely. In such cases, most countries have a system of judicial review. In Britain, environmental groups are increasingly using this to ask the courts whether the government or some other public body has misused its administrative powers in making decisions with harmful environmental consequences. Greenpeace used this approach to challenge (unsuccessfully) the commissioning of THORP, British Nuclear Fuel's (BNFL) thermal oxide nuclear-waste reprocessing plant, at Sellafield, in Cumbria in 1993. BNFL tried to argue that Greenpeace had no right – no *locus standi*, in legal terminology – to bring the case. The judge, however, took the view that it was good to have the public interest in the case presented in a professional way. This utilitarian approach reflects the tendency of the courts generally to take a liberal approach to *locus standi*.

The judge in the THORP case made two further important points. He argued that the principle of justification, derived from EU law, applied in Britain. The principle says that the issuing of a

license for a polluting activity such as the release of radiation had
to be justified as being in the public interest. The principle has
forced a rough-and-ready cost-benefit test on other British nuclear
plants when applying for operational licenses. Secondly, he decided
that Greenpeace should bear only its own costs and not, as is usual
for the loser in such a case, those of BNFL as well. That decision
may encourage other non-governmental groups to resort to the
courts more often.

Despite the existence of private rights to sue for environmental
damages, Britain and most other countries have an increasing body
of environmental legislation. Common law cannot, for example,
readily deal with damage that has not yet taken place. Statutes, on
the other hand, can establish a system of licenses or permits, so that
those activities which may cause pollution can be regulated before
they do so. Common law also cannot cope with situations where
many polluters are involved: pedestrians can hardly sue every
motorist who pollutes the air.

In Britain, the Victorians, rich and dirty, grew more interested in
green issues as their air grew blacker and their rivers smellier. The
Alkali Act of 1863 broke new ground by establishing the concept
of government regulation of industry. Legislation augmented the
concept of civil liability for infringing the rights of an individual with
that of criminal responsibility for pollution. For instance, the Rivers
Pollution Prevention Act of 1876 was the first act to make it a
criminal offense to pollute any British river. The Victorians also
developed the use of the common law of nuisance, and of liability
for personal injury. Lawyers in Victorian courts engaged in vigorous
philosophical debates about the right to enjoy property, free from
the pollution that the century's breakneck industrial development
so frequently caused.[3]

British legislation to protect individual species also dates back
to the last century. Some of it was intended to help farmers, by
protecting birds that destroyed pests. But the most important piece
of environmental legislation in Britain this century was arguably the
1947 Town and Country Planning Act, passed by the post-war
Labour government under Clement Attlee, giving the protection

of the countryside a statutory framework. The legislation is concerned with regulating land use and new developments, rather than protecting the environment as such, but the controls can be a powerful tool of environmental policy, influencing where polluting activities might be put and so helping to protect water from contamination and cities from industrial air pollution. It also embedded the concept of public participation in the planning process. In the 1990s, planning legislation has begun to be used in a more ambitious environmental way: John Major's government announced that it would discourage applications for out-of-town superstores, partly because they encourage the growth of road transport. If that principle is extended, planning law could become an even more powerful instrument of environmental policy in Britain.

CIVIL LIABILITY FOR ENVIRONMENTAL DAMAGE

One of the most difficult issues for environmental policy is that of liability for past environmental damage. Throughout the developed world, governments are trying to decide who should pay to clean it up. Until now, many have relied on the courts to decide what to do. That approach is proving increasingly unsatisfactory.

A basic question is whether polluters should be liable for damage, irrespective of the care or negligence they have shown: whether, in legal jargon, liability should be fault-based or strict. The legal position in the United States is simple but brutal: polluters are liable for past damage caused by the way they dispose of hazardous waste, even if they have taken proper steps to try to prevent it. One Californian company rejected a suggestion by local officials that it deposit waste in a municipal dump and insisted that the materials be disposed of, at higher cost to itself, in a specialized site. This worthy decision was later used to charge the company part of the cost of cleaning up that site.

In Britain, environmental cases have also increasingly driven a wedge between moral responsibility and legal liability.[4] But up to now, the courts have not taken as ruthless a line as those in the United States. In 1993 England's Court of Appeal decided that a leather company should pay almost £1 million in damages to the Cambridge Water Company for contaminating one of its boreholes as a result of spillages of solvents at its factory – even though the spills had taken place some 17 years earlier and it was accepted that nobody at the time could reasonably have predicted that they would eventually contaminate the borehole. The case was overturned in the House of Lords on appeal at the end of the year. The Lords said, reasonably enough, that Parliament should decide whether Britain was to have strict liability for environmental damage. The question should not be resolved by a quirky interpretation of an obscure Victorian legal case, upon which the Court of Appeal had relied. But they also discussed at length the principle of "foreseeability". At least one law lord argued that, since the 1970s, times had changed; companies should have begun to foresee that long-lasting pollution would become less publicly acceptable.

European countries have found it extremely difficult to define civil liability for environmental damage, for good reasons. The intention of American legislation was to get polluters to pay: a reasonable and long-established principle. But the principle is difficult to enforce in two situations: where damage was not caused by negligence, and where no individual polluter was principally responsible. In the United States, the problem of allocating responsibility – and clean-up costs – for land contaminated by past dumping of hazardous waste has led to notoriously expensive and long-drawn-out legal battles. These have been fought mainly by the insurance companies of businesses billed with the costs of remediation. A 1992 study by the Rand Corporation, a think-tank in California, found that insurers spent $470 million on legal fees and other paperwork costs in 1989 alone: enough to finance the treatment of 15 contaminated sites.[5]

In Europe, governments have tended to get taxpayers to carry the costs of cleaning up environmental damage. In practice, precious little cleaning up has taken place. Now, the contraction of manufacturing industry has left a growing number of sites in need of remediation. Moreover, the public has become more anxious to see contaminated land cleaned up, rather than left to be cleaned only when (if) a new use for it is contemplated. In Britain, a report by the House of Commons Environment Committee in 1990 recommended that "urgent attention" be given to creating a statutory liability for damage caused to property and the environment by land contamination. The government argued that, for the time being, the principles of common law were adequate. By the mid-1990s, that attitude was starting to change, in part because of developments in Brussels (see below).

The problem of defining civil liability for past contamination has been most severe in Eastern Europe and the former East Germany, where it has been a serious barrier to foreign investment. A survey of some 1000 big North American and West European companies conducted by the World Bank in 1992 found that more than half of those firms that had got as far as evaluating sites in Eastern Europe rejected them at least partly on environmental grounds. Governments in the region want investors to revive existing enterprises; but foreign investors worry that local law often does not clearly define whether they will be liable for past pollution. Governments are also ambivalent: many would love foreign money to clean up their environments, but even if they assure investors that they do not need to clean up to Western standards, investors are still cautious, reasoning that, as East European countries seek to join the European Union, clean-up standards will rise and they will be sent the bill.

The European Commission has also been wrestling with defining civil liability for environmental damage. In March 1993 it published an extremely tentative paper on the issue. It appeared to favor strict liability, at least for future damage, and some kind of joint compensation scheme, financed by enterprises whose activities were "most closely linked to the type of damage needing restoration" – and, perhaps, the taxpayer.

Meanwhile another international body, the Council of Europe, drew up a convention on civil liability for environmental damage caused by dangerous activities, completed at the end of 1992. The convention takes a tougher line than Brussels or most European governments. It extends the concept of liability, which is strict, to damage to the unowned environment, such as landscape and even cultural heritage. It also specifically extends the right to bring an action for damages to non-governmental organizations in specified circumstances. The British government, for one, has said firmly that it will not ratify the convention.

In developing a regime for statutory civil liability, governments must make a decision on two key issues:

1 Who should pay? This question in turn raises at least three more issues:
    a) Can a past polluter be identified? If not, or if the past polluter has gone bust, or if many polluters have been involved (as at a communal dump), the only sensible answer may be for the taxpayer to meet the costs of cleaning up. However, if a bank has taken possession of a property as security for a loan, or finances a polluter, governments have to consider whether the lender should incur some of the liability. If a past polluter is clearly to blame, then governments must look at a further question:
    b) Was the pollution the result of negligence or of breaking the law? If not, governments must decide what defenses against strict liability should be allowed. All countries are increasingly moving towards extending strict liability for pollution damage.
    c) Should governments use different policies for past damage and future damage? If so, how difficult is it to determine when contamination occurred, especially if the pollution took place gradually over many years?
2 How much does pollution need to be cleaned up? While Brussels has been transfixed by the first set of questions, the second – how clean is clean? – has become more important in the United States. If land is to be used for housing, it obviously needs to be cleaned to a far higher standard than if it is to be used for a petrol station. Under Dutch law, land is supposed to be cleaned to a set standard, regardless of future use, although the wisdom of doing

so is increasingly being questioned. In the United States, regulators are beginning to take a more realistic approach, and the British government proposed in 1994 that the level of cleanliness should be appropriate to future use.

THE BRUSSELS INFLUENCE

The fact that Brussels, in 1994, was considering a directive on civil liability for environmental damage means that Britain may, in time, have to legislate on the issue. Membership of the EU has an important influence on the development of environmental law in Britain. The Treaty of Rome did not specify the environment as an area of Community competence. But Brussels gradually extended its power to make environmental policy, building mainly on Article 100 of the Treaty of Rome, which set out the basis for forging a common market. Only with the passing of the Single European Act in 1987 did the European Community formally acquire responsibility for environmental policy. Since 1987, Brussels's environmental policies have been covered by two new articles in the amended Treaty of Rome, Article 130R, and Article 100A. The first, which needs Europe's governments to be unanimous, covers purely environmental measures; the second, which deals with harmonizing standards, allows some countries to out-vote others. That leaves much scope for dispute.

The Single European Act has given Brussels wider scope for environmental policy. It has created a tension between Brussels and London: the British government argues for the doctrine of "subsidiarity", meaning that policy should be taken at the lowest appropriate level. The government says that Brussels has no business to determine the standard of British drinking or bathing water, or even possibly what Britain does with its contaminated land. The doctrine of subsidiarity, though, has not stopped the British government from continuing to implement those European policies to which it has already agreed, or from trying to influence policy discussions in Brussels. Meanwhile some countries, such as Denmark and Sweden, have been keen on a different version of the subsidiarity argument: that Brussels should not stand in their way if they wished to apply higher environmental standards than the rest of the EU.

The development of Community environmental policy has had a broader impact on British environmental law. For one thing, it has encouraged the government to accept the new principles of prevention and precaution. For another, it has changed the shape of legislation.

The Single European Act adopted the preventive principle: action should be taken if an environmental risk was known to exist, even if damage had not already occurred. The Maastricht Treaty of 1993 went a step farther, and incorporated into Community policy the precautionary principle: the deeper concept that action should be taken even if an environmental hazard could not be proved to exist – as in the case of global warming, for example. Both these principles have been increasingly reflected in British environmental legislation. The precautionary principle, in particular, was set out in the 1990 White Paper on the environment (*This Common Inheritance*). It had previously been used to justify the introduction of differential excise duty on unleaded petrol. The Royal Commission on the Environment, in a report on lead in the environment, had argued that there was no firm evidence that children's health was affected by atmospheric lead, but that the government should, as a precaution, take steps to reduce it.[6]

The influence of Brussels has also made British environmental law more detailed. Britain had tended to develop a framework in its legislation and then spell out the details in circulars – advisory documents without the strict force of law. In the early 1980s the European Court of Justice ruled that European directives must be transposed into law in the member countries. European directives tend in any case to be highly detailed, because of the need to influence policy in countries with federal governments and different legal systems and enforcement policies.

Even without directions from Brussels, the courts in most

countries are likely to remain a key component of environmental policy. They will increasingly be required to interpret an ever more complex body of statutory law. Besides, as environmental legislation expands, enforcement issues will become more important. The courts offer the environmentally conscious citizen one of the few routes to put direct pressure on polluters, and on enforcement agencies that are reluctant to use their powers properly. Future governments may expand this role. The environmental strategy of Britain's Labour Party is to create "a situation in which all citizens can act as environmental watchdogs". It calls for a charter of statutory environmental rights, including the right to compensation for environmental damage, legally enforceable through the courts. Such a charter would have enormous consequences for public- and private-sector polluters. But it would also give the courts an unprecedented say over environmental policy. It may never happen, but it shows which way the political wind is blowing.

Chapter 8

National Accounts

Much of the argument about the impact of environmental policies on the economy turns on the way in which growth and development is measured. The basis for such measurements is the United Nations' System of National Accounts (SNA), an internationally agreed framework for recording what is happening to a country's wealth, income and expenditure. But the way in which national accounts have traditionally been compiled tends to ignore some important aspects of a country's changing prosperity. In particular, conventional national-income accounting is a poor guide to the way a country is caring for its environment.

The failure to reflect environmental quality was criticized almost as soon as the SNA came into being, in 1947; economists such as Kenneth Boulding and JK Galbraith complained that increases in a country's income as recorded in the SNA might actually mean a decrease in welfare.[1] Such arguments were early versions of the "growth or greenery" debate.

Most of the pressure to revise national accounts has been concentrated on gross domestic product (GDP), the most widely used measure of economic activity. As every student of economics learns early on, GDP is an imperfect indicator of the quality of life. But then, that is not what it is intended to record. Its purpose is mainly to measure transactions that pass through the market. It does not, for example, reflect the contribution made by output that is not marketed, such as the unpaid work of running a home, a point that has annoyed feminists.

The 1980s saw increasing agitation to alter the SNA to take account of changes in environmental quality. The environment, argued the agitators, provides productive economic resources (such as the capacity to absorb waste or to renew supplies of fresh water) and goods which consumers value (such as unpolluted air or fine views). Such economic information is missing from national accounts. As a result, policy makers may receive incomplete information about the way their policies are affecting an economy. Worse, they may aim for targets that can be measured by national-income accounts, ignoring the fact that their policies may harm the quality of life in ways that the accounts do not reflect.

Faced with such complaints, the United Nations spent much of the 1980s thinking about ways to improve the SNA. It eventually decided not to make a fundamental revision, although the SNA was tweaked enough to include some environmental points. For example, national balance sheets will now make a more careful distinction between cultivated and non-cultivated productive natural assets and will record changes in their stock. Instead of changing the basic SNA, the UN published in 1993 new guidelines for "satellite" integrated environmental and economic accounts. The guidelines, tested in Mexico, Papua New Guinea and Thailand, include suggestions on ways to treat the depletion of natural capital (through logging and mining, for instance) and the costs of degradation (by pollution of air and water, or soil erosion). The guidelines also suggest ways to measure those environmental assets that have no market prices.

The UN's caution is understandable. Many of the changes that environmentalists want to see in national accounts are more difficult than they initially appear. Some would not necessarily strengthen the case for environmental policies. But many environmentalists are disappointed by what they see as the UN's timidity. They have persuaded politicians to look again at the way national accounts are compiled. On Earth Day in 1993, President Clinton announced that the United States would examine ways to makes its national accounts look greener. At much the same time, the EU began a Community-wide exercise of the same sort. The question for the next few years will be whether such experiments can move beyond the UN's cautious approach, and integrate environmental factors into the heart of national-income accounts, so that the headline figures for economic growth (measured as changes in GDP) really do reflect changes in environmental quality.

PROBLEMS WITH NATIONAL ACCOUNTS

Conventional national accounts have, in the eyes of environment-alists, three main drawbacks:

1 They fail to reflect the full value of the services that environmental assets provide. They take no account of unmarketed natural assets such as clean air or unpolluted rivers.

2 They treat the use of natural capital differently from that of manmade capital. The use of natural capital is generally treated as consumption. So a country that exhausts its manmade capital without replacing it clearly grows poorer; one that exhausts its fish stocks or destroys its forests appears, by conventional measures, to grow richer. The result is to make policy makers behave as though natural wealth were limitless.

3 They often record the costs of cleaning up environmental damage as an addition to national product; they do not subtract the environmental loss caused by the damage in the first place. Conventionally, cleaning up oil spills or buying catalytic converters counts as final expenditure and so increases GDP. This is unreasonable, in green eyes: if pollution does not count as a reduction in GDP, cleaning it up should not count as growth.

While many economists accept the need to do something about

such shortcomings, they have found it hard to agree on useful changes. One of the most fundamental difficulties is that of valuing non-marketed resources. Even when the depletion of natural capital can be measured in the market – as with coal-mining, say, or logging – its valuation raises difficulties. When oil is $20 a barrel, a country may have no reserves worth measuring; when the oil price rises to $50 a barrel, it may suddenly find that oil is worth recovering. But such valuation problems are simplicity itself, compared with putting a value on clean water or virgin forest.

Another difficulty is the treatment of "defensive" spending on, say, pollution prevention. Many economists dislike the idea of adjusting national accounts to remove pollution-prevention spending as an item of economic activity. Many other sorts of spending are treated the same way: expenditure to prevent crime, or repair wrecked cars, or treat sick cigarette smokers is, in each case, measured as an addition to national wealth. Moreover, to exclude spending on pollution prevention would be perverse: countries that cleaned up their dirty rivers and polluted air would not appear to grow richer, while countries that spent the same sums on polluting activities would appear to be better off. The point has an important implication: if environmentalists argue that pollution-prevention spending boosts jobs and incomes, there may be some virtue in recording environmental clean-ups as a contribution to growth.

RESOURCE DEPLETION IN DEVELOPING COUNTRIES

The earliest attempts to incorporate environmental information into national accounts were relatively simple and confined to the industrial countries. Several developed countries have long collected information on their physical stocks of natural capital. Norway and France, for example, both have programs – in Norway's case dating back to 1970 – to collect data on the physical stock of natural resources such as forests and fisheries. Such accounts measure the stock of natural resources in terms of hectares or cubic metres or

other non-monetary units. Not surprisingly, it is harder to measure changes in the quality of natural capital (water or air pollution, for instance) than to measure quantity. It has also proved hard to use the data for planning or policy analysis.

However, the 1980s saw an increasing interest in accounting for the way developing countries used their natural resources. Typically, the environment is what such countries live off. In poor countries primary production – farming, fishing, forestry, mining – often accounts for more than a third of measured economic activity and more than two-thirds of employment. Natural resources are their main assets. In such countries, the concept of sustainable development is particularly appropriate: if they run down their stock of natural assets, they may become poorer, even though conventional figures for economic growth suggest that they are becoming richer.

While the United Nations was working on its guidelines, Robert Repetto and a team of economists at the World Resources Institute (WRI) looked at possible ways to adjust GDP for the depletion of natural resources. They carried out two large natural-resource accounting studies, of Indonesia and Costa Rica.[2] Such natural-resource accounting is a more limited exercise than true environmental accounting, which attempts to adjust a country's entire national-income accounts to reflect what has happened to a wide range of environmental resources.

The WRI exercise concentrated on one main aspect of national accounts: the way they treat the depreciation of natural resources. National accounts apply the concept of depreciation in their treatment of manmade capital, such as factories and machinery. As their value declines, it is written off against the value of production. If a country's manmade assets depreciate faster than they are replaced, it is clearly living beyond its means.

No such concept applies to natural capital. As it is used up, national accounts show no charge against current income, to reflect the fall in future potential production. When Britain discovered oil in the North Sea, its accounts did not register a huge increase in its assets. Britain's exploitation of its oil has been measured in terms of barrels sold – as an income gain, rather than a drawing down of capital. Had the national accounts treated North Sea oil as a stock of capital, they would have concentrated attention on the extent to which that asset had been drawn down to provide income, or to pay for reinvestment in manmade capital.

True national income, Repetto argues, is "sustainable" income. He draws attention to the definition of income used by Sir John Hicks, a British Nobel Prize winner: income is the most that can be consumed within a given period without leaving a person or country worse off than before. Income generated by depleting natural resources may well not be sustainable.

By conventional measurements, for example, Costa Rica's economy grew on average by 4.6 per cent a year between 1970 and 1989. Repetto's study argued that more than a quarter of this apparent growth disappeared when adjustment was made for the depreciation of forests, soils and fisheries. It valued the loss of natural resources as more than an average year's GDP during the period. Huge losses took place in fishing, when catches of some valuable species collapsed in the mid-1980s. The driving force behind the country's losses of natural productivity was deforestation, which the study estimated to account for 85 per cent of the total depreciation in the value of Costa Rica's natural resources in 1989 alone.

Accounting for the depletion of natural resources raises a number of difficult questions. For example, what happens to the proceeds from selling natural resources? If Saudi Arabia counts all its oil output as capital depreciation, it may appear to have no net income at all, even though it not only enjoys a high level of consumption but also invests some of the proceeds of the oil in ways that guarantee a continued stream of future income. What if Costa Rica had invested the proceeds of deforestation in educating its children? Conventional national accounts are just as bad at capturing improvements in human capital – in the ability of people to work more effectively – as they are at capturing declines in natural capital. Yet a country that traded its natural capital for human capital might well be thought to become richer, not poorer.

At the heart of this debate is an important issue in the greening of national accounts. To what extent are natural capital and manmade capital substitutes for each other? If a country chops down all its trees and uses the proceeds to build factories, it may indeed enjoy a sustainable flow of income. In that sense, the two kinds of capital are substitutable. But if the impact of deforestation is a succession of devastating floods, then clearly they are not. In any case, at some point, it will become impossible to continue to substitute manmade capital for natural capital: a certain natural-resource base is essential for human survival.

Another central issue is that of valuation. When measuring the depletion of natural resources, Repetto and his colleagues stick to values which, even when not measured in the marketplace, at least approximate market values. Costa Rica's loss of trees, for instance, is reckoned as the marketable value of standing timber and future timber revenues lost when the forest is cleared. This approach does not include other values which are harder to deduce from market transactions, such as the value a forest may have as a home for wildlife or a place for recreation.

But the Costa Rica study showed that even marketable natural resources posed valuation difficulties. On the face of it, deforestation gathered pace through the period Repetto studied. As a result, in the final six years of the period, annual depreciation of Costa Rica's natural-resource base was 70 per cent greater than the average of the previous 12 years. In fact, rises in the price of timber greatly exaggerated the impact of the physical loss of trees.

A similar difficulty arose with a study of environmental accounting in Papua New Guinea by Peter Bartelmus, who worked on the revision of the SNA.[3] He found that an environmental adjustment to the country's accounts for the years from 1986 to 1990 would indeed reduce net domestic product (a measure that expresses GDP minus the depreciation of capital, including natural resources). But the extent of the reduction varied wildly, from 1 per cent to 10 per cent, depending on the year chosen and the method used. Calculations were impeded by the absence of figures for spending on environmental protection. Only sketchy information existed on the stock of some natural resources, such as fish; and nobody knew much about the pace at which others, such as forests, might replace themselves. Where relevant knowledge did exist, much of it was confidential, as was much of the information about sales revenues and extraction costs in the mining industry.

To make calculations even harder, prices of raw materials produced by Papua New Guinea changed considerably. Until 1989, most of the way through the accounting period, some 35 per cent of the country's export earnings and 8 per cent of its gross domestic product (conventionally measured) came from the Bougainville copper and gold mine. In 1989 the mine was shut down by sabotage and rebellion. But even when the mine was operating, the minerals it produced were subject to massive price fluctuations. In 1987–88, for instance, the average gold price fell by a third. Not only did that affect the island's conventionally measured national accounts; it raised the question of what a "sustainable" strategy for the disposal of natural wealth should be in such circumstances.

APPLYING GREEN ACCOUNTING

The economists who developed the guidelines for satellite accounts for the UN took a broader approach than the WRI team. They focused on the whole national-accounting process and attempted to calculate not just the use of resources included in the economic system, but changes in environmental quality, such as increases in air pollution or loss of wild species. Like the WRI team, though, they concentrated on developing countries, partly because they assumed that these would be the most difficult places to apply the technique. If it could be made to work in the "worst" cases, the UN's experts reasoned, it might also work in the best.

In some ways, that view may be mistaken. The relationship between the environment and economics differs enormously between the developed world and poorer countries. Not only does the exploitation of natural resources account for more of national output in most poor countries; damage to the natural environment is also likely to impose more obvious costs. There is a further distinction. In developed countries, the scale of industry and transport means that environmental degradation (pollution, for instance) tends to matter more than the depletion of natural resources. But most statisticians feel that it is easier to put monetary values on depletion, if only because depletion usually extracts something that is sold.

The main problem for attempts to "green" national-income accounts is to devise a common measure of value. The work of the WRI and the study in Papua New Guinea demonstrated the difficulties of taking account of the depletion of natural resources whose value can be established in the market place. Much greater difficulties arise when something that is never remotely likely to be bought or sold – such as the ozone layer or a clean river – has to be put into the same accounts as the car industry or the housing market.

Not only is it hard to make measurements, but there is controversy over what should be measured: the cost of restoring the environment to its previous condition (which greens prefer but which may be nonsensical if restoration is impossible), or the amount that consumers might be willing to spend to improve environmental quality (which is usually smaller, and may underestimate the value of the environment to future generations). Such controversies, hard enough to resolve in the case of one aspect of the environment, become hideously difficult when the figures have to be consistent for the entire accounting system of a country. And even if such problems could be overcome for a single country, they are utterly impossible to solve when devising a standard to be applied in all the member countries of the UN.

Incorporating environmental values into conventional national-income accounts may turn out to be simply too difficult to do on a large scale. It will be hard to produce enough consensus on valuation techniques, and to devise figures that can be recorded over a period of time – an essential aspect of useful national-income accounts. But there may still be limited areas where environmental information can be incorporated into national accounts. After all, the environment is not the only area where a value has to be found for unmarketed services. National-income accounting has sometimes found ways to measure the value of these services – as in the case of, say, policemen (based on their salaries) or of the services provided by owner-occupied homes (imputed from the price of rented housing). But sometimes, too, it has failed, as in the case of valuing the work done by burglars or by stay-at-home spouses.[4]

An alternative approach has been suggested in The Netherlands. In May 1993 the Dutch Central Bureau of Statistics published satellite accounts which break down the economy by industry and households, and show how each contributed to a variety of environmental problems in 1989. The results show that, for example, agriculture contributes little to employment or exports; but – with the world's highest application of nitrogen fertilizer per hectare – it contributes mightily to acidification and eutrophication (both caused by the pollution of water with nutrients).

This exercise annoyed Dutch farmers, who claim that they are only part of a larger industry. The crops they raise are transported to factories, processed, distributed and sold. Why should the environmental damage done by the production of food be measured at the farm? The farmers would have been on stronger ground if they had made a different point: why should the costs of agricultural pollution be attributed to the producer rather than the consumer? Anne Harrison, an economist at the OECD, points out that if people travel on a polluting bus, it is not clear that the emission from the bus should be ascribed to the transport company rather than the passengers.[6]

But the Dutch study does offer a way to examine the effects of economic activity on environmental degradation without trying to value it. Indeed, the Dutch statisticians argue strongly against attempts to incorporate monetary values for environmental damage into estimates of national income, on the grounds that such exercises do not compare like with like. Steven Keuning, head of the Dutch national-accounts research division, argues that green accounts are not true national accounting but rather an exercise in posing hypothetical questions. "If the (substantial) costs subtracted in these approaches had been charged in reality," he says, "we would have lived in a totally different world, and it is quite naive to assume that all economic subjects would have swallowed these costs without an adjustment of their behavior."[7] That, though, is precisely the reason environmentalists have so often chivvied politicians to introduce green national-income accounts.

Environmentalists hope that, if environmental loss can be shown as an economic cost, people's behavior will change. It makes good sense to ram home the point that natural-resource depletion and environmental degradation can impoverish a country, and to encourage voters and politicians to think about the consequences. But finding ways to incorporate the costs of environmental damage into national statistics is not a magic cure for bad environmental policies.

Part III

POLICIES IN ACTION

Chapter 9

The Greenhouse Effect

The environmental issues that attract most public attention in the developed world are not necessarily the ones that matter most to humanity. An absence of clean drinking water or adequate sewerage kills far more people than nuclear radiation or toxic waste are ever likely to do. But the wealth of the first world means that its environmental preoccupations are the ones that attract most money and the most expensive solutions. This part of the book looks at the way these rich-world preoccupations are handled. Three issues are related to the use of energy: global warming, energy efficiency and nuclear power. These topics are interlinked: the two obvious answers to worries about the build-up of atmospheric carbon dioxide and its possible effect on climate are measures to use energy more efficiently, or a switch to non-carbon fuel, of which easily the largest currently in use is nuclear fuel. One later chapter deals with waste, which has become an increasingly pressing worry in rich countries; and another with conservation, which many people in rich countries see as the most pressing environmental problem in the poor world.

In each case, the themes are the same: can countries use the power of the market to make wiser decisions, or to design more effective policies? The costs of measures to protect the environment need constantly to be set against the benefits, and against the other ways in which societies want to use their limited economic resources (including education and health care). Moreover, the more environmental policies can work with the grain of the market to influence behavior, the more likely they are to achieve their objectives without greatly inhibiting economic growth.

These points matter most of all in the case of the greenhouse effect, which some think likely to be the most damaging of all the environmental consequences of human activity, and which would undoubtedly be the most costly of all to prevent. No other environmental issue presents as big a challenge to policy makers. And, it must be said, no other environmental issue has attracted so much intellectual curiosity and research support. The sheer intricacy of the problems involved in climate change give the issue a special appeal. In recent years it has attracted more research, from a greater variety of disciplines, than any other green problem. The latest work on the subject is the product of 30 months of work by a large group of experts in preparation for the first meeting of the conference of the parties to the Climate Convention, in the spring of 1995.[1]

The basic mechanism of the greenhouse effect is relatively uncontroversial. Gases accumulating in the atmosphere appear to trap the sun's returning rays, like the glass in a greenhouse, causing the planet to warm up and the climate to change. Nature has always given off plenty of such gases. But human beings are adding rapidly to the total. The four main gases implicated – carbon dioxide, methane, nitrous oxides and chlorofluorocarbons (CFCs) – are released by a broad range of activities, from burning fossil fuels to deforestation to farming. Such activities occur not in one or two countries, but all over the planet, so the origins of the greenhouse effect are truly global. So are its effects. In this, it is unlike almost any other environmental problem. The same is true of its timescale. While most kinds of pollution are felt within a few years – or at least a human lifetime – the greenhouse effect may last for several centuries. It is thus virtually irreversible.

But effective policies to combat it face enormous obstacles. To slow down the build-up of the main greenhouse gas, carbon dioxide, requires measures to reduce the use of fossil fuels. Yet not only is the world's population (and thus its demand for energy) growing rapidly; energy prices have been low for almost a decade. They may well remain low, as new technologies increase the efficiency with which oil can be extracted, and as Russia and the former Soviet republics earn hard currency by increasing their energy exports. Low prices will not only encourage faster growth in energy consumption; they will also discourage the development of energy generated by non-fossil fuels, such as nuclear power or solar energy.

THE IMPACTS OF GLOBAL WARMING

One of the main difficulties in the development of policies to deal with the greenhouse effect is the sheer level of uncertainty. While temperatures seem to have risen over the past century, they have not risen by as much as the best climate models predicted. An increase in tropical storms between 1949 and the mid-1980s, which some took as an effect of global warming, seems to have been caused mainly by more accurate observation techniques. As a result, the scale and geographical extent of global warming are a matter of scientific debate.

The middle ground is held by scientists on the Intergovernmental Panel on Climate Change (IPCC), set up by the World Meteorological Organization and the United Nations Environment Programme in 1988. They argue that a doubling of the atmospheric concentration of carbon dioxide will lead to a rise in mean temperatures of between 1.5 and 4.5 degrees Celsius.[2] The effects, they think, will be a rise in sea level as the higher temperatures cause sea water to expand and glacial ice to melt, possibly with little warning. Warmer weather will lead to a number of other changes: some species will become extinct as they fail to adapt quickly enough to changes in the climate; rainfall may diminish; weather may become stormier; some regions will no longer be able to grow food.

The IPCC's views appear, since then, to have become rather more gloomy. Its report for the 1995 Berlin conference argues that the global-warming gases have a greater potential effect than had previously been thought (though with a margin of uncertainty of plus or minus 35 per cent!). On the other hand, some predictions seem more sanguine: forecasts of the rise in sea level have moderated over time, for instance. But there are two important caveats. First, some scientists have suggested ways in which warming, once it passed a certain threshold, might trigger a dramatic catastrophe. Were the West Antarctic ice sheet to melt suddenly, two million cubic kilometres of ice would slide into the sea, causing a rise in its level of between five and six metres[3] and sharply reducing its salinity.

Secondly, the IPCC projections look only at the effects of doubling the concentration of carbon dioxide from pre-industrial levels. But the Earth's known reserves of fossil fuels are enough to allow humanity to go on burning them long after the doubling point is reached. William Cline has pointed out that, if humanity continues to burn fossil fuels fast enough to exhaust reserves over the next 300 years, the atmospheric concentration of carbon dioxide would peak at six times the pre-industrial level about the year 2200. It would then gradually decline as the gas was absorbed into the deepest parts of the oceans.[4]

It will take at least two decades to be sure about the severity of these threats. But by then, many more tons of warming gases will have been spewed into the atmosphere. Does that matter? A report by the US Office of Technology Assessment argues that a delay of 10 to 20 years would have little effect on the concentration of gases in the atmosphere.[5] But the report also points out that, if countries then have to take rapid and significant action, it would be more expensive to do so from a standing start. In the intervening years, many countries will have invested in technologies that increase the output of global-warming gases, instead of learning how to prevent them. Policy may therefore need to precede proof.

THE IMPLICATIONS FOR ENERGY

If global warming is to be limited, the world simply cannot afford to burn all the fossil fuel now known to be economically recoverable – let alone the greater quantity that might become so. Indeed, most climatologists argue that the world cannot afford to release much more carbon dioxide than it already does each year. The question then becomes an allocation problem: any internationally acceptable solution implies sharing out that carbon dioxide budget. If the developing countries need a bigger share to accommodate their growth, the rich countries will be obliged to accept less.

The dilemma has only to be put in this way for its intractability to be obvious. Two factors complicate it further. First, the growth in future energy demand will come largely from the developing world. That is where almost all the 2 billion extra people of the next twenty years will be born. It is also where energy use is currently lowest. The average person in a developing country uses the equivalent of one or two barrels of oil a year for fuel (apart from what is scavenged directly from forests and fields); the average European or Japanese uses the equivalent of between 10 and 30 barrels a year; the average American, 40 barrels.

Second, coal, which accounts for 70 per cent of the heat content of the world's fossil fuel reserves, will remain the Earth's main source of fuel, apart from wood (and for the time being, oil and gas), and the main fuel for electricity generation. As other fuels run out and become more expensive, coal's importance may increase.

But coal will remain particularly important in the two most populous nations: India and (even more) China, which has one-third of the world's known reserves of coal. To persuade the Chinese to leave their vast coal stocks unburnt in the ground, any alternative source of energy will have to be cheaper than coal (especially in terms of capital cost) and easier to use. At present, economies of scale mean that a large conventional coal plant with no pollution controls is cheaper to build than any rival technology.

Might technological change provide a way to burn coal, and still release less carbon dioxide into the air? After all, that is what the rich world has achieved with sulphur dioxide, which is now frequently scrubbed from coal gases before they escape from a power station. Unfortunately, with global warming, the options for reducing the output of carbon dioxide are more limited than those for removing most other pollutants. No satisfactory technology can strip the carbon dioxide, as a scrubber can strip the sulphur dioxide. For the moment, there is an alternative to coal, although it is not nearly as plentiful, and more expensive for some countries: natural gas. The world is about to see a switch from coal to natural gas, driven by a leap in the efficiency with which gas can be converted into electricity. Because gas produces almost half as much carbon dioxide relative to the energy it gives off as coal, this is the brightest single hope for curbing the growth in the world's output of carbon dioxide. In addition, advances in technology will continue to improve the efficiency with which existing sources of energy are used – as they have already done. But in the long term, it will be necessary to develop generating plants that burn no carbon: nuclear, hydro, solar and other still experimental technologies.

At present, these options have problems of their own. The next two chapters consider some of the barriers to improving energy efficiency, and the economic and political drawbacks to expanding nuclear power. Non-carbon fuels face other difficulties. Hydro projects have environmental drawbacks, making them controversial in some countries, and may involve shifting large numbers of people in others. Solar power, though becoming rapidly cheaper, is still expensive and experimental. The biggest problem of all, though, is the problem of plenty. As long as fossil fuels are cheap, it will be extremely expensive to provide incentives to improve energy efficiency or to develop non-fossil alternatives.

ESTIMATING COSTS AND BENEFITS

The costs of slowing down climate change are hard to measure. But given the many unknowns, measuring the *benefits* of action – the costs of the damage that the greenhouse effect may cause if nothing is done – is even harder to do.

Some action to slow down climate change is likely to be virtually costless, because it delivers other benefits, or because it makes commensurate savings. The most striking example is that of electricity generation in developing countries. Power prices are, on average, barely one-third of the cost of supply and roughly half those in developed countries. Petrol prices average about $1.25 a gallon (compared with $3–4 per American gallon in Europe and Japan). Few have more than rudimentary energy taxes. Given the rapid increase in local air pollution from power generation and traffic, many developing countries would be better off economically and environmentally if they priced fuel at rich-country levels.

Smaller but similar gains could be made in the rich world. For instance, measures that improve the fuel efficiency of buildings would have an effect on other sorts of pollution that go with the production of heating fuels, and might earn a rapid return for those who pay heating bills. In the run-up to the 1995 Berlin meeting, work by the IPCC suggested that some policies to deal with global warming might have benefits that are three times as great in reducing other environmental problems as in reducing climate change.

Such free lunches are far and away the best hope for reducing the growth of carbon dioxide output over the next half century. The OECD estimates that, if non-OECD countries removed all energy subsidies over the next decade, world emissions of carbon dioxide would be 20 per cent lower in 2050 than would otherwise be the case. Moreover, removing distortions in energy taxes delivers cuts in emissions as well as faster economic growth. No other strategy offers these double benefits.

But the costs of action are likely to rise rapidly after the first, most sensible steps have been taken. They might be offset by a technological breakthrough, which sharply reduced the cost of carbon-free energy. But such a breakthrough is just as likely to take place in the exploitation and use of conventional fossil fuels, which are so much more widely extracted and used than, say, solar power or wind power. Besides, as long as energy prices remain low, the market gives no incentive for energy-saving innovation.

Projections that run far into the future must be treated cautiously. A tiny change in assumptions can have an enormous cumulative effect. But the broad consensus among models of the costs of slowing down climate change is that a worldwide freeze on output of carbon dioxide would cost about 1.5 to 2.5 per cent of world GNP in the first half of the next century, and about 3 per cent in the second half.[6]

As for the benefits of action – or the costs of damage from climate change, which amount to the same thing – the most detailed study, by Cline,[7] suggests that, for the United States, the effects of doubling carbon dioxide in the atmosphere might impose costs of 1–2 per cent of American GDP. If warming were to continue, he argues, the costs over the next 250 years might be 6–12 per cent of GDP. Such figures do not allow for some sudden catastrophe, which might lead to much higher costs. The largest elements are the cost of lost farm output and the need to generate extra electricity for air conditioning, although losses from species extinction might turn out to be considerable.

If such figures apply worldwide, the damage caused by global warming over the next fifty years may be quite modest. However, in some poor countries, the impact of damage might indeed be much greater – if the gloomiest predictions of sea-level change turned out to be true, for instance, Bangladesh would be swamped and the Maldives would vanish from the map. But because of the harsh fact that property prices are so much lower in the poor world than the rich, the worldwide economic costs of climate change may not be substantially different.

Over the much longer term, the costs of climate change for both rich and poor countries may well be greater still. But for the next half century at least, the costs of preventing global warming may be slightly higher than the costs of living with a changing climate. Only in about 2150 are the gains from slowing global warming likely to overtake the rising costs imposed by climate change.

Even then, there are two mitigating points to bear in mind. For some countries, global warming may actually bring benefits. The regional effects of climate change are particularly hard to predict, but it seems possible that some places may find that they can grow more crops, or have a more comfortable climate. Certainly a change of such magnitude is unlikely to bring only losers; yet the losses have been more closely studied than the possible gains. Secondly, a large part of the costs that climate change seems likely to inflict will involve the loss of species that fail to adapt. Again, some species may flourish rather than fail. But a more important point is that other aspects of human activity are already wiping out species at a terrifying rate. Many of the species that climate change might threaten in the second half of the twenty-second century will, on present trends, long since have vanished from the face of the Earth.

SHARING OUT THE COSTS

Globally, the costs of taking action to prevent climate change are not much higher than the benefits that might be expected. But the costs for individual countries are likely to vary considerably. In particular, many developing countries, faced with fast-growing populations and economies, are likely to be unenthusiastic about taking action to stabilize their carbon dioxide output, the goal that many environmental campaigners urge.

While developing countries will incur costs because of their desire to develop, another group of countries will incur costs if the world buys less of their products. These are the big energy producers. Two-thirds of the world's coal reserves are split between the United States, China and the former Soviet Union; three-quarters of its oil reserves are in the OPEC countries; three-quarters of its natural gas is split between OPEC producers and the former Soviet Union. All these countries stand to lose revenue if there is a decline in world demand for fossil fuel.

The OECD estimates that the average loss of real income to the non-OECD countries of stabilizing their output of carbon dioxide at 80 per cent of 1990 levels would be almost 5 per cent during 1995–2050: considerably higher than the costs to the rich countries, with slower-growing populations. Yet stabilization by the OECD countries alone will be a policy of diminishing value. By the middle of the next century, calculates the OECD, stabilization by its members at current levels would reduce world output of carbon dioxide by 11 per cent from the level it would otherwise have reached.[8] Unless the developing countries could be persuaded to follow suit, their output would swamp that achievement. On some estimates, the carbon dioxide output of China alone would exceed that of the entire OECD.

Not only will the costs of action vary between countries. So – in ways that are at present hard to predict – will the benefits. Some countries will suffer disproportionately from climate change. They will not necessarily be the countries that do most to cause it. On the other hand, some countries may gain. Russia and Canada, both large energy producers, might be delighted if global warming made it possible to grow food in their inhospitable northern wastes.

Towards Agreement

The uneven distribution of costs and benefits means that one of the most awkward problems for the international convention on climate change will be how to allocate the costs of curbing carbon dioxide output. Because the greenhouse effect is a problem with global origins and global implications, it is likely to be managed effectively only with global agreement. That consideration led 153 countries to negotiate and sign, at the Earth Summit in 1992, a treaty to try to slow down climate change. Their commitment was modest: to stabilize greenhouse gases in the atmosphere at a level "that would prevent dangerous anthropogenic interference with the climate system" (but the treaty specifies no date or quantity). Countries agreed to draw up inventories of their greenhouse-gas output.

The rich countries agreed to go further, and prepare plans to show how they might reduce their output of greenhouse gases to 1990 levels. Several countries voluntarily promised to achieve such a goal, but then some began to have second thoughts. The Norwegians, one of the first countries to promise to stabilize carbon dioxide output, said (quite rightly) that a flat target for stabilizing output was economically inefficient. The EU, having agreed an overall target, failed to agree on how to share it out; much hope is pinned on the scope for energy efficiency in eastern Germany. The United States initially refused to set a target on the grounds that it would be legally binding on the administration, in a way that is not true in other OECD countries. One of President Clinton's first moves after his election was to reverse this policy. He may regret it, given the failure of his attempt to push through a big increase in energy taxes. Not surprisingly, the US objected at the first formal meeting of the climate treaty's signatories in April 1995 to taking measures beyond 2000. Meeting the millemial target will be hard enough.

The climate convention is only a first step. To put flesh on its few bones, countries will need to take some difficult decisions over the next few years. In particular, the costs of implementing the agreement and the way those costs are shared will be greatly affected by the way the targets are defined and by the mechanisms for payments between countries. That in turn will determine how likely countries are to make commitments and then abide by them.

As the Norwegians realized, flat targets are indeed inefficient. They are the international equivalent of command-and-control measures in domestic environmental policy: they inflict the same reduction in emissions on high-cost and low-cost producers alike. That is likely to be vastly more expensive than concentrating reductions in those countries that can make them most cheaply. Rough calculations for the EU by Scott Barrett of the London Business School suggest that the most cost-effective distribution of reductions might be 50 times less expensive for the EU than achieving the same goal by stabilizing emissions from each member country individually.

One way to share the costs of action is to concentrate reductions in carbon dioxide output in countries that are least energy-efficient, and to persuade other countries to carry part of the cost. Some such schemes have been undertaken voluntarily by power companies. In 1988 Applied Energy Services, an American independent power company, decided to plant 52 million trees in Guatemala, to soak up carbon dioxide equivalent to the gas produced by a new coal-fired plant it had just opened in Connecticut. A few other American power stations have done something similar, as has the Dutch state-owned electricity board, which charges consumers a small levy to pay for overseas tree-planting.

Such deals acquired official blessing in the Climate Convention, and the Global Environment Facility, the treaty's financing arm, has the power to help to finance them. But there are obvious dangers. The trees may die and not be replaced, for instance; and subsidized planting may disrupt the local economy.

THE CASE FOR ADAPTING

As it stands, the climate treaty has little chance of making a significant change in the world's output of fossil fuels over the next century. Does this matter? On the basis of the likely costs of damage, at least for the next century and a half, the honest answer is no. It would, of course, be wise for countries to introduce measures that would pay off in any case – such as raising energy prices to economically efficient levels and reducing other kinds of pollution. It might be wise to go beyond that point, in the interests of buying insurance against nasty surprises – although it is impossible to know how large a premium would be right.

Beyond that, adapting to climate change, when it happens, is undoubtedly the most rational course, for a number of reasons. Most countries will be richer then, and so better able to afford to build sea walls or develop drought-resistant plants. Money that might now be spent on curbing carbon dioxide output can be invested instead, either in preventing more damaging environmental change or in creating productive assets that will generate future income to pay for adaptation. Once climate change occurs, it will be clearer – as it now is not – what needs to be done and where. Most of the decisions involved in adapting to change will be taken and paid for by the private sector rather than (as with curbing greenhouse-gas output) by government. Above all, adapting requires no international agreements.

Adaptation is especially appropriate for poor countries, once they have taken all the low-cost or no-cost measures they can find. Given the scarcity of capital, it makes good sense for them to delay investment in expensive ways to curb carbon dioxide output. Future economic growth is likely to make them rich enough to offset those effects of climate change that cannot be prevented.

Many people find such arguments unpalatable. To many environmentalists, climate change seems to be nature's revenge on humanity for economic growth. The idea of adapting to it, rather than struggling to minimize it, will sound wilfully irresponsible. Yet the harsh reality is that plenty of other kinds of environmental damage deserve greater priority. Water pollution kills more people than global warming is likely to do; soil erosion leaves more people hungry; the loss of species is just as irreversible; deforestation has locally (and perhaps internationally) more dramatic effects on climate. The world has only so much wealth to devote to solving environmental problems. Many of these deserve greater priority than global warming.

Chapter 10

Saving Energy

Many kinds of environmental damage are caused by the use of energy. As a result, many environmental policies are intended to curb energy-related pollution. The most dramatic reductions have come about in one of two ways: through technological advance, or through switches to other fuels. The second – in particular a switch from coal to natural gas – will dominate the environmental impact of energy use in the developed world in the near future. But environmentalists are more interested in a third option: increasing energy efficiency. Together with the development of non-fossil fuels (by which they mean solar and wind power, rather than nuclear and hydro power), environmentalists believe energy efficiency holds out the best long-term answer to most energy-related pollution problems.

Will using energy more frugally cost money or save it? Economists and environmentalists disagree. The argument is important, and not just for the discussion about global warming. For if energy efficiency brings benefits in its own right, then policies to foster it are worth pursuing for their own sake. If not, the world may decide the price is too high, and choose instead to adapt to the changes in climate that the greenhouse effect may cause.

THE SCOPE FOR CONSERVATION

As economies develop, their demand for energy, relative to GDP, tends to rise rapidly and then to peak. The ratio of energy demand to GDP has been falling in Britain since 1880 and since the early years of this century in most other industrial countries. In the 1970s, in the wake of the first oil-price shock, the fall in energy intensity shifted gear: during 1973–85 total energy use per head in the OECD countries fell 6 per cent, while GDP per head rose 21 per cent. In some countries the figures were even more impressive. Energy intensity in the United States fell by 24 per cent and in Japan by almost 32 per cent.

What happened? Some energy savings come from changes in industrial structure; some from improvements in the efficiency of existing uses of energy. The first steps of manufacture – the initial conversion of raw material to cement or steel – are the most energy-intensive. *Scientific American*, in a special issue on energy in September 1990, cited a vivid example: "An aluminum smelter spends $1.20 on energy for every dollar spent on wages and capital; a manufacturer of inorganic chemicals, such as oxygen or chlorine, spends 25 cents. But a maker of frozen foods spends only five cents on energy for every dollar spent on wages and capital, and a computer maker only 1.5 cents."[1] As people grow richer, the processes that use a lot of energy gradually account for a dwindling share of consumer spending. The most energy-intensive industries simply shut down, or move to cheaper countries. Both seemed to occur in the industrial countries of the OECD: industry's share of their GDP fell sharply in the 1970s and 1980s.

Such structural changes account for some energy saving, but more significant gains have come from the introduction of more energy-efficient technologies. For instance, in new electric power stations, thermal efficiency (the proportion of energy input converted to energy output) rose from under 5 per cent in the early part of this century to 25 per cent by 1950 and stands at nearly 50 per cent today. In general such refinements occur gradually, as companies replace old machinery or find better ways to control existing processes. Sometimes a technological leap takes place. Once invented, such processes spread at varying speeds. China and Eastern Europe still make much of their steel using the open-hearth technique, which Europe, Japan and the United States began to abandon in the 1960s.

In the late 1970s and early 1980s the sharp rise in fuel prices led to a spurt of investment in more energy-efficient ways of doing things. The British insulated their lofts; the Americans switched to smaller cars; companies gave their energy managers bigger budgets. At the same time, structural change accelerated, as basic industries shut down. Steel is an example of both trends at work in Europe: the energy needed to produce a metric ton fell from just over 21 gigajoules (GJ) in 1980 to 19 GJ in 1988, but consumption of steel per person had already leveled off in the 1970s and in the 1980s it began to fall. A study by the Office of Technology Assessment of what happened in the United States during 1972–85 found that changes in efficiency played the biggest part in reducing energy intensity; structural changes were only about half as important.[2]

After 1986, when the price of oil collapsed, energy efficiency stopped improving, or swung into reverse. This effect was least apparent in manufacturing, but dramatic among car buyers. In 1980 one-third of American car-buyers said fuel economy was the most important feature of a new car; in 1987, only 3 per cent considered this. In Japan the average new car logged only 27.3 miles per gallon in 1988, compared with 30.5 mpg in 1982. That made Japan's new cars bigger gas guzzlers than America's, where legally backed standards   for fuel efficiency (corporate average fuel economy, or CAFE) have squeezed new cars up to about 28 mpg.

Much more energy efficiency is technically possible. As a rule of thumb, most countries could reduce their energy consumption by at least 10–20 per cent simply by adopting the most efficient technologies currently on the market. Amory Lovins, an ebullient American apostle of energy efficiency, argues that his country's electricity use could be cut by three-quarters by employing the most efficient new lighting, motors, appliances and insulation currently available – "at a cost", he likes to tell admirers, "below that of just operating an existing coal or nuclear-power plant, even if building it cost nothing."[3]

Lovins achieves his eye-catching results by assuming that every device for saving energy is used. That sounds relatively easy. But it would be a triumph for conservation if America would simply use energy as efficiently as Western Europe or Japan. In almost every use of energy, the United States is more lavish than Western Europe or Japan. Industry provides plenty of examples: in 1986 a ton of paper took 19.1 GJ of energy to produce in North America, 14.7 GJ in Europe and 8.8 GJ in the Pacific region. (The low figure for the Pacific reflects in part differences in process and in part more extensive use of recycled paper.) Work by Lee Schipper and his colleagues at the Lawrence Berkeley Laboratory in California suggests that American industries use 10–25 per cent more energy per unit of activity than other industrial nations.[4]

Schipper finds the same story in the home. Energy use, for heating, appliances and cars, is typically 20–33 per cent higher in the US than in Europe. One reason, of course, is the sheer difference in scale. Americans enjoy some 80 per cent more living space per head than Europeans; their vast kitchens have room for vast refrigerators, washing machines and clothes driers. Lots of space needs lots of heat in winter and air conditioning in summer. Even allowing for such differences, Schipper still reckons that American homes are significantly less energy-efficient than homes in Europe and Japan. Domestic energy use could, he says beguilingly, be cut by 25–30 per cent using measures that would pay for themselves in five to seven years.

As at home, so on the road: Americans use larger cars to criss-cross their vast country, and use them more often, than do Europeans or Japanese. Car ownership and miles driven have been rising faster in Europe and Japan than in America, and the efficiency of new cars growing more slowly (or not at all). Yet Americans still drive half the world's vehicle-miles. Unlike their newest cars, their average car uses almost three times as much petrol per year as the average car in Europe. And unlike Europeans, they increasingly commute to work in light pick-up trucks, which account for a fifth of all passenger vehicles but use almost half as much petrol as the total for all of America's cars.

The scope for greater efficiency is particularly large in Eastern Europe and the former Soviet Union. The Soviet Union was (after the United States) the world's second-largest energy consumer – but used that energy to produce far less wealth. Developing heavy industry, regardless of cost, meant that the communist block wasted energy on a gigantic scale. In Hungary in the first days after communism, 70 per cent of energy was used to process raw materials which provided only 15 per cent of GDP. In Poland, which until the start of 1990 priced electricity at a quarter of the world market level, coal production swallowed almost a tenth of electricity output. In these countries, with mature but misshapen economies, the energy savings won as industry restructures will easily offset any growth in demand that increased wealth may bring in the 1990s.

In the developing world, great inefficiencies also exist; but there the growth in population and in demand for energy is likely to be so strong that improvements in efficiency will only diminish, not prevent, a large rise in energy consumption. The average African household uses five times as much energy as a European family to cook the evening meal. In China inefficiency is truly dreadful. In 1982 it used twice as much energy to produce a unit of GNP as the Soviet Union, and four times as much as Japan. Removing such inefficiencies would reduce the need for increasing power supplies.

THE COSTS OF CONSERVATION

Environmentalists understandably yearn to give energy efficiency a shove in the right direction. Economists, by contrast, argue that many of the purported savings from energy efficiency are illusory. If they were not, companies and individuals would need no government pressure to undertake them.

Every plan to encourage investment in energy efficiency finds plenty of what the industry calls "low-hanging fruit": projects with succulent returns. Robert Ayres, in a paper at a conference on energy and the environment in the twenty-first century at the Massachusetts Institute of Technology in 1990 drew attention to the "energy contest" begun in 1981 by the Louisiana division of Dow Chemical, to find capital projects costing less than $200,000 with payback times of less than a year.[5] In 1982 the contest yielded 27 projects in which Dow invested $1.7 million: the return averaged 173 per cent (a payback period of about seven months). The contest continues, with more projects backed each year.

Compared with the cost of building new generating capacity, such returns look unbeatable. Indeed, at the margin, saving a kWh almost always costs less than generating one. Moreover, investing in energy efficiency can be done in small chunks, unlike building new generating capacity. The technology is often relatively simple – as simple as mending leaks in gas mains or insulating houses. No tiresome planning permission is needed, no furious residents demonstrate. And the technology is, generally speaking, safe. Conserving energy never caused a Chernobyl.

So why are people and companies so reluctant to behave as Amory Lovins urges? Studies repeatedly confirm the curious fact that people demand higher rates of return to invest in energy-saving equipment than utilities are willing to accept to invest in building new power stations. Investments in new energy supplies typically need to show a real rate of return of 5–10 per cent. By contrast, companies tend to look for paybacks on energy-saving investments in one to three years. Individuals are every bit as demanding. They are generally willing to pay more for energy efficiency only if the extra cost is covered by savings within less than three years. Some surveys find that people want paybacks within a few months. Indeed, some people may not want efficiency even if it is free. A conservation project at Hood River, on America's west coast, in the early 1980s offered to pay the entire cost of weatherproofing local homes. Only 85 per cent of those eligible agreed to have it done.

Environmentalists argue that part of the explanation for this curious behavior is a number of factors which, they argue, discourage the market from working properly. Undoubtedly the market fails to capture the full environmental costs of energy use. But even in simpler ways, the impact of price may be diluted. People may not have the right information. A home buyer, for instance, may not know how well a house has been insulated. Discovering how to save energy is complicated, even for companies: what works for one industrial process will not necessarily work for another. Though energy-saving is often low-tech, it is not always simple.

Moreover, the market may be distorted in other ways. Those who pay energy bills may not always choose the equipment that determines them. The builder of a new home usually chooses not only the level of initial insulation, but also the heating system and the air-conditioning. Reducing the running costs of such equipment may not increase a builder's profits. Institutional barriers have similar effects. People who rent their homes do not install double glazing, from which their landlords would benefit too. School and hospital administrators find it easier to get a budget for current heating bills than for improving insulation, which counts as a capital cost. The structure of fuel tariffs may add yet another distortion: the higher the fixed charge relative to the variable cost, the smaller the savings from reducing energy use. In the case of large users, the energy supplier may offer power at a lower unit price if more is consumed.

But market distortions do not entirely explain the unwillingness of people and companies to pay for energy efficiency. There are other explanations that may be more important. Even if investing in energy efficiency looks a wonderful buy, there may be real costs: the costs of disruption, for instance, while light fitments are changed or insulation is installed. Besides, energy efficiency is likely to be only one – relatively unimportant – quality that people consider when buying a house or a car or a cooker. They may even prefer inefficient models if they cost less to buy. Thus they may install a cheap central-heating boiler, even if it is expensive to run, because they plan to move house next year.

For many people and businesses, faced with limited cash, investing in energy-saving will not be a priority. Even for those whose cash is not limited, energy efficiency will frequently be only one of the considerations in buying new equipment. It is always possible to design a washing machine that is extremely energy-efficient but does not get the clothes terribly clean (the author has just such a machine), or a car that has low running costs but is not safe on the road. Quite a lot of people choose washing machines mainly to clean their clothes, and cars mainly to be safe. Businesses are even more likely to base decisions on such considerations. Moreover, the lower that energy prices fall, and the more energy-efficient that technology becomes, the smaller a part of total costs energy will be, and the less important such costs will be in the initial purchase decision – especially if the more energy-efficient product costs more than the inefficient sort.

Making the Market Work Better

Some genuine barriers undeniably exist. Policies that dismantle barriers, and thus make the market work better, make good sense. Other interventions, though, may simply be politically convenient ways to avoid setting proper energy prices. As always, politicians may find it simpler to set standards or dream up ingenious regulatory devices than to ensure that energy customers pay the marginal cost of generating an extra kilowatt.

Clearly, the market will work better if provided with better information – although that is not always as easy to provide as its sounds. Britain has two schemes for calculating the energy efficiency of buildings: one simple, one elaborate. Which should the government support?

From better information to minimum energy standards is a short step. In the case of buildings, where the effectiveness of insulation may be hard for a buyer to judge, it makes sense to use building regulations to drive standards up – and to apply them to alterations, as well as to new homes. For cars, it does not. Most people know with some accuracy the fuel consumption of the model they buy. Yet the American government has in the past been keen to raise CAFE standards from today's 27.5 mpg to 40 mpg by 2001.

Straight fuel-efficiency standards override consumer preferences. That has a cost, though not an obvious one. In Europe petrol prices are two to three times those in the United States, and yet the fuel-efficiency of new cars is not much over 30 mpg. What fuel tax would lead consumers to buy cars with an average of 40 mpg? The answer tells you what tougher CAFE standards would have cost in lost freedom of choice.

If Americans paid European levels of fuel taxes, their driving habits might be more frugal. Where efficiency is the result merely of tougher standards – or indeed of taxes on gas-guzzlers – consumers will always be tempted to use up part of the gain in driving their cars farther, or turning up the thermostat. An American study of households whose homes were insulated in 1982 found that 49 per cent of them did not use less energy as a result.

The simplest way to increase investment in energy efficiency is to increase energy prices. The relative energy efficiency of American and European industry bears that out. So does the fall in energy intensity that followed the price rises of the 1970s. The change may take time, especially if all energy prices rise together, rather than the price of one fuel relative to other possible substitutes. Change will be least painful if people can be persuaded that a succession of stepped price rises lies ahead, and so make changes gradually. It can be eased and guided by good information, by judicious use of standards and by attempts to break down some of the market's many imperfections. But to rely on intervention as an alternative to price changes is a mistake.

DEMAND-SIDE MANAGEMENT

The assumption that markets cannot be trusted to deliver greater energy efficiency has led to the development of demand-side management projects by electricity utilities in the United States. The idea grew out of a campaign against the Pacific Gas and Electric Company (PG&E) by the Environmental Defense Fund (EDF) in California in the late 1970s. The EDF argued that promoting conservation was cheaper than building new power stations, yet had the same effect: a utility's customers were interested not in buying kilowatts but in keeping warm, or cool, or running their appliances.

But how to persuade a utility to sell less of its product? Fortunately for environmentalists, America's energy industry is highly regulated. A series of changes in the states where environmental pressure is strongest have gradually made it more profitable for some utilities to invest in energy conservation than to supply more power. A first step was to decouple profits from sales volume. That came in 1978 in California. The next step was to link energy efficiency to profits. As Ralf Cavanagh of the Natural Resources Defense Council (NRDC) in California says, "You've got to give the rats some cheese."[6] So, starting in 1989, state regulators and environmentalists devised a variety of incentives for utilities to invest (in Lovins's catchy phrase) in "negawatts", not megawatts. Some incentives simply aim to allow utilities to recover the costs of investments that cut their customers' fuel bills; others go further, and allow the cost of such investments to be included in a utility's rate base, so that it makes a return – increasingly, a higher return than on supply-side investments.

Such policies have undoubtedly changed the behavior of utilities. PG&E, the main electricity company in San Francisco, hoped to negate 75 per cent of the load growth that would otherwise need new plants. By spending $160 million in 1991 and up to $260 million in future years PG&E intended to avoid building any new power stations in the 1990s. The utility offers incentives to refrigerator salesmen who boost sales of energy-frugal appliances; provides rebates to builders whose building are at least 10 per cent better insulated than California's building code requires; and offers free weatherproofing. The general aim is to cut the payback period on such investments to two years.

This example inspired regulators in Massachusetts, New York and

Vermont, chivvied by environmentalists, to look for ways to make the electricity market take account of environmental costs. That tilts the arithmetic still further towards conservation. But how should such externalities be priced? Unhelpfully, each state uses different numbers.

A second set of regulatory changes has encouraged a move to competitive bidding: utilities buy power from whomever can generate it most cheaply. In a few states – notably New York, Maine and Massachusetts – regulators and utility companies have tried to combine the two ideas, allowing bids for energy-saving along with bids for generating new power. Companies have sprung up to offer both, including a subsidiary of PG&E that does so in partnership with Bechtel. "We can sell them negawatts, megawatts – you name it," says its boss.[7]

The next stop along this curious track is fuel switching. If gas releases less global-warming carbon dioxide, why not require utilities not only to sell energy efficiency to their customers, but also to persuade some to switch from electricity to gas? In Massachusetts in 1991 a gas company tried to persuade New England Electric System, an electric power company, to pay for its customers to convert to gas, on the grounds that it was cheaper than generating extra electricity. In Vermont, two of the big electricity companies do audits to tell their customers what they might save by switching to gas, but have been understandably reluctant to pay for conversions.

BETTER WAYS

Ought American utilities to be in the energy-efficiency business? After all, it means that some electricity consumers (those who do not want to save more energy, perhaps because they have already insulated their homes and bought their efficient fridges) are subsidizing others. Some of those consumers might eventually have bought their efficient fridge even without an incentive.

Utilities making money from energy-efficiency programs dismiss such cavils. PG&E claims that complaints about cross-subsidy come "not from the customers but from the economics professors." But the professors have a point. An article in *Science* magazine in 1993 reported that the costs of saving energy through utility conservation programs were surprisingly high. Much of the investment in conservation that they made benefited industrial users, who might be expected to be less affected by the various market barriers that purportedly deter households from investing in energy conservation. And up to 60 per cent of the energy-saving investments that electricity utilities had made for their customers under demand-side management schemes would have taken place in any case.[8]

One powerful argument against relying on conservation subsidies to clean the environment was put forward by Larry Ruff of lawyers Putnam, Hayes & Bartlett, at the 1990 MIT conference.[9] Put a charge of 25 cents a pound on sulphur dioxide emitted from power plants, and emissions would surely fall by at least half. The higher prices would also encourage consumers to save electricity; but the total cost of getting rid of half of emissions and paying the charge on the other half would be less than 1 cent per kWh. Use the same money to foster energy conservation directly, and the effect would be much weaker. Even if only very dirty kilowatt-hours were conserved, the fall in sulphur dioxide emissions would be only one-tenth that achieved by attacking the problem directly.

What holds for sulphur dioxide holds equally well for carbon dioxide. If a subsidy of 4 cents per kWh is needed to conserve one kWh, then it could well cost $200 for each ton of carbon dioxide prevented through energy-efficiency measures. If society is willing to pay that sort of money to curb global warming, why not levy it through a carbon tax of $200 a ton? The effect would be to encourage a shift to low-carbon fuels, and to induce some energy conservation as a direct response to higher electricity prices. Overall, the $200 carbon tax might cut carbon dioxide output by four or five times as much as $200 devoted to subsidizing conservation.

The moral of the story is simple. Proper pricing matters more than fancy gimmicks. American utilities have frequently been encouraged by their regulators to charge less than the marginal cost of their product. Britain's privatized industry, in the course of the 1990s, is moving closer to marginal-cost pricing, with higher tariffs for customers who buy at peak periods, than any other industry in the world. Will customers respond, by investing in conservation without the help of their local distributor? Over the next decade the two countries will prove a fascinating experiment in two approaches to encouraging efficiency.

Chapter 11

Nuclear Power

Concern about global warming has come at an important moment for the nuclear power industry. It provides 17 per cent of the world's electricity – 5 per cent of its total energy use – from about 420 plants, mainly in the rich world. It is thus by far the biggest source of non-fossil commercial energy. (Oil is the largest source of energy worldwide). If global warming is to be curbed at a bearable cost, nuclear power appears to offer the only commercially viable option that can help to meet the world's growing demand for energy.

Nuclear power confronts environmentalists with a special dilemma. Any move to tax the carbon content of fossil fuels, or to restrict their use in electricity generation, would make nuclear power more attractive. Increasing the output of the nuclear power industry might be one of the less painful and expensive ways to engineer a reduction in the use of fossil fuels, because switching between fuels is likely to be less expensive than reducing the growth in the use of all fuels. Yet to rely on nuclear power raises some of the same issues posed by allowing global warming to occur: today's energy consumers benefit, but at the possible expense of future generations. In the case of nuclear power, the penalty on posterity will be the need to live with an accumulation of radioactive waste.

The nuclear debate has up to now tended to be mainly about safety. Yet other issues are just as important. Is nuclear power likely to be less expensive than fossil fuels, if all its costs, including environmental ones, are properly accounted for? If so, would it be better to burden future generations with the certainty of inheriting our nuclear waste rather than the possibility of living with a climate that had altered in harmful ways?

A BROKEN PROMISE

Nuclear power was once seen as the energy of the future. In the early 1950s, when the world seemed to be facing a growing energy shortage, nuclear technology appeared to offer energy that was safe, cheap and abundant. Right through to the early 1970s, it attracted extravagant hopes. In 1972 the Nuclear Energy Agency (NEA), the nuclear information arm of the OECD, predicted that OECD countries would have more than 1000 gigawatts (GW) of nuclear capacity by 1990. In fact, by the end of 1992 capacity was some 260 GW, and the NEA was forecasting less than 300 GW by the end of the century.

Today, fewer and fewer countries are ordering new nuclear plants. In the United States, where a quarter of the world's nuclear plants operate, no new plant has been ordered, without subsequently being canceled, since 1974. In Europe, every nuclear country but France had a moratorium on new plants in place by the early 1990s: either official (as in Britain, awaiting the outcome of a long-drawn-out nuclear review) or de facto (as in Spain) although a few plants (such as Britain's Sizewell B) were still under construction. Several developing countries had built plants that were not yet running, or had canceled projects halfway through. Even the French program was slowing down. Having ordered six plants a year between 1974 and 1981, France started work on only five in the decade after 1984. Only in Japan and South Korea does the future of nuclear power still seem promising.

One reason for nuclear power's slow growth is that rich countries have repeatedly found they needed less electricity than they had forecast. But that is not the only explanation. Nuclear's share of total electricity generation has been falling almost everywhere. Among OECD countries, only Canada, France and Japan were still generating a rising share of electricity from nuclear fuel in the early 1990s. Only Japan expected nuclear's share to go on rising into the next century.

Why? Part of the problem is, as it has always been, public unease. No matter how often the industry argues that coal mining has killed many more people than nuclear plants have, most people fear a technology that they find hard to understand and associate mainly with bombs. Accidents at Three Mile Island and Chernobyl frightened them even more, although in the first case the safety procedures successfully contained overheating and in the second, where the consequences were graver, the failure was human, not technological.

Paul Slovic, an American professor of psychology, once asked four groups of people to rank various risks. A group of experts put nuclear power twentieth in order of risk, well below surgery, X-rays and private aviation. A group of business executives ranked it eighth. Two groups – members of the League of Women Voters and college students – rated nuclear power worst of all.

Ill-founded or not, such fears will not easily be overcome. They are encouraged whenever public authorities turn out to have misled the public. They may increasingly spread to new nuclear countries. Even in South Korea, public agitation has led to higher safety standards.

Worries about safety affect costs. They make it harder and more time-consuming to find sites for new plants or for storing waste. Complex safety devices mean complex plants, which are more expensive to build (and to re-license when they grow old). Such worries will also, in time, increase the cost of shutting down redundant plants. But even without the remorseless rise in safety requirements, nuclear plants in many countries will find it increasingly difficult to compete with those using conventional fossil fuels.

THE COST OF NUCLEAR POWER

Even without trying to include environmental costs, the true economic cost of nuclear power is hard to calculate. The equation includes the costs of capital, of operation and maintenance, of fuel and – a huge imponderable – of decommissioning a plant. Such figures are uncertain even for conventional fuels. For nuclear power, all except the cost of capital are greatly influenced – decommissioning costs, indeed, are almost dictated – by government safety standards.

The capital costs of nuclear power stations are high. As a rule of thumb, capital accounts for over 50 per cent of the lifetime costs of a nuclear plant, only 25–35 per cent of those of a comparably sized coal-fired power station, and even less for a gas-fired plant. The result is that the costs of nuclear power are highly dependent on the level of interest rates. The public inquiry into Britain's Sizewell B found that, if money cost 5 per cent to borrow, the plant would pay; at 8 per cent it would not. Roughly speaking, that holds true for most plants in most countries.

In practice, the capital needed for nuclear plants is often borrowed, or at least guaranteed, by government. That is also true, in some countries, for plants using coal, oil or gas. But because nuclear power is so capital-intensive, anything that reduces the cost of capital is disproportionately helpful. Now, however, developed countries are increasingly demanding realistic rates of return from private enterprises, and some countries (including India) are increasingly turning to private capital to finance new power stations. Private investors shy away from the risks of nuclear power.

The sheer scale of nuclear plants brings other problems. It forces countries to predict accurately the speed at which electricity demand will grow. But that, over the years, has proved a mug's game. That is a good reason for preferring technologies that promote the building of smaller generating units.

Because of high capital costs and interest bills, nuclear plants need to be built fast. They are vulnerable both to the usual vagaries of large projects involving complex technologies and to delays caused by public hostility. These factors have much affected the building of nuclear plants in the two countries that publish solid figures for construction costs, the United States and Britain. In both countries, nuclear plants have succumbed to that common disease of big projects, "appraisal optimism". Projections of their cost, on the drawing board, invariably turn out to be far lower than the eventual figures. One survey of the costs of American plants found that the final costs of projects were far above – sometimes double – those estimated not just at the start but even when the plant was half-finished.[1]

Britain's nuclear program has suffered terribly from political blight. Political meddling meant that the country's seven advanced gas-cooled reactors (AGRs) were built to four different designs, a sure way to drive costs through the roof. A standard design, once approved, is far more likely to get faster approval second time around, and to be quicker and cheaper to build. Lord Marshall, a distinguished scientist who chaired Britain's Central Electricity Generating Board, says: "Economies will come from repetition. Don't let a scientist get anywhere near the plant. All we want is production engineers who will meticulously reproduce what's there."[2]

The masters of this art have been the French and the Japanese. Électricité de France, the French state-owned power company, squeezed construction times, from first concrete to grid connection, from 75 months in 1977 to 60 months by 1985. The Japanese appear to have done even better, with the time from first concrete to first electric current typically only four years. Unlike the French, they have never ordered more than three or four plants a year, so that supply has kept pace with demand. Japan has also stuck to a couple of American designs, mastering and refining them, rather than launching grandiose national models of its own. In nuclear power, modesty pays.

Once built, nuclear plants must pump out power around the clock, to service their huge capital costs. Reliability is all-important. Pressurized-water or boiling-water reactors (the most common and most reliable types) run on average for about 70 per cent of the time – much better than the 60 per cent or so of the early 1980s. Britain's Nuclear Electric, the state-owned nuclear-generating company, has seen the key to improving its finances as increasing the reliability of its unreliable AGRs.

FUEL COSTS

In the 1970s, as worries about safety increased, the capital costs of nuclear plants rose too. But in the 1980s, the rise leveled off. By far the biggest change in the economics of nuclear power since then has been the collapse in the price of fossil fuels. In the early 1990s, world recession sharply cut the prices of coal, oil and gas. Uranium prices tumbled, too – but uranium is only a small part of the overall cost of generating nuclear power. Now, fossil fuels seem likely (with perhaps the occasional hiccup, as in the mid-1970s) to be plentiful and cheap for at least the next thirty years.

The effects of the recession were accentuated by changes in regulation and advances in technology. In both Europe and America, legislation that had previously banned the use of natural gas to generate electricity (on the bizarre grounds that it was too good to waste) has been scrapped. At the same time, the newish technology of combined-cycle gas turbines has created a revolution in the design of gas-fired power stations. They can now be built in smaller units, at lower cost, they require less maintenance and fewer staff and they generate power at higher levels of efficiency than ever before. When Britain's electricity companies were privatized, they embarked on a vigorous program of switching from coal- to gas-fired plants.

In many parts of the world, not least much of the United States, coal is still nuclear's main rival. Coal has not benefited from technological advance as much as gas has: in its case, the main changes have been in ways to reduce its environmental impact. These tend to make coal costlier, not cheaper. But the recession, and in some countries the dash for gas, have helped to reduce the price of coal. Lord Marshall, an energetic supporter of nuclear power, sums up the position in many countries: "You can't make nuclear power economic until natural gas has started to run out. Anywhere where there is natural gas, nuclear power will have to mark time."[3]

THE DILEMMA IN THE FORMER SOVIET BLOC

There is one part of the world where Lord Marshall's dictum is in abeyance for the moment. That is the former Soviet bloc, much of which is more dependent than Western Europe on nuclear power for its electricity. Hungary gets half its electricity from four nuclear reactors; Bulgaria a third from one plant; Ukraine a quarter from 14 reactors.

Since the end of communism, Western Europe has been extremely nervous of another Chernobyl. The state of reactors in some of the former Soviet countries is alarming. In Eastern Europe, those in Bulgaria are generally regarded as the worst. The six reactors at Kozloduy were all built by the Russians. But while the Czechs and Hungarians made much of the equipment for their Russian-designed reactors, making them as safe as many reactors in the West, the Bulgarians did not. Their plants are badly built and have been badly managed. When inspectors from the International Atomic Energy Agency visited the reactors in 1990, they found holes in the walkway gratings in the reactor room of one of the older stations. "After one of the experts had fallen through one of these holes, badly bruising his leg," complained their report, "one of the guides commented that others had fallen through that hole and other holes and that they should be fixed so that no one breaks his leg."[4]

However dangerous their nuclear plants, though, the ex-communist countries cannot afford to shut them down without financial help from the West. Several countries that were at first determined to close their plants subsequently changed their minds. Lithuania is one: its vast Ignalina reactors, the world's biggest, provide more than enough electricity for the tiny country. Ukraine is another: in mid-1994 it decided to keep open the two surviving reactors at Chernobyl, instead of closing them down as it had previously planned to do.

The problem for these countries is that they have little alternative. Those (such as Russia) that have supplies of coal, oil and gas want to sell them for hard currency; those (like Lithuania) that have no indigenous source of fuel find it much cheaper to buy uranium than coal or oil. Besides, the biggest cost of a nuclear plant in the rest of the world, the cost of capital, is not a problem in those countries whose plants were built by the Russians. Since the capital is free, the wisest policy is to squeeze as much power as possible from it.

If the Western countries want to persuade the former communist countries to close their plants, they will need to offer just as good a bargain: not only free plants, but plants that cost as little in terms of fuel imports as does the existing nuclear stock. It is hard to see that happening. It would certainly be foolish to persuade these countries to replace their nuclear plants with more nuclear plants, if they had to shoulder the bill themselves. It would be foolish for these countries to build the most capital-intensive kind of generating plants. The wise policy is therefore for the West to help to make sure the existing plants are run as safely as possible. That means giving money, to be spent ideally in the local engineering industry, training, and advice.

THE DIFFICULTIES OF DECOMMISSIONING

Nuclear plants in the West are starting to grow old. In the United States, 49 of the country's 112 plants are now at least 20 years old. They were originally licensed to run for 40 years. The question facing regulators is whether to spruce them up so that they can carry on, with new licenses; or to shut them down. Regulators now encourage utilities to compare the costs of continuing to use an existing plant with other ways of increasing supply or reducing demand. Compared with energy-efficient light-bulbs – or indeed, even compared with coal – nuclear suffers. Though the operating and maintenance costs of American nuclear plants vary widely, the average in 1993 was higher than the costs for fossil-fuel plants.

Some American utility companies have already decided to close elderly plants early, rather than spend money to refurbish them and get their licenses extended. Other countries will soon face the same problem. As they do, another issue will become urgent: what to do with an unwanted nuclear plant?

The need to dispose of unwanted radioactive waste has always been an issue for the industry. As of early 1995, no country had made a final decision on where to put its high-level waste; indeed only one, Sweden, has built a special site to store its medium-level waste. Plant closure will greatly aggravate this problem and raise the power companies' costs.

When a plant is on the drawing board, decommissioning seems unimportant. This is the magic of discounting: a dollar spent in 30 years' time is worth far less than a dollar spent today. When a plant is decommissioned, its highly radioactive core has to be disposed of. So does lots of less radioactive but still dangerous waste. Once the core has been removed, there are basically two choices: take the plant to pieces at once and store the bits somewhere, or bury the site in concrete or sand and leave it alone for a very long time. The second choice is much cheaper, but might be less politically acceptable.

Since no commercial plant has yet been decommissioned, no country has squarely faced this choice. But the debate has been under way in Britain. In 1998 Nuclear Electric will lose the huge subsidy that it draws from a levy on all electricity bills. Nuclear Electric has eight ancient Magnox plants which account for most of Britain's nuclear waste and will soon have to be decommissioned. The company is eager to persuade the state to take these liabilities off its hands, and the government is eager to privatize the company. Freed from the liability of the Magnox reactors, Nuclear Electricity thinks it could make a profit.

The British government has therefore been forced to consider future decommissioning policy. The Treasury is keen to see old power stations entombed: that will be cheaper in the short term, but it will cost money to maintain them in the future. The Department of the Environment worries about how the public will feel about the idea of concrete tombs littering the countryside. It would rather spend money now, to build a deep repository for waste, which will cost less to run in the years to come. The argument is a classic environmental debate: should the costs of dealing with an environmental problem be carried by this generation, or left to future, possibly richer generations? Whatever the answer, it is by no means certain that today's generation, even if it were willing to do so, could dispose of waste in a way that was notably safer than keeping it where it is visible and easy to monitor.

NUCLEAR'S FUTURE

Having once decided to generate electricity from nuclear power, this generation has in effect pre-empted the choice. Future generations will have to continue to store the waste that our electricity consumption has created. Such a burden might reasonably be passed on if nuclear power could make a large difference to the ability of people living today to combine prosperity with environmental protection. If nuclear power offered a cost-effective alternative to fossil fuels – or, every bit as important – if it offered a way to halt the deforestation caused by the third-world hunger for fuelwood, then posterity might think the trade had been worth making. Nuclear power fails on both counts.

For developing countries, where much of the future demand for electricity will arise, nuclear power is rarely an appropriate technology. It is complex and difficult. Countries with well-educated workforces manage it well: South Korea and Taiwan are obvious examples. Many other industrializing countries have managed it appallingly badly. Mexico, Brazil and Argentina have all been driven by rising costs to shelve their ambitious nuclear programs. In India and Pakistan, nuclear power appears to have been as badly run as in the worst parts of the former Soviet Union. Because nuclear power is capital-intensive and needs a lot of highly trained people to run it safely, it is not yet an appropriate source of energy for most developing countries.

It is hard to see what might improve its prospects, in rich countries or poor ones. The world cannot simply abandon overnight a technology that produces a sixth of its electricity. But future nuclear power stations will need to be radically different from today's. They will need to be safe, available in small units and simple to build and operate. They must not use or create materials that can be used in weapons. Ideally, they would not create waste at all.

Is that possible? Vast sums have been spent on nuclear research: OECD governments alone spent about $90 billion (in 1991 prices) between 1980 and 1991, without getting anywhere much. Over $1 billion a year has gone into research into nuclear fusion, technology that has not yet generated a joule of electricity. It is hard to imagine such sums going into any other form of electricity generation with such horrendously small results. Meanwhile the pace of technological advance in nuclear plants has been painfully slow, and gets slower as governments become more reluctant to order new ones. Most of the efforts of big manufacturers has gone into trying to improve the safety of nuclear reactors. Such refinements have tended to raise the capital cost of plants, not lower it.

Measures to tackle global warming will, to some extent, make nuclear power appear economically more attractive. If governments want to slow down the world's output of carbon dioxide, they may eventually impose a tax on the carbon content of fossil fuels. That would tip the balance some way from coal to nuclear power.

But such a price rise would also tip the balance from coal to natural gas, which gives off less carbon dioxide, and to new technologies that reduce the carbon dioxide given off by coal. And indeed towards energy conservation. Governments might decide that some of those billions spent on nuclear research would be better put to finding ways to extract more power from coal. Developing countries have plenty of coal. It cannot be used in bombs. Its wastes, though dirty, do not inspire public terror. Had nuclear power become, in the past half century, really cheap and really reliable, then it would have established a clear advantage over coal. In fact, it has barely kept abreast. For the sake of both present and future generations, it will be better to continue the search for economic alternatives to fossil fuels than to regard nuclear power as the right response to global warming.

more hazardous waste than other industrial countries is that its definition is wider.

Even without the definitional problem, rubbish is extremely hard to measure. But the figures show that, at least in the richest countries, municipal waste is growing more slowly than the economy as a whole. In western Germany, for instance, OECD figures suggest that industrial and municipal waste was lower in 1990 than a decade earlier, in spite of growth in GDP per head of 1.8 per cent a year over the period. Even in America, municipal waste grew on average by 0.5 per cent a year in the 1980s, while GDP per head grew by 1.9 per cent. Such figures indicate that rich societies throw away progressively less of their total economic output. That makes sense: a growing proportion of consumer spending goes on services, such as insurance, education and entertainment which create less waste than buying food or household goods.

Not only does generation of municipal rubbish seem to be growing more slowly than many people imagine; the components that appear to be increasing are not the ones that have attracted most political attention. People often assume that plastic packaging takes up the most room in rubbish dumps. In fact, the excavations of a remarkable researcher prove that is not so. Working out what goes into landfills is usually a matter of extrapolation from what people buy. Bill Rathje, a professor of archaeology at the University of Arizona, is one of the few people who has burrowed into America's landfills and weighed and measured their contents – a treatment usually reserved for the dustbins of rock stars. By far the biggest component of the landfills he has examined is paper and board. Easily the biggest single item is newspaper, which has taken around 18 per cent of America's landfill volume for 30 years. The fastest growth has been in other kinds of paper, and particularly paper packaging, which now takes up 19 per cent of the space in landfills. The volume of plastics, which grew in the 1960s, has remained steady at about 12–13 per cent since the early 1970s.[1]

A SHORTAGE OF SPACE?

While municipal waste seems to grow more slowly than income in rich countries, it still grows. It still has to be put somewhere. Waste policy in several rich countries has been much influenced by the fear that they may run out of space for rubbish dumps. The shortage of landfills, illusory even in the 1980s, vanished by the early 1990s.

It was always largely an invented shortage. Environmental pressure has gradually closed off the easy options for getting rid of waste and raised the cost. For instance, one low-cost way to dispose of large quantities of bulky waste is to dump it in the sea. The ocean might seem a thoroughly sensible place to dispose of rubbish. After all, why not put it as far as possible from human beings?

But now the sea is off-limits, and the land is also increasingly unpopular. People have become ever more hostile to the idea of living near a rubbish dump. Opening a new landfill has therefore become a big political problem. In the United States, the rigmarole of getting a permit to develop a site can easily cost perhaps $500,000, even before the expense of acquiring land, according to estimates by First Analysis, a Chicago-based consultancy, produced in 1989.[2] Some of that money goes on public relations in the local community; and the risk is high, as permits are often refused or issued only after three to five years of arduous negotiations.

The costs of opening a landfill are also aggravated by the higher standards that rich countries tend to demand. Dumps – especially new ones – need to use special liners to stop moisture from seeping out; to collect and treat any ooze that does escape; to monitor the waste that is added to a dump; and to provide for shutting down the landfill at the end of its life and for cleaning up any environmental damage that may occur thereafter.

As a result, in the most environmentally conscious countries, new landfills have been opening more slowly than old ones have closed. Does that amount to a crisis? In 1986, America's EPA spread much alarm by estimating that the 6034 landfills then open would decline to about 2000 by 1992. In fact, nothing of the sort seems to have happened. Estimating landfill space seems to be almost as hard as estimating the volume of rubbish. However, a meticulous article in May 1992 in *Waste Age*, an American magazine, collated the results of five separate surveys (which had reached five widely differing conclusions) and estimated that the total number of landfills in the United States might be anything from 4462 to 10,467.[3] A best guess would be about 6600 – a figure, the article pointed out, that was higher than the EPA's estimate for 1986, let alone for 1992.

Besides, even though American states between 1986 and 1991 appear to have shut four landfills for every one they opened or expanded, new landfills are generally larger than the small ones which close. The few states that actually measured what was happening to landfill capacity reported that it was increasing, in some cases because more waste was being diverted to recycling or waste-to-energy plants. By the early 1990s, as the recession reduced the amount of rubbish that needed to be disposed of, there were clear signs of a glut of landfill space in the United States.

In Europe, the availability of landfill space varies enormously. Britain has plenty. While the United States discourages the use of quarries as rubbish dumps, Britain does not, and a survey of waste management in Britain by First Analysis reported in 1989 that the country was extracting aggregates three times faster than it was landfilling waste.[4] The bricks from which the Midlands and south-east England are built come from clay pits which make splendidly impermeable rubbish dumps, although some of these convenient holes are in inconvenient places, far from the cities that generate the most waste.

Generally speaking, the availability of landfill space is more a matter of politics than geology. Peter Daley of Waste Management International pointed out in a lecture to Britain's Royal Academy of Engineering in 1993 that landfills, at the present rate of waste generation in Europe, use about two square metres of land per person per century. Even for The Netherlands, that represents an area only twice the size of Schipol airport. Clark Wiseman of Gonzaga University in the state of Washington estimates that, if

America continues to produce municipal solid waste at present rates for the next 1000 years, the whole lot will still be containable in a pit 120 feet deep and 44 miles square.[5] Given that America's 48 contiguous states have 3 million square miles between them, this is hardly a problem of scarcity.

CREATING INCENTIVES

Environmentalists argue that, whether or not there is a shortage of landfill space, the pricing of waste disposal does not fully reflect the environmental costs involved. How to impose those costs? In the case of large waste-disposers the answer is relatively easy: they are billed directly. Big companies also face penalties for waste dumped in inappropriate ways. The costs and penalties are higher, the more dangerous the waste.

Such financial incentives have been effective. Big firms have become, in the course of the late 1980s and early 1990s, more conscious of the advantages of minimizing the amount of waste, especially hazardous waste, that they create. But, while large industries and offices usually pay to have their waste collected, households rarely do so. It costs them nothing more to put out an extra binfull, although the community as a whole will have to pay more; conversely, they save nothing if they recycle or compost or simply buy more carefully. It has proved much harder to devise policies to influence their behavior.

In looking for alternatives to conventional rubbish collection, governments have considered two main ways to reduce household rubbish. One is to devise financial incentives. The other is to force companies to take responsibility for the waste their products create.

The oldest sort of financial incentive to reduce waste, the **refundable deposit**, has mainly been used to encourage people to bring back their drinks bottles. Some governments have experimented with deposits on car hulks and used car batteries. The difficulty is to pitch the deposit at the right level. If it is too low, it will have little effect; if too high, it may deter people from buying the product in the first place (or encourage fraud or theft).

The most direct incentive is to charge people by the amount of rubbish they put out. Such **pay-to-throw** schemes are run in perhaps 2000 American cities. The EPA has analyzed 109 of them. Most charge a fixed fee for a basic service and another – say – $1.35 for each extra bin of rubbish. Such programs have obvious snags. Collectors rarely weigh the rubbish. Households have perfected a maneuver known as the "Seattle Stomp", after the largest American city with a pay-to-throw scheme. The bills tend to be relatively small, so chasing defaulters is disproportionately expensive – and default rates can run at up to 40 per cent of households. Charging people who live in apartments is especially difficult.

A number of studies are trying to add up the effectiveness of pay-to-throw schemes. One, by Don Fullerton of Carnegie Mellon University and Thomas Kinnaman of the University of Virginia, weighed the rubbish of 75 households for four weeks before and after the introduction of a pay-to-throw scheme charging 80 cents a bag, in Charlottesville, Virginia.[6] They found that the volume of rubbish put out weekly by the average household fell – by 37 per cent – but the weight fell by much less – 14 per cent – as citizens perfected the Seattle Stomp. Much of the reduction was achieved by extra recycling. But a large part was untraceable. Households may have put it in the garden compost bin – or in the skips and dumpsters of local businesses.

If a household chose only between the rubbish bin and recycling, Fullerton points out, then a pay-to-throw scheme might indeed be the best way to capture the external costs that household rubbish imposes on the rest of society. But there is a third choice – illegal dumping, or burning rubbish in the back garden – whose social costs may be even higher than the social costs of landfills. Local businessmen in Charlottesville, noticing a mysterious increase in unidentified rubbish in their skips, have no doubt which routes many of their fellow citizens chose. Fullerton therefore advocates taxing consumption, not disposal, at a rate which reflects not the disposal cost of a good but the costs that would be inflicted on society if it were illegally dumped. The tax should then be returned as a subsidy on all recycling and all proper rubbish disposal, leaving a tax only on illicit dumping.

Another option is a **landfill tax**. Such a tax is imposed in New Jersey and Pennsylvania, applied in France and will be introduced in 1996 in Britain. A landfill levy can raise large amounts of cash (which in Britain may go to cut business taxes). But it generally falls not on the individual household, but on whichever public authority is responsible for waste collection and on companies that bring their rubbish straight to the dump. It is therefore less likely to discourage the absolute amount of waste than to encourage a shift to other disposal routes. A study for the British government by Coopers & Lybrand, a consultancy, argued that the main effect of a levy would be to encourage incineration.[7] Even at £20 a ton ($32), the study claimed, half of all domestic waste would still go to landfill, 38 per cent would be incinerated (compared with 15 per cent today) and 12 per cent of domestic waste would be recycled (compared with 2 per cent now).

The most ambitious scheme for discouraging waste would be a **virgin-materials tax**. In theory, that should make new materials more expensive to use and so provide an elegant incentive to recycle more. But the practical difficulties are so large that no country has yet attempted such an option. The obvious difficulty would be what to do about imports. GATT rules make it hard to levy a tax on the estimated value of the virgin materials incorporated in an import. There would be other difficulties. If the tax is intended to discourage landfill, should it be based on the volume of a product? If it were based on a narrow range of products, would it not merely encourage substitution?

The truth is, devising financial incentives that reduce household waste is extremely difficult. Governments have therefore tried to hand over the whole problem to industry. Companies have been told to create products that minimize waste – or (which is not always the same) that are easy to recycle. Moreover in Europe, following the lead of Germany, governments are increasingly compelling industry to run recycling schemes, arguing that the cost of doing so is the best way to force companies and their customers to reduce the amount of waste they create.

THE ECONOMICS OF RECYCLING

Pushed by environmentalists, governments have seized on recycling as the best way to reduce the amount of rubbish. Voters appear to love recycling. It seems to meet some deep human need to atone for modern materialism. Unfortunately, people do not seem to feel quite the same craving to buy products made of recycled materials. And not everything in the dustbin is equally recyclable.

Governments have frequently set over-ambitious targets for recycling. Usually, they have failed to draw up a proper baseline first, or to lay down exactly how they will measure success. Invariably, they have failed to work out what the economic cost of achieving those targets will be, or to foresee the consequences of a huge and rapid increase in the collection of supposedly recyclable materials.

Recycling, even with higher landfill costs, is still an extremely expensive way to get rid of municipal waste. Of course, the economics depend in part on the money that can be made from selling recycled materials. But that is rarely profitable. And recycling saves some of the costs of landfill, but then, so does incineration.

The arithmetic, as spelt out by Bill Brown, director of environmental affairs at Waste Management, America's biggest waste-management company, is discouraging.[8] "We lose money on recycling," he admits. "It costs $175–200 a ton to collect from the curbside, sort and recycle typical household refuse. We might make $50 a ton from selling waste materials, and we might avoid $30 a ton of landfill charges. But the bottom line is that it's not profitable."

Similarly dismal conclusions came from a study for the British government by ERM, an environmental consultancy.[9] The costs of running a recycling scheme ranged from £196 a ton, if everybody took part, to £285 a ton if only 60 per cent of people participated.

Deduct modest revenues from sales of old bottles and newspapers, which might be even more modest if an increase in the supply caused their price to fall, and the slender savings from the avoided cost of disposing of rubbish in other ways (slender because British landfill prices are between £5 and £30 a ton). It is clear that meeting the government's official goal of recycling half the reusable waste in household bins could cost roughly £50 a household – or twice as much as ordinary rubbish collection.

Some recycling pays for itself, and always has done so. Precious metals are recaptured from industrial processes. Printers and offices recycle white paper. Re-use also sometimes pays: British milkmen retrieve milk bottles, and bartenders return crates of empty soft-drinks bottles. In poor countries, re-use is commonplace: markets in Bangladesh display selections of secondhand Coke bottles, and little boys in Ouagadougou sell cast-off plastic bags.

Viable recycling depends on a happy coincidence of materials costs, labor costs and technology. Over time, fewer materials have come to be re-used or recycled. One reason is the rise in the price of labor, relative to the price of raw materials: returning soft-drinks bottles through supermarkets to be refilled is dearer than using new ones each time. Moreover, industries tend to prefer virgin raw materials: they are more likely to be of consistent quality and in dependable supply.

Waste materials may be contaminated or laborious to separate. This is particularly true of household rubbish, especially if the household does not separate rubbish reliably. Companies, generally speaking, produce relatively few kinds of waste – mainly paper, say, or mainly metal scrap – which makes recycling easier.

In promoting recycling as the best answer to waste disposal, environmentalists are swimming against the forces of the market. The main constraint on recycling is not the difficulty of persuading people to sort their waste: they are surprisingly eager to do so. The problem is that there are not enough markets to absorb the waste that is available for recycling. This is partly a matter of technology – as more paper mills have been built with the capacity to take old paper instead of new pulp, the demand for recycled paper has increased and its price has risen. But mainly it is simply a matter of what producers want. As a result, the more recycled materials are collected by enthusiastic governments, the more their price declines until in some cases it is negative: to persuade a company to recycle waste plastic, a large cheque has to be attached to each consignment. In the case of household waste, the price rarely covers more than a fraction of the cost of collection and sorting.

THE GERMAN EXAMPLE

It therefore becomes necessary to rig the market. That is precisely what the Germans have done. Klaus Toepfer, the federal environment minister until 1995, capitalized on his country's environmental angst by developing a bold principle: that companies should have a legal obligation to take back – and to recycle – their product at the end of its life.

So far, this principle has been applied only to packaging (though legislation on cars and electronic goods may one day follow). Environmentalists hate the amount of packaging that finds its way into the household rubbish bin. Not surprisingly, the packaging industry disagrees. It argues that good packaging reduces other kinds of waste (by preventing food from rotting or goods from getting broken in transit, for instance). Anyway, say packagers, their wrappings have become lighter over time.

The German government rejects such claims. In 1991, it passed a packaging ordinance which makes companies take back the packaging in which goods are transported and sold. Manufacturers and packagers have been compelled to set up a parallel waste-collection scheme, called the Duales System Deutschland (DSD). Recyclable packaging is collected from households and returned to the manufacturers, who are responsible for recycling it. The scheme is backed up with tough quotas, both for the amount of each kind of packaging to be collected, and for the amount to be recycled. Incineration with energy recovery, which accounts for much German waste disposal, is not counted as recycling.

All this is expensive. Part of the cost falls on consumers who now, in the city of Bonn, wash their rubbish and sort it into four separate bins. Bigger costs fall on companies. Those that take part in the DSD are charged for each package, which must be approved by the organization as recyclable. The package can then carry a green spot, to show retailers that they can leave its recycling to the DSD. Understandably, retailers are unenthusiastic about stocking goods whose packages bear no green spot. The DSD levies transfer some DM3–4 billion a year from the consumer's pocket into the waste-management industry.

In its early years, the German scheme caused havoc in neighboring countries. Inadequate domestic recycling facilities meant that much German packaging waste was exported, disrupting local recycling schemes. The British government was lobbied by increasingly frantic waste-paper merchants and plastics recyclers, protesting that their markets were being destroyed by the backwash of German rubbish. The solution that many countries adopted was a version of Germany's plan: to make companies subsidize at least part of the cost of packaging recycling. In 1994 a Brussels directive set common goals for recycling, of between 25 per cent and 45 per cent of packaging by 2000. It also insisted that countries should not collect for recycling more waste than they had the domestic capacity to dispose of.

Easily the best way to recycle most municipal waste is to incinerate it and recover the energy. The financial costs of incineration, even with high environmental standards, are usually lower than the costs of conventional recycling. Most of the unpleasant gases from incinerators can now be scrubbed from their smoke. Above all, incinerators produce electricity: a single product, of predictable quality, for which a market already exists, with stable prices. If developed countries want to reduce the waste that goes to landfill, rather than simply make green gestures, incineration with energy recovery is the best way to do it.

GOING ABROAD

Compulsory recycling in rich countries has harmed some of the poorest people in south-east Asia, for whom scavenging is a source of income. In Indonesia the scavengers have found their incomes cut by the arrival of shipments of plastic rubbish (mainly from the United States). In November 1992, after demonstrations by the scavengers, Indonesia imposed a ban on rubbish imports.

In a rational world, such trade would be welcome. Indonesia would have taken the money and put the scavengers to work sorting rich people's rubbish. Waste processing ought to be an industry like any other. After all, importing the West's rubbish is not inherently more demeaning or environmentally harmful than making fertilizers or building golf courses. But many countries are deeply unhappy about importing other people's rubbish, and scruples are not confined to poor countries. Even within rich countries, cities and states increasingly keep their waste facilities to themselves.

But controlling the movement of waste is a legal quagmire. The central problem is separating the concept of a waste from the concept of a raw material. Trade in recyclables is a large industry – worth, on OECD estimates, 32 billion Ecu (US$43 billion) a year. Much of the trade is in scrap metal or waste paper. Governments have found it extremely difficult to find a way of separating this legitimate trade from the sort they want to ban.

One test is whether a material has an economic value. But whether, say, used office paper has an economic value may depend on whether it has been collected and sorted. Value may also depend on the price of other raw materials: when the price of oil was high, companies in America would pay to collect and clean used lubricating oil. Once the price of oil fell and the business collapsed, was used oil a waste?

The American courts have resisted controls on interstate transport of all kinds of waste. That is an easier position to implement than that of the Basle convention, agreed in 1989 and in force since May 1992. This international treaty tries to limit transboundary movements of hazardous waste. It insists that signatories should aim to treat their own hazardous wastes at home. They should not export such wastes without first getting permission from the importer, and making sure that the receiving country is equipped to dispose of them properly. And movements of hazardous waste between parties and non-parties to the treaty are banned, unless both countries have a bilateral agreement that meets the terms of Basle.

The main practical problem has been to define hazardous waste. Most of the wastes that countries ship abroad are not intended for final disposal but are "recovery" wastes, exported in order to have something useful extracted from them. These wastes are by definition the raw material for another process, so stopping trade in them between parties and non-parties interrupts trade more severely than preventing a few drums of something nasty being dumped across national borders. But if recovery wastes are regulated more lightly, a loophole could open up for drum-dumping.

The Basle convention fails to offer a watertight definition of hazardous waste. Each country has its own definitions, some much more comprehensive than others. Basle's basic principle is that if the country exporting a waste does not regard it as hazardous, it does not need to ask consent of the importing country in order to ship it. The trouble here is that some countries – such as Germany – do not regard a waste as hazardous if it is intended for recycling. So if a German company wants to ship a load of slag from a steel plant to Brazil, purportedly for recycling, and German law regards slag intended for recycling as non-hazardous, the German firm does not need to ask for consent before shipping it – even if the slag is considered hazardous under Brazilian law. Under Basle, it is up to the importer to get permission from the Brazilian authorities.

Controlling trade in waste will not get easier. Indeed, waste-smuggling will become one of the growth industries of the early twenty-first century. What are the alternatives?

One is to try to raise waste-disposal standards everywhere. If developed countries do not want their rubbish to end up in the third world, they must help developing countries to build better treatment facilities and police higher standards. Conversely, if developing countries dislike being used as illicit rubbish dumps, they must improve the quality of their own waste-disposal facilities, and prevent illegal dumping.

That is a tall order. There are better options. First, developed countries must accept that high standards and high costs for waste disposal will always increase the incentive to dump and cheat. They must take this into account when devising their own waste-management policies. It is vital to take only those measures whose costs match their likely benefits. Expensive gestures will mean more waste dumped in the wrong places.

Second, rich countries should accept the fact that they do not and never will have the facilities to recycle more than a fraction of the rubbish they create. Instead, they should offer to pay other countries handsomely – and openly – to take the stuff off their hands. Legalized export of waste from rich countries to poorer ones is much better than a black market. Poor countries, instead of banning imports of hazardous waste, should accept it and legalize it. That way, they can make sure that the fees benefit the whole country, rather than slipping into the pockets of a few.

Waste prevention will always be a difficult policy goal. Hypocrisy and wishful thinking will not make it easier. The best way to reduce the rubbish that goes into the domestic bin is not to persuade people to sort out unwanted recyclables. It is to persuade them to buy less and to buy differently. That may be more difficult, but it is ultimately more likely to lead to a cleaner environment.

Chapter 13

Protecting Nature

One of the most painful sorts of environmental damage is the loss of natural beauty. For many people, the extinction of species, the destruction of habitats and the ruin of precious views and landmarks arouse much deeper passion than city smog or global warming. Moreover, while it is possible to clean up city air and perhaps even to slow down global warming, the loss of species and habitats will be more difficult to arrest. For pollution problems can sometimes be solved with technology, while the protection of nature may require changes in human behavior, which are much harder to achieve. Economic growth may be more difficult to reconcile with effective conservation than with a decline in pollution.

Yet answers need to be found. At present, some of the richest natural habitats exist in some of the countries where economic growth is slowest: sub-Saharan Africa, the former Soviet Union, Latin America. As development occurs in those countries, people will log and farm and build over the land which, up to now, has often lain undisturbed. Such countries are not likely to restrict their freedom to develop unless they can see that it is in their interest to do so. In trying to preserve natural beauty and diversity, some environmentalists have therefore begun to look for ways to combine conservation with exploitation. Such strategies call for a balance to be struck between those who want the environment protected for its own sake and those who feel that local people must see a financial return from conservation, if they are to co-operate.

THE CONSEQUENCES OF EXTINCTION

The worst damage to nature results in the extinction of species and a consequent reduction in the earth's biological diversity (commonly dubbed "biodiversity"). But nobody is sure how fast extinction is occurring or what has so far been lost. The number of species on the planet is a matter of conjecture: estimates range from about 5 million to 30 million. Only 1.4 million have even been named or briefly described. Beyond a doubt, extinction is taking place more rapidly than it has done for 65 million years, when the collision of a comet with the earth during the Cretaceous period is thought to have wiped out perhaps 60 per cent of all the species then living. Some argue that, if natural habitats continue to vanish at their present rate, one-third of the earth's species may be wiped out by 2050, and half to two-thirds by 2100. But without a clear idea of the baseline, such estimates are partly guesswork.

The primary cause of extinction is the destruction of tropical forests, in which live most of the world's species, counted and uncounted. Some forests are being logged by commercial foresters, but most are being converted to farmland and plantations. Farming – the clearing of land that was once wilderness, or the use of chemical insecticides and pesticides – accounts for the loss of many species, especially in developed countries. A few species are being wiped out by hunting (elephants and rhinos, for instance) and by fishing (several species of whale). Others, such as New Zealand's many flightless birds or Britain's red squirrels, are threatened by introduced species.

Given that most of the species being lost have never been identified, except perhaps by a few indigenous people, does their loss matter? It is not easy to defend the economic value of biological diversity. Individual species are valued because of the services they perform or simply because of the aesthetic pleasure they provide. But such values are fragile, and hardly a justification for preserving biological diversity in general.

People often argue that forests in developing countries should be protected because unmodified genetic material found there may turn out to be useful. In particular, forests may be future sources of drugs and new kinds of food. Perhaps the best-known example of such a drug is that extracted from the rosy periwinkle, a medicinal plant from Madagascar discovered in the early 1960s to be useful in the treatment of several kinds of cancer.

In the past, it has been difficult to reward developing countries for preserving their natural gene pool, in part because of the difficulty of patenting natural resources. Some botanical institutes, including those in New York and at Kew, in London, have therefore insisted that royalties for any commercially useful discoveries of plant research carried out on behalf of large companies should be paid to the countries from which the genetic material comes. In 1992 Merck, a large pharmaceutical company, agreed to pay Costa Rica a flat "prospector's fee" of $1 million, and royalties on any products developed from genetic materials discovered there.

The trouble is, international drug companies have not devoted much of their vast research budgets to hunting for new medicines in the rain-forest. They may be shortsighted, or feel that it is easier to design new drugs than sift through the vast numbers of species in search of miracles. The most notable exception, the Merck program, has remained just that – an exception.

Another difficulty arises with defending biological diversity as an insurance against the risks that over-bred plants or species will succumb more readily to pests and diseases. Wild strains are periodically bred back into domestic ones to strengthen and protect them. That might be a good reason for establishing an international fund to make payments to countries that protect certain natural species or habitats. But it is a flimsy reason for arguing for the conservation of biodiversity in general. If a plant or species has no useful relatives, does that mean it needs no protection? Neither pandas nor cowslips would survive long with such arguments.

A stronger argument for conserving forests is that they provide a large part of the food, fuel and fiber that poor people need in order to survive. This essential role means that, where property rights are strong and clearly defined, forests are likely to be protected by their owners, who stand to make a profit from them. But where forests are owned by the state and badly policed, or where communal property rights break down, they will be vulnerable. Even this argument for protecting forests works only up to a point. If farm yields are high enough, the rational economic course may be to convert a forest into farm land, rather than scavenging among the trees.

It is always risky to argue for preserving biological diversity solely on the basis of the economic usefulness of natural resources. Even the newest recruit to these arguments, the fact that trees mop up carbon dioxide and so provide a sink for global-warming gases, has its drawbacks. Trees are efficient sinks only when they are growing. So the most efficient way to create a carbon sink is to plant a fast-growing forest, chop it down at maturity and burn the wood for fuel instead of coal or oil. Maximum biological diversity is rarely compatible with efficient commercial forestry. As always, it is a mistake to pursue two goals with one policy instrument.

Arguments set purely in terms of ethics or aesthetics are also problematic. Ethical views of nature change, and vary from one culture to another. The United States, which forced the Japanese to open their ports to American whaling fleets in the last century, now threatens them with trade sanctions for continuing to whale long after the last American boat has gone out of business. People may fight for the snow leopard's right to survive because the beast is lovely to look at, but are less likely to do battle for beetles, which make up a large share of the world's endangered species. And the ethical case for preserving biodiversity is unlikely to protect the mosquito or the guinea worm from attempts to wipe it out, or to resolve the argument about whether people in overcrowded parts of Africa have more right to land than elephants or lions.

The strongest reason for protecting biological diversity is simply the vague but universal human feeling that the existence of the natural world matters and enriches the context of life. The best way to persuade developing countries to take more interest in nature conservation will be to combine an appeal to such emotions with more utilitarian arguments. If countries can be convinced that conservation can enrich them, they will be more likely to protect their biodiversity.

WHAT TO SAVE?

What matters to many ecologists is the "web of nature" (the phrase of EO Wilson, author of the best-known book on extinction)[1]. Each species is dependent on others in little-understood ways. Indeed, the fashion in conservation has shifted from saving individual creatures (the panda, the tiger) to saving entire ecosystems, especially in such conservation "hot spots" as New Zealand and Madagascar – countries where diversity is greatest.

Andrew Solow, a mathematician at the Woods Hole Oceano-graphic Institution, and some colleagues, offer a different guide-line.[2] They developed a measure of diversity: the amount of evolutionary distance between species. Close relatives have many genes in common. If those genes might be medically or agricult-urally useful, then saving one species may be nearly as good as saving its (perhaps more endangered) close cousin. On this principle, the endangered species most in need of saving are those with no relatively unendangered close cousins. If an endangered species that shares many genes with another, less endangered one does become extinct, most of its genes will still be saved.

That pragmatic view is taken a step farther by Martin Weitzman, an economist at Harvard University.[3] He argues that conservation policy needs to take account not only of which species are most worth saving, but also of the costs of preserving them. Where species are equally important in genetic terms, policy-makers who have to choose where to spend scarce cash should plump for saving the less endangered species. In practice the choice rarely presents itself in such conveniently stark terms. But the approach is sound:

biologists and policy-makers need to be ruthlessly pragmatic in setting conservation priorities.

MAKING NATURE PAY

The loss of biological diversity is often the result not of a policy failure but of a deliberate decision. In papers for the Centre for Social and Economic Research on the Global Environment in London, Timothy Swanson, the center's biodiversity director, points out that most countries have converted their naturally diverse assets into specialized plants and animals that grow quickly and are cheap to harvest – such as wheat and cows.[4] That conversion, more or less completed in the developed world, raises the productivity of the land.

Combating such powerful economic forces has led some conservationists to change their approach. In the past, conservation policy has tended to concentrate on creating parks and setting rules. Increasingly, policy-makers are seeking to make nature pay, in two main ways: by extracting value directly from nature, and by paying people to manage conservation.

The first approach often involves developing tourism. If travelers come to look at natural beauty, local people see a stronger case for conserving it. In Japan, environmentalists have helped to start up a whale-watching industry, employing some of the fishermen in the region of Ogata who once hunted the creatures. At the 1993 meeting of the International Whaling Commission in Kyoto, members of the Whale and Dolphin Conservation Society, a British group, could point out to delegates that whales could be more profitable in the sea than on the table. A Bryde's whale, they reckoned, fetched about 33.4 million yen ($300,000) in the local fish market. But the 16 Bryde's whales that swam off the Ogata coast would, over the next 15 years, bring local boatmen some 675 million yen, and nearly eight times that in hotel accommodation and souvenirs.

Another way to make conservation pay is to sell natural products, harvested in sustainable ways. Jason Clay, an American eco-entrepreneur at Cultural Survival, a campaigning group, has devoted years to building markets in the United States, Canada and Britain for the harvest of the Amazon rainforest. His successes include "Rainforest Crunch", an ice cream produced by Ben & Jerry, an eccentric but upmarket Vermont company, and various perfumes and preparations developed by The Body Shop, a British company. He hopes to build similar markets for rainforest nuts and fruit.

Such projects inevitably have drawbacks. If harvesters (or, worse, tourists) roam around a forest, they may well trample or frighten away some biological diversity – and not only in poor countries. In New Zealand, a country that earns as much from nature tourism as from its meat exports, the Department of Conservation has been torn between the Treasury, which wants it to raise revenue from trekkers and geyser-watchers, and environmentalists, who argue that its main job is to protect the country's natural beauty. Another problem, pointed out by John Browder of Virginia State University, is that the benefits from converting sustainably managed natural products are sometimes too small to make much difference: only 60,000–70,000 families make their living from extractive activities in the Amazon region, he notes.[5] It would be better to concentrate on helping the 1 million households who live on environmentally damaging agriculture there to farm in less harmful ways.

Where countries market their wildlife directly, they need to squeeze the full value from their resources. Exported wildlife often brings only a tiny fraction of its worth in rich markets to those who capture or kill it. For instance, parrots from Irian Jaya, exported from Indonesia for $2 each, sell in the United States for $500 wholesale. Swanson has suggested that wildlife producer organizations are needed to act as nature's OPEC, ensuring that the maximum value is extracted from the consumers of sustainably produced natural resources. Such organizations would need the backing of importing countries to ensure that a black market did not develop in unsustainably produced wildlife.

Environmentalists would like to apply similar ideas to the trade in tropical timber, which is an important factor in the inexorable disappearance of tropical forests. They have been trying to develop a certification scheme for well-managed forests. In the past, developing-country timber exporters have attacked the idea as an attempt to put their tropical products at a competitive disadvantage to timber from temperate countries. So environmentalists want certification to apply to temperate producers as well as tropical ones.

Malaysia and Indonesia are both beginning to see advantages in a certification scheme, provided that they set the rules. Both countries, as of 1995, were looking for ways to increase the return on their timber: they have tried, so far without much success, to develop domestic furniture industries. If Western consumers are willing to pay a "green premium", then certification would allow timber producers to make more money from what they chop down. The evidence suggests that most shoppers would not pay extra, but rough sums by economists at the World Bank suggest that timber producers could still benefit from an effective certification scheme. To be credible, a certification scheme would need to cut out middlemen and put timber importers in close touch with producers. That approach would raise the return to producers. So would regaining the markets that have been lost in Europe and the United States where some local authorities have banned the use of tropical timber. Together, reckon the Bank's economists, the two factors might bring timber producers an extra $100–$120 million a year in revenues.

Subsidizing Sustainable Practices

The second approach to conservation is to pay people to manage it. In rich countries in particular, governments have increasingly been looking for ways to encourage private landowners to be better conservationists. The slow – extremely slow – liberalization of world trade in agriculture will help: subsidies for food production are an incentive for landowners to squeeze more from each acre of land they own. In the Scottish highlands, for instance, the fact that farmers can earn a subsidy from the EU for each sheep on their land is an invitation to put more stock on the hills than the fragile vegetation can cope with. Governments now want to pay farmers to be conservationists rather than agriculturalists.

In the EU, farmers are paid to "set aside" grazing land. In Britain, they receive extra money for farming "environmentally sensitive areas", and separate payments to encourage them to rebuild old stone walls or to create bogs or flower meadows. The drawback of such plans is that the administration is immensely labor-intensive; and preventing fraud leads to highly specific rules, which then fail to allow for the individual eccentricities of conservation.

In the United States, the legislation to protect endangered species has been skillfully used by environmentalists to protect a number of habitats from development. In the early 1990s this provoked a bitter row between loggers and environmentalists over the virgin forests of the Pacific Northwest, which were said to be the last hideout of the spotted owl. In fact, spotted owls turned up in Californian forests, too, and appear to be less endangered than many environmentalists had argued.[6]

The Endangered Species Act and other environmental legislation has also come under growing attack from another quarter. Land-owners have denounced regulations that force them to undertake nature conservation on their own property as an unconstitutional interference with their private property rights. They draw attention to a clause in the Constitution which says, "private property shall not be taken for public use without just compensation", and argue that attempts to control the use of private property amount to "takings" and required compensation. In March 1995 America's House of Representatives passed a bill requiring the government to compensate property owners for regulations reducing the value of their propety by 20 per cent or more.

Accordingly, some environmentalists have begun to look for ways to give landowners incentives to be conservationists. Defenders of Wildlife, a conservation organization based in Washington DC, has undertaken a number of experiments. The group set up a Wolf Compensation Fund, financed by voluntary contributions, to compensate landowners in Montana whose livestock was killed or injured by wolves. In 1992 another program was started to pay landowners who could prove that wolves had successfully bred and raised pups on their land. Hank Fischer, the group's Northern Rockies representative, told a congressional hearing in October 1993 that the program was "designed to make wolves an asset rather than a liability for private landowners". The group also published a collection of other bright ideas for using the market to create conservation incentives for private landowners.[7]

Making such incentives work on a national level will not be easy. All subsidies can cause distortion and fraud, although subsidies administered by voluntary groups are likely to be much less vulnerable than state subsidies. But subventions are the simplest way for society to compensate those who give up direct economic rewards in order to protect nature. If people draw pleasure from knowing that, out in Montana, wolves still run wild, then they should be willing to pay for that pleasure. Paying poor countries for the costs of conservation is even more important, as Part V of this book explains.

Part IV

THE ROLE OF
INDUSTRY

Chapter 14

The Greening of Companies

The increase in the world's wealth and population means that the impact people have on the environment will also increase. It can be restrained only in two ways: by changing people's behavior, or by changing the technologies they use. Changing behavior is difficult and likely to have only a modest effect: think how slow people have been to learn not to drop litter, one of the most basic acts of environmental self-discipline. Changing technology is far easier, and may allow large and rapid reductions in the throughput of environmental resources.

Technological change needs the co-operation of industry. That requires environmentalists to change their view of industry. In the past, they have often seen industry as the enemy. That is hardly surprising: industry has often been the immediate cause of environmental degradation. But, given the right policy incentives, industry can also be a friend to the environment. As some environmentalists, and some industrialists, now realize, industry can also help to reduce environmental damage.

The key lies in technological change. For centuries, new technologies have been saving resources. The closed stove delivers the same amount of heat for less fuel than does the open hearth; seven times as much electricity can be generated from a ton of coal today as at the start of the century. In the past, such advances have usually been driven by the desire to cut costs. Now, they need an extra impetus: the pressure of government policy and of industry's perception of its environmental responsibilities. The challenge is greater than ever. For while technological ingenuity has reduced the impact of many activities on the environment, it has not kept pace with the rate at which human demands on the planet's resources have grown. More than ever, industry needs incentives to produce products and devise processes that make as little impact as possible on the environment.

WHY COMPANIES CARE

Corporate attitudes to environmental issues have changed significantly. For many years, most companies regarded environmentalists as enemies and environmental regulation as something to be fought off as long as possible and then complied with reluctantly. This bad-tempered approach began to change in the late 1980s, first among large companies in the most polluting industries, such as chemicals and oil. By the time of the 1992 Earth Summit, some businessmen had embraced green philosophy in a big way. Under the chairmanship of Stephan Schmidheiny, a charismatic Swiss with a private business, they formed the Business Council for Sustainable Development (BCSD). Its 50 members put together guidelines on environmentally friendly behavior for companies and held their own conference in Rio the week before the world's leaders assembled.[1]

The BSCD is now only one of a proliferation of industry organizations which voluntarily set higher environmental standards for their members. One of the earliest was the "Responsible Care" program set up by America's chemical manufacturers. Under it, companies committed themselves to tracking the fate of their products through their life cycle, from manufacture to final disposal, and to adhering to a set of basic environmental principles. The European chemical industry council (known as CEFIC, from its

French name) has been especially energetic in supporting the scheme. The mix of "product stewardship", life-cycle analysis, measurement and public accountability in the Responsible Care program is typical of the way the most thoughtful companies have presented their environmental policies.

Why did some firms do an about-turn in their attitudes to the environment? A number of factors played a part. They included:

- management morale – managers, especially those of the post-Stockholm generation, often want to have an environmental record they can be proud of; some feel it improves the quality of management too;
- staff morale – in many companies, the pressure to adopt sound environmental policies came initially from the workforce;
- consumer tastes – shoppers suddenly became more interested in the environmental pedigree of the products they bought;
- desire for good publicity – companies began to see value in a reputation for good environmental citizenship;
- fear of incurring the costs of environmental damage, which have risen dramatically as regulations have tightened and also become increasingly unpredictable;
- savings – companies found that reductions in their use of raw materials and energy, and in the amount of toxic waste they produced could yield savings, partly because of the rising costs of waste disposal.

Some of these motives would have driven companies to behave in an environmentally responsible way even without government intervention. Others were essentially defensive measures to avoid unpleasant alternatives. This chapter discusses the first kind of motive; the next considers the second. Both have created big markets for environmental goods and services.

GREEN CONSUMERISM

A change in consumer tastes – dramatic in Britain – took place in the late 1980s. It was bolstered by *The Green Consumer Guide*, written by John Elkington and Julia Hailes and published in September 1988, which shot within a week to the top of the best-seller list.[2] The book was novel in two ways. Its basic message was reassuringly in tune with the wealthy, worried years of the late 1980s: even if people were not willing to consume less (and most of them patently were not), they could still improve the environment by using their purchasing power discriminatingly. Its other novelty was to name names: to tell people which companies' products to buy, to use their money to the greenest effect. Surprisingly, *Which?*, the magazine of Britain's Consumers' Association, had failed to spot this market. *The Guide* was followed by a host of imitators with titles such as *50 Simple Things You Can Do To Save the Earth*, but none had quite the same impact.

Well before green consumerism hit Britain, it had been effective in northern Europe, where a number of companies had successfully promoted the environmental attributes of their products. For instance, Henkel, a German household-goods giant, developed an alternative to the phosphates normally used in detergents, called zeolite. Henkel's phosphate-free detergents swept the board in Germany, encouraging the German government to ban detergents that contained phosphates, and blew a large hole in the French detergent market. In vain, the phosphate manufacturers tried to publicize research that suggested that zeolite formed a nasty sludge in sewage works while phosphates, soluble in water, flushed through.

During the 1980s, other detergent manufacturers began to find ways to use the environmental properties of their products as selling points. One was Procter & Gamble (P&G). In the early 1980s a technician at its French division came up with an innovation still regarded with awe in the detergent trade: the flexible plastic "dosing" ball. It had two merits: it stopped detergent from gumming up the dispenser and therefore being wasted, and it allowed a highly concentrated washing solution to engulf the clothes for the first ten minutes of a wash. The ball allowed P&G to develop concentrated liquid detergent that could be sold in a plastic container. Plastic is a material environmentalists dislike. But it can be recycled. P&G has been careful to use a lot of recycled plastic in its containers.

Better yet, it hit on the idea of the refillable container. P&G's decision to sell its fabric softener in refillable pouches and promote it as a way to reduce household packaging waste helped to revive sales so successfully that it became a Harvard Business School case-study. There were other benefits to the company: savings in manufacturing, packaging and transport costs. Liquid detergents rapidly increased their market share, and refillable containers proved popular with supermarkets, in part because they take up, on some calculations, a quarter as much shelf space per wash as concentrated powders.

THE McDONALD'S EXPERIENCE

Often, companies have embraced green consumerism to ward off bad publicity. That was the case with McDonald's, America's biggest fast-food chain. The company does not use greenery to sell hamburgers, but it has consciously used environmental policy to improve its image. This approach began after the company found itself, in 1988, the target of a vociferous campaign by environmental groups against the enormous amounts of rubbish it produced. Environmentalists in the United States attacked the polystyrene "clamshells" in which its hamburgers were sold as a symbol of the throwaway society, and the company's high profile made it a natural target.

The attack caught the company by surprise. With schoolchildren demonstrating outside its shops and letters pouring into its Chicago headquarters, the company was approached by the Environmental Defense Fund. EDF saw a chance to use McDonald's plight to educate consumers, by helping to develop ways to reduce the amount of rubbish the company produced. The company cautiously agreed: "We're good at running restaurants, but we don't know much about the environment," was how one of its managers put it. "We're close to our customers, and we knew they wanted us to be environmentally responsible."[3]

Encouraged by EDF, the firm switched (initially just in the United States) from the hated clamshells to a quilted paper wrap, made from a layer of tissue sandwiched between a sheet of polyethylene and a sheet of paper. The wrap is no more biodegradable than the clamshell, but it takes up one-tenth as much space in a rubbish dump. EDF had hoped to persuade McDonald's to switch from disposable containers to washable plates and cutlery. But the company pointed out that dishwashers use hot water and detergent: not necessarily an environmentally friendlier combination than throwaway packaging, carefully designed.

The legacy of this unusual partnership has been a continued drive by McDonald's to look for ways to cut waste – by using recycled materials in packaging and restaurant fittings, for instance, and transporting products such as ketchup in reusable crates. Another impact has been educational. With 18 million customers a day, McDonald's is in a much better position to make people think about environmental issues than EDF with 200,000 members – or any other environmental organization, come to that. Just as the promotions of toothpaste manufacturers eventually persuaded thousands of people to brush their teeth, so too does the advertising of environmentally conscious companies provide an important public service – education.

A PREMIUM PRODUCT

One of the advantages of green consumerism, from a company's standpoint, is that people are willing to pay a premium for goods they regard as better for the environment. Some companies – Tesco, a British supermarket chain, is a classic example – have used environmental concern as a way to reposition themselves upmarket. But there is some evidence that the size of the green premium declined in the recession of the early 1990s. In the United States, according to Bradley Whitehead of McKinsey, a management consultancy, the average premium fell from 6.6 per cent in 1990 to 4.5 per cent in 1992.[4]

Consumers continue to tell market-research companies in surprisingly large numbers that they use their buying power to help the environment. An annual poll of 2000 adults in Britain by MORI found that 23 per cent claimed in 1990 to avoid buying the products or services of companies with poor environmental records; as did 22 per cent in 1993. In 1990, 40 per cent bought products made from recycled material; as did 50 per cent in 1993. In 1990, 38 per cent bought "environmentally friendly" detergents; as did 36 per cent in 1993. The greenest of these green consumers are also the richest: more than half of those earning £25,000 a year or more are classified by MORI as "environmental activists", compared with only 18 per cent of those earning £11,500 a year or less. The identification of green thinking with the top end of the market will continue to press some companies to watch their environmental performance.

But, with the exception of a few niche companies, such as The Body Shop, green consumerism will never be the main driving force behind corporate environmentalism. For one thing, it simply does not penetrate far enough. As Whitehead points out, 66 per cent of American consumers cannot name a single "environmentally conscious" company.[5] Companies farther away from the super-market shelf may care even less about their environmental image: who monitors the company that bottles the beer or makes the forklift truck? When an environmentally favorable product does not do as good a job as its rivals, consumers may grow bored with it: Ecover, an environmentally conscious washing powder, emerged in a survey by the British Consumers' Association in July 1994 as particularly bad at removing stains. Moreover, green consciousness affects only a narrow band of goods. Hardly anybody shopping for a television set or eating in a restaurant thinks about the environmental implications of that particular purchasing decision.

Even if people did think that way, they would often find the answer impossibly complicated. Take the humble yogurt. Without chemical preservatives, it may go bad more quickly; it will therefore need to be transported in more frequent small batches (using ungreen lorries) and stored in chillier refrigerators (using extra energy). What kind of yogurt should the environmentally caring customer buy?

ECOLABELING

To help people wend their way through the green maze, governments and (in the United States) private organizations have tried to develop ecolabels. The earliest such scheme, Germany's Blue Angel, dates back to 1978; a 1988 poll found that 79 per cent of German consumers recognized its label. Japan's Eco-Mark scheme was launched in 1989, and Canada's Environmental Choice in 1990. A study of ecolabeling by the OECD in 1991 found that 22 countries had or were planning such projects.

Ecolabeling, however, is a difficult concept. Few products actually benefit the environment. So labelers first have to decide whether to exclude whole groups of products, such as household chemicals, on the grounds that even the best cause too much harm, or whether to encourage consumers to pick the least harmful. If they follow the latter course, they may need to decide how far to go in comparing various substitutes. The German scheme gives ecolabels to aerosol deodorants which do not contain ozone-depleting CFCs, but none to the roll-on kind. They are friendlier to the environment, but do not qualify for a label because officials treat them as a separate product.

Traditionally Germany's Blue Angel looked only at one or two criteria in comparing the environmental qualities of a product. In the early 1990s, ecolabeling became broader, and generally tried to consider a product's impact throughout its life, or "cradle-to-grave".

But life-cycle analysis is fiendishly complicated. Where does the life of a product begin? When the raw materials are extracted? Or when the materials to make the machinery that extract the raw materials are assembled? How does one compare the impact of water pollution with that of air pollution or solid waste? Does it matter where the pollution associated with manufacture arises: is it better to make products in places where waste disposal does little environmental harm, or where it does a great deal? What about the way the product works: if a dishwasher is energy-efficient but breaks down frequently, causing endless visits by a repair man in a vehicle, is it environmentally preferable to one that is less efficient but more reliable?[6]

Some of these problems became apparent when the Dutch environment ministry asked which were more environmentally friendly: china coffee-cups and saucers, polystyrene mugs or paper cups? The report, published in 1992, ran to 123 pages, complete with appendices, charts, tables and chemical equations.

The answer, it transpired, was inevitably: it depends. Two things tipped the balance: how many times the china cup and saucer were used, and how often they were washed. If the china was washed after each drink, it had to be used 1800 times before it had less impact on the environment than a polystyrene mug. That still gave china the edge: Dutch caterers reckon to use a china cup and saucer 3000 times. But the edge was dramatically increased by a refill: two drinks from the same cup meant that a china cup had to be used only 114 times before it beat polystyrene on energy use and only 86 times before it did less damage to the air. Paper cups did more harm than polystyrene on every count except their impact on water.

The finding – an incentive, surely, to avoid the washing up – draws attention to another important point: how the customer uses a product may be every bit as important for its environmental impact as how the product is made or disposed of. This emerged even more clearly from an analysis of washing machines undertaken by PA, a consultancy, for the European Commission. It found that almost all the variations in environmental impact among different models resulted from the way they were used, rather than the way they were made. Julia Hailes, a co-author of *The Green Consumer Guide* and a member of Britain's National Advisory Group on Ecolabeling, argues that clear instructions can be as important as clever techno-logy. Companies may make more progress towards cleaning up if they educate their customers to use their products correctly.

A further difficulty with ecolabeling is that of deciding how sparingly to award labels. Award too many and the concept is quickly devalued. Award too few and the important goal of educating consumers may not be met. Moreover, companies may feel that their efforts go unrewarded. Schemes have tended to award labels first for products whose use environmentalists want to promote (biodegradable engine oil in Canada, building materials made from waste paper in Germany). Testers usually neglect more common items, whose effects on the environment may worry shoppers but are difficult to measure or simply do not interest environmentalists. While examiners mulled over the pros and cons of labels for home composters and soap made from used cooking oil, detergents, dishwashing powders and disposable nappies languished untested.

IMPRESSING OTHERS

A desire to impress consumers is not the only reason companies would care about their environmental record, even if legislation did not force them to do so. They may wish to influence potential neighbors, or planning authorities. A company that has a good environmental record will find it easier to get permission to expand a plant or build new premises than one with a reputation for messy accidents. Companies may also want to impress future recruits. Who wants to work for a company with a reputation for doing wilful environmental damage? Above all, they may want to impress their staff.

To see how mixed the motives of companies may be, consider two companies on either side of the Atlantic.

Monsanto, a large American chemical company, knew that legislation passed in 1986 would require it, like all such firms, to publish its annual output of 320 hazardous chemicals. The day before the first figures were to be released, Richard Mahoney, Monsanto's chairman, announced the "Monsanto Pledge". The company would reduce its worldwide air emissions of the 320 chemicals by 90 per cent by the end of 1992. It would then "continue to work toward the ultimate goal of zero emissions." The announcement deftly turned what might have been bad news – Monsanto was a large emitter of toxic chemicals – into a bonus. (In 1993 Monsanto enjoyed a further bonus: it announced that it had indeed achieved the 90 per cent reduction.)

One benefit was publicity. Mahoney argues that the strategy was aimed partly at the company's employees, especially those under 40. They share the background and values of many members of environmental groups; some may well be members themselves. Another has been a reduction in the risk of accidents, and in being the hostage to fortune that waste disposal now represents. But Monsanto also had the good luck to be protected from competing rivals with lower environmental standards by its patents (its best-sellers include Roundup, a herbicide, and NutraSweet, an artificial sweetener) and by the high costs of entry into its main businesses.

Another company, which has also tried to pursue a responsible environmental policy is B&Q, Britain's biggest do-it-yourself retailer. Chivvied by Bill Whiting, the marketing manager, the company developed its own certification scheme for some of the tropical woods it uses; became more careful about the origins of the peat it sells; looked for ways to improve the disposal of waste, both by its stores and by its customers; and tried to persuade its suppliers to follow tougher environmental guidelines.

Whiting sees his company's interest in environmentalism not as a business opportunity but as a discipline:

I don't suppose the mine owners ever saw that the end of using children was a business opportunity, but there comes a time when the community feels that an industry's policy is no longer acceptable. The kids who work in our stores – and our own kids – ask questions. Sometimes a company needs to feel that its influence on the community is beneficial, and not just profit-driven.[7]

A MORAL DUTY OR A COMMERCIAL IMPERATIVE?

Some people, seeing the behavior of companies such as Monsanto and B&Q, argue that businesses can be trusted to behave in environmentally responsible ways, without government intervention. Many economic liberals (in the American sense of the term) want to believe this; so do many companies, disliking the whole business of regulation.

In fact, as the next chapter argues, a great deal of corporate environmentalism has been driven by regulation as, indeed, it should be. Companies are not individuals, with a moral obligation to be good environmental citizens, even in situations where that is not in their commercial interest. They are owned by their shareholders; and their overriding duty is to do what is in the long-term commercial interest of their owners. It is the job of government to set the regulatory framework in which companies operate; it is the job of companies to obey the law (in spirit as well as letter). To rely on companies to set their own environmental standards is not merely naive; worse, it is unfair to companies that genuinely want to pursue sound environmental policies. Left to regulate themselves, the most responsible companies may well follow such policies. But not all their competitors will copy it. Pressure from consumers is not sufficiently universal or coherent to ensure that dirty firms are driven out of business, and environmentally responsible ones prosper.

Chapter 15

Business Opportunities and the Environment

When companies introduce good environmental policies, they often do so because their managers have a strong sense of corporate responsibility. Sometimes, they know that a good environmental reputation gives them a competitive edge. But sometimes, their motives are essentially defensive. They know that tough environmental goals will help to protect them from law suits, losses or regulatory pressures. In the late 1980s, companies learned to respond to such pressures more imaginatively: to turn them to advantage. The danger with their success is that politicians start to assume that regulation is costless – or even profitable. In the hunt for ways to reconcile growth with a cleaner environment, politicians may persuade themselves that regulation increases industrial competitiveness.

One reason politicians reach this conclusion is that companies have done a great deal to foster it by publicizing the view that tough environmental policies save them money. Some American companies go in for acronyms to underline the point: 3M has a scheme called Pollution Prevention Pays, Chevron has SMART (Save

Money and Reduce Toxics), Texaco has WOW (Wipe Out Waste) and Dow Chemical has WRAP (Waste Reduction Always Pays). Firms themselves often found, when they first introduced measures to tackle pollution, that they made big improvements in their environmental performance. Between 1989 and 1991, for instance, Texaco reduced its output of dirty air and water and solid waste by 40 per cent, and its toxic emissions by 58 per cent.[1] Often, such changes were accompanied by striking savings. 3M's Pollution Prevention Pays claims to have saved some $500 million since 1975.

Another reason why politicians associate corporate greenery with profitability is that so many large companies have participated in voluntary programs to reduce pollution. In the United States, the Environmental Protection Agency introduced a program in February 1991 called "33/50". It invited 555 companies which released large amounts of chemical pollutants (and a further 5000 in July that year) to make a voluntary commitment to reduce releases of 17 of the nastiest chemicals by 33 per cent by the end of 1992 and by 50 per cent by the end of 1995. The aim was to give companies plenty of freedom to decide how best to make such reductions: whether to use filters for "end-of-pipe" clean-ups, for instance, or whether to change the way they made their products and the materials they used in order to prevent waste from arising in the first place. Within a year, 734 companies signed up.

An even more ambitious voluntary program has been undertaken by the Dutch. Under the 1989 National Environmental Policy Plan (NEPP), the environment ministry set tough targets for reducing pollution. It then talked to individual industries, asking them to produce plans to meet the targets. By the end of 1993, detailed plans had been hammered out with sectors that account for a total of 60–70 per cent of Dutch pollution. For example, agreements with oil refineries in Rotterdam cut smog and emissions of sulphur dioxide. In 1992 deals with packaging companies contributed to the first decline in the volume of municipal waste since the 1930s. Output of ammonia also fell sharply.

The Netherlands' experience says something about the strengths and weakness of such projects. Its second NEPP, drawn up in 1993, proved more difficult to devise and implement. The first plan had been published when the economy was growing at 4 per cent a year; in 1993, growth was flat. Besides, the sectors which signed up the first time were the well-organized ones with lots of large companies. The second plan has had to get to grips with The Netherlands' fragmented retailers, split among 250,000 outlets, and its equally divided building industry. All this has made it harder for officials to bargain with companies, as they bargained with the first bunch of industries, trading flexibility in implementing controls for stiffer standards.

Behind both voluntary experiments, though, lurks the threat of regulation. Past experience with environmental legislation led both American chemical companies (the main signatories of 33/50 agreements) and Dutch polluters to prefer flexibility to pick their technology and timing to the rigidities of the law. Government offered industry a trade: agree to voluntary measures, and you can work (more or less) at your own pace and in the way that suits your industry best. But without the threat of legislation, it is unlikely that either group would have co-operated. Moreover, if the industry does not believe the government, it may not co-operate. The British packaging and newsprint industries, told by government to find voluntary ways to increase recycling, dragged their feet, confident that the government would find it difficult to legislate.

WHEN REGULATION PAYS

The argument that tough environmental policies are in the commercial interests of businesses, and that strong environmental regulation may improve national competitiveness, was put most persuasively in a famous one-page essay by Michael Porter, a Harvard Business School management guru.[2] The burden of Porter's thesis was that inadequate environmental regulation in the United States was losing the country a wonderful opportunity to break into markets abroad. Other countries, notably Germany and

Japan, were stealing competitive advantage by imposing more stringent environmental regulations. The message was clear: America needed to set stiffer environmental standards in order to improve its competitiveness. "Properly constructed regulatory standards", he commented, "will encourage companies to re-engineer their technology. The result in many cases is a process that not only pollutes less but lowers costs or improves quality."

Porter's essay had an enormous political impact, because it appeared to offer that economic oxymoron: a free lunch or, to use the more fashionable term, a "win–win" strategy. The same measures could give a country a cleaner environment *and* a more competitive economy. No wonder this argument appealed to politicians as diverse as Al Gore in the United States and Jacques Delors, casting around in the final months of his European Commission presidency for ideas to stimulate employment in Europe.

Indeed, there are situations in which strong environmental regulation may benefit companies. Some industries have always known this: waste-management companies like to tell one another that the more government interferes in business, the more money business makes. Their industry is particularly influenced by government regulation. But the kind of situations in which companies benefit most from environmental rules are not those that Porter or most politicians have in mind.

First, environmental regulations may reduce the costs of a company's inputs. A food-processing company might gain from higher standards for the water supply it used. A business renting holiday cottages along the south coast of England might benefit if tighter rules on sewage dumping cleaned up the local beach. The German paper industry has benefited from the country's recycling laws, which have increased the supply of cheap recycled pulp.

Secondly, regulations may create markets for a company's products. Johnson Matthey campaigned to make catalytic converters compulsory in Britain[3] (the company mines platinum and palladium, key ingredients in a catalyst). Britain's nuclear electricity generators have been keen on carbon tax: not surprisingly, as they are the main commercial source of carbon-free energy. Shanks &

McEwan, one of Britain's biggest waste-management companies, campaigned in 1993–94 to persuade the waste-regulation authorities to tighten the rules on what could be put in landfills, arguing that some hazardous materials should be incinerated or treated instead. Given that Shanks & McEwan put such materials in landfills that it ran, the campaign might appear odd. But its logic was sound. The company foresaw that tighter controls on importing hazardous waste would cut the turnover of its incinerators by around 40 per cent. Incineration is so much more expensive than landfill that few companies would voluntarily choose it as a disposal route. So Shanks wanted tougher rules to bring it new domestic customers. So far it has failed: but a new Brussels directive on landfills will eventually help by restricting the extent to which Britain can put hazardous waste in landfills.

Third, regulation may drive some companies out of an existing market, often by increasing the capital requirements. Again, an example from waste management. In the United States, tougher standards for landfills were repeatedly promised in the early 1990s and then postponed. Part of the reason was the extra costs they would inflict on cities; part, the threat they posed to small landfill operators, who lobbied furiously against them. The delays infuriated the larger companies. Waste Management, the largest, "helped to develop the rules and then spent many tens of millions of dollars to put our own facilities into compliance," according to Bill Brown, the company's director of environmental affairs.[4] Waste Management finally teamed up with several environmental groups, including the National Audubon Society and the Sierra Club, to push the legislation through. They finally began to take effect in October 1993. The higher standards will mean profits for those waste managers who have invested enough to meet them. The source of the profits will be the higher charges that the companies will be able to pass on to the communities which use their dumps.

In all these cases, regulations are a way to protect a market. They have the same effect as, say, tougher rules on the financial stability of banks or the promises made by travel agents. They protect the scrupulous companies from being undercut by the unscrupulous.

The cost (though often well hidden) is borne by the customer.

Regulation can even be used this way to protect companies from foreign competition (a theme explored in Chapter 18). The most famous instance is Denmark, which has many small brewers and environmentally conscious consumers. Denmark imposed a deposit on soft drinks and beer containers, which also had to be refillable and to meet approved standards for size and design, a condition the government claimed would facilitate re-use. Foreign companies pointed out that glass was relatively expensive to transport; that Denmark was a small market, for which it was hardly worth designing special bottles; and that the rules unfairly protected Danish industry. In 1988 the European Court of Justice ruled that the insistence on certain designs was an interruption of trade, but allowed Denmark to keep the other rules. Germany, which also has lots of small brewers (which find it easy to collect and refill bottles), has since imposed similar rules.

Environmental regulations can give one company or industry a lead over its rivals. Used judiciously, such regulations may create a community of interest among companies, government and environmentalists. The Montreal Protocol, the treaty to reduce the use of CFCs, was possible because governments and environmentalists were backed by the big CFC producers. They reasoned that the United States would eventually ban CFCs on health grounds (or that they would be sued by people who claimed that the damaged ozone layer had caused their skin cancers), and that the alternative chemicals were so expensive to make that they needed a global market. The best way to secure that was through an international treaty, banning the use of their own rival – but less expensive – product. While the CFC manufacturers, such as DuPont and ICI, were present in force at the international meetings to negotiate the treaty and its subsequent tightenings, their customers were not. The companies that use CFCs – refrigerator manufacturers, air-conditioning servicers, dry-cleaners – are often small-scale, fragmented businesses. But they and their customers, not the CFC manufacturers, will carry the main costs of the change.

A company that develops a technology to meet high environmental standards has an interest in pressing government to mandate those standards, and in allowing environmentalists to lobby on its behalf. American waste managers invested heavily in the early 1990s in tightening the controls on hazardous-waste incinerators. The Hazardous Waste Treatment Council, a trade body, then joined forces with environmentalists to urge the government to outlaw the burning of such waste in industrial boilers and cement kilns, which can charge less because they must meet less stringent standards for air emissions. Government, for its part, will find that higher environmental standards cost society less if appropriate technologies to meet them already exist.

WIN–WIN OR TRADE-OFF

In his famous article, though, Porter was not talking about environmental regulations as a form of protectionism. He appeared to claim that environmental regulation would encourage companies to make profitable innovations that would not otherwise have occurred to them, and that would make them more competitive in foreign markets. His claim is, to say the least, an unusual one. Generally, businessmen grumble that environmental regulation undermines competitiveness. Economists tend to agree, while arguing that businessmen usually exaggerate the importance of the effect.

Environmental economists were baffled and indignant that a mere management consultant could have such an impact with a single article, especially when he appeared to out-green them. They marshaled some hefty counter-arguments. Heftiest of all is the argument that Porter's basic claim is wrong. One group of economists pointed out that the United States spent a larger share of GDP on environmental compliance than any other country in the world; that it ran an increasing trade surplus in environmental-protection equipment between 1989 and 1991; that it was well ahead of Germany as an exporter of air-pollution control equipment (the area Porter assumed to be the biggest lost opportunity); and that it had overtaken Germany in 1991 as the country with the largest trade surplus in environmental-protection equipment.[5]

The Porter hypothesis assumes that companies have large unexplored opportunities to save money and improve products; that government regulations are likely to force companies to make savings and product developments that they would not otherwise have done, and that these innovations will pay better than the investments they would have made of their own accord.

The first of these assumptions is greatly encouraged by slogans of the "pollution prevention pays" sort. The trouble is, it does not always pay – or it may pay simply because it avoids an even higher cost, such as a fine or a bill for cleaning up toxic waste, that would otherwise be imposed not by the commercial market but by regulators or the courts. Even when pollution prevention or energy efficiency appears to yield genuine savings, a nagging question remains. Were companies really too stupid to see such savings before? Others may cariacature this doubt, as does the famous joke about two economists walking down the street who see some money lying on the pavement. "Look," says one, "there's a £10 note." "It can't be," says the other. "If it were, somebody would have picked it up."

The real costs of some apparent savings may not be easy to spot: they may, for instance, arise because good managers are diverted from making and selling a company's basic product to improving its environmental performance. But they will still affect the company's competitiveness.

Most of the savings that really pay have almost certainly been made. Further steps will become increasingly expensive. An article by two McKinsey consultants, Noah Walley and Bradley Whitehead, vividly outlines the way in which the costs of environmental protection are rising in the United States. They describe:

> One large chemical company, anxious to capitalize on its early successes, committed to a program to reduce emissions of hazardous wastes. The company soon found that it was starving other important projects, like plant upgrades, and that roughly two-thirds of its capital budget went

to environmental spending. Perhaps even more alarming, nearly 80 per cent of plant engineers' time was being consumed by environmental projects. Managers at this company are just beginning to understand that all their relatively easy environmental problems have already been solved and that the economic forces at work in the industry are making it increasingly difficult to find win–win solutions.[6]

The company shares some of the characteristics of Monsanto, where Richard Mahoney admits that the costs of doubling investment in environmental protection in the late 1980s was to wipe out not just waste but most of the improvement in profit margins the company might otherwise have enjoyed in that period. Other companies are equally burdened. Texaco plans to invest $1.5 billion a year for five years on environmental compliance and emission reduction. The total investment will be three times the book value of the company and twice its asset base. Yet such projects will provide little revenue.

To believe that environmental regulations improve corporate competitiveness, it is necessary to believe that the average company routinely misses profitable opportunities to develop environmental products or install anti-pollution processes. Moreover, it is necessary to believe that these missed business opportunities are likely to be more profitable than opportunities that companies overlook for other reasons. Otherwise, competitiveness would presumably be best improved by regulating in other, perhaps non-environmental areas.

HIDING THE COSTS

And what about international markets? "[We] can prosper by leading the environmental revolution and producing for the world marketplace the new products and technologies that foster economic progress without environmental destruction," says Al Gore, America's vice president, in a foreword to the new edition of his book, *Earth in Balance*.[7] In the early 1990s several countries hoped that they could develop new markets for environmental technology. Japan's Ministry for International Trade and Industry, for example, wants Japanese companies to develop a range of energy-efficient technologies. And the Clinton administration has launched a research program to try to build an environmentally friendlier car.

There is a thin line between this familiar sort of government-directed (and, often, government-subsidized) research on the one hand, and the more novel idea that regulation should be used deliberately to set the pace of technological advance. Environmentalists were introduced to the technology-forcing capacity of environmental regulation by the experience of the Montreal Protocol. When it was signed, commercial alternatives to CFCs in many of their uses did not exist. Within a few years of the agreement, alternatives for most uses were in production. A more recent attempt to repeat this experiment has so far been unsuccessful. The Air Resources Board of California's Environmental Protection Agency has insisted that 2 per cent of vehicles sold in the state will have to be "zero-emission vehicles" from the start of 1998 (and 5 per cent from 2001). A dozen states in the north-eastern United States voted in 1994 to adopt California's standard too. That potentially expands the zero-emission rule to 40 per cent of the market for vehicles in the United States. Yet progress to develop a commercially viable electric car has been slow. Sometimes, technologies cannot be forced.

There are other risks in using regulation to force the pace of technological advance. Governments may bet on the wrong technologies: arguably, it would have been better for the American car industry if California and its imitators had decided instead to foster breakthroughs in conventional car design. And regulations will not guarantee that the gain benefits domestic industry: some of the most striking advances in the development of electric cars have been made in Britain, and it is perfectly possible that the main beneficiary of the rules will once again be Japan.

There are ways to have both environmental improvement and greater economic efficiency at the same time. But regulating industry is not one of them. It is wrong to pretend that the environment can be cleaned up for nothing. The "win–win" argument breeds the view that pollution prevention is costless. A 1993 public-opinion poll in the United States found that over two-thirds of Americans did not believe that their country had to choose between environmental protection and economic development. Yet pollution takes place because polluters force the rest of society to carry the costs of their polluting activities; so preventing pollution involves forcing polluters to carry their share of the costs.

Those costs will be substantial. In some rich countries, they have been growing faster than the economy for two decades. Walley and Whitehead point out that a 1991 worldwide survey of several hundred chief executives by McKinsey found that most expected environmental spending to double as a percentage of sales in the course of the 1990s.[8] In some pollution-intensive industries the rise will be particularly dramatic. They cite estimates that America's Clean Air Act will cost petroleum refineries $37 billion: over $6 billion more than the book value of the entire industry.

These immense numbers may turn out, like many previous industry estimates of environmental costs, to be an exaggeration. But while they are not necessarily an argument for abandoning environmental policy, they are a good reason for companies and government to spend much time and effort on the design of policy, so that it can be implemented in ways that achieve the maximum environmental improvement for the minimum economic cost. Companies need to think hard about ways to keep down environmental costs when they take investment decisions. That is the point when they have most freedom to meet regulations before they become a burden.

It is worth repeating that it is usually a mistake to use one policy instrument to try to achieve two different goals. The best policies to improve competitiveness certainly do not involve tougher environmental regulation. Some of the best ways to improve the quality of the environment will make countries less competitive, not more. A cleaner environment is worth having for its own sake, and industry is more likely to help to deliver it if politicians do not oversell the case for high environmental standards.

Chapter 16

Environmental Investment and Reporting

How can anybody tell how green a company is? To measure their impact on the environment, some companies have developed the environmental audit. To communicate their findings to the world at large, they have developed the environmental report. Such management tools and the information they generate have been a powerful stimulus for corporate environmental policy. When companies have measured the amount of energy they use or pollution they create, they have often been astonished – and abashed – by the results. Information also gives them a baseline by which to measure improvements. But information in public hands is an even more powerful instrument.

Measurement can be used for many different purposes. When companies collect information about their environmental performance, they understandably want to control the way it is used. Environmentalists, for their part, see environmental reporting as a way to put pressure on corporate policies. In particular, some hope it will increasingly be used by investors to steer cash to the greener companies. Such divergent expectations have led to confusion about what information companies should publish and why.

THE ORIGINS OF ENVIRONMENTAL AUDITING

The original purpose of the environmental audit, when it was first developed in the United States, was to allow American companies to be sure that they were complying with the complex legislation that governs their responsibilities for avoiding pollution. Specialist environmental auditors therefore check compliance and examine sites or plants being bought or sold to ensure that they carry no surprise liabilities. The technique was pioneered for chemical and petrochemicals companies, and in the early 1980s, these companies were overwhelmingly the main customers for such auditing services.

Since the establishment of the Toxics Release Inventory (TRI) in 1986, American companies in the most polluting industries have had a legal obligation to publish details of their 307 most hazardous air emissions. They must also tell the Securities and Exchange Commission, the country's share-trading regulator, about prospective environmental liabilities, usually for cleaning up contaminated land. As a result, a growing number of American companies include some kind of environmental information in their financial statements.

Such obligations are virtually unknown in Europe. There, the concept of the environmental audit was introduced by American multinationals, concerned about the danger of acquiring environmental liabilities across the Atlantic. Europe's liability legislation is more relaxed than America's. But the growth of green consumerism in Europe in the late 1980s encouraged companies to call in the environmental auditors, in order to find out what they should tell inquisitive environmentalists. Ron McLean, who runs environmental management for Arthur D Little in Europe, reckons that by 1990 European companies accounted for 30–40 per cent of his business.[1] Two years earlier all of his clients had been the European subsidiaries of American firms.

Because legal obligations to report environmental information are still rare in Europe, European companies use auditing differently. Audits have typically examined production processes for environmental friendliness, and have looked especially carefully at where their raw materials come from. A survey of environmental reporting in Europe undertaken for the European Commission in 1993 thought that "the disclosure levels in Germany are far higher than for any other country." Now, European governments are also starting to mandate the publication of environmental information. Since 1989 Swedish companies have been obliged to report their environmental performance in relation to government regulations. In The Netherlands, some 30 companies now issue environmental reports, and the Dutch government has announced that it will make them a legal requirement. Further away, India in 1992 became the first country in the world to require environmental audits by law, insisting that the results be reported to state Pollution Control Boards.[2]

The collection of information provides an internal discipline, and gives the corporate environment division greater clout than it might otherwise have had. But without some follow-up action, the mere collection of information is not a very useful activity. One obvious use for environmental data is to improve the quality of management. Companies approach this in two ways. First, some deliberately use data collection to train or to help staff in one part of the group become familiar with other parts. Allied-Signal and Union Carbide both put their high-flyers to work with consultants when conducting audits. BP, one of a number of companies that uses its own staff for audits, creates teams of people drawn from different parts of the group in different countries.

Secondly, companies develop a system of following up problems that the initial audit has identified. Union Carbide, scarred by the awful Bhopal disaster of 1984, has become especially good at that. Its auditors, often retired senior managers, look not only at subsidiaries but also at some facilities used by the company, such as overseas terminals. The tough follow-up procedure makes sure that findings are translated into action. British Gas classifies the findings of environmental audits under headings ranging from "essential" (activites that break the law or company policy) to "desirable" (activities where a more active approach is needed).

ENVIRONMENTAL REPORTING

A growing number of companies publish an environmental report. This usually (but not inevitably) contains information gleaned in the course of an environmental audit, although the audit takes on a different shape if its primary purpose is to assemble data for publication. Sometimes the environmental report is a by-product of the audit: Ciba-Geigy, a Swiss pharmaceutical company, regards its report as one of the outputs of its Safety, Energy and Environmental Protection reporting system.

The pioneers of environmental reporting were Norsk Hydro in Europe and Monsanto in the United States. Norsk Hydro, a chemical and fertilizer manufacturer, published in 1990 a report full of detailed figures on emissions and discharges, measured against authorized limits. Monsanto, in 1991, published an "Environmental Annual Review" which gave details on its toxic air emissions for its operations in Canada, Britain and Belgium as well as the United States and set out quantified goals for improvement.

Since then, more than a hundred companies worldwide have published some environmental information. The most striking feature of such reports is their diversity. With financial reporting, countries have strict rules on the information that must be published and the form in which it should be presented. No such conventions exist for environmental reports. Companies are free to publish whatever they wish (or whatever they think they can get away with). Reports can thus be almost anything printed on recycled paper with a few nice pictures of birds and flowers (an approach that is particularly popular in Japan). Quite a few companies simply carry a few rather general paragraphs on environmental performance in their annual report and accounts.

Among businesses that take such reports seriously, most publish an essay of sorts on the environmental impacts they perceive their business to have. An example of this approach done well is British Gas, whose environmental review describes the company's approach to such subjects as contaminated land and energy efficiency, although it also sets some targets and reports on their achievement. About a third of the companies that publish environmental reports concentrate on numbers rather than text. Some use information that they are in any case obliged to publish (such as the TRI data in the United States) as the basis of their reports.

Some companies ask an outside body to sign off on their report, in the hope of giving it extra credibility. This verification process, like everything else about the reports, varies enormously in rigor. Some canny firms of accountants and environmental consultants have spotted the exercise as a new market opportunity. (Ecover, a manufacturer of environmentally benign washing powder, uses Greenpeace.) The independent experts rarely visit sites and check data directly. The general practice is to take a company's numbers on trust.

That is not necessarily wise. Most reports use quantitative data, but none, as of early 1995, indicated the relative reliability of the data they produced. Ron McLean thinks that perhaps 5 per cent of the statistics in a typical environmental report emerge from continuous measurement.[3] Another 30 per cent or so come from frequent measurements. Some of the remainder may come from a single reading; others from estimates. He picked up this point in the statement that accompanied the 1993 environmental report of Ciba-Geigy. He commented on the relative quality of the data used to report emissions of gases and discharges of hazardous wastes. In some cases, he pointed out, emissions are estimated from relatively few observations. He questioned the reliability of such estimation methods, and urged Ciba to request information on the quality of the data from its sites in order to improve future reports.

WHAT TO MEASURE

Among companies that publish figures in their environmental reports, two broad styles are emerging. One – the Anglo-American model – might be typified by Dow Europe. It tabulates pollutants to air, water and soil from its individual plants and lists the extent to which they have been reduced or increased in recent years. It reports company-wide figures beside detailed breakdowns of emissions for individual plants. It is possible to learn the amount of hazardous waste going to landfill from the company's plants in Tarragona, in Spain, and to compare 1988 with 1995; or to discover the amount of CFCs produced by its Danish operations. In each case, there is a manager's name and a contact telephone number. Another version of this approach, that of Union Carbide, tracks performance against the "Responsible Care" program of the American chemical industry. It gives details of pollution prevention and safety, and sets targets for future improvements.

The other model – the Teutonic, perhaps – tries to capture the difference between what companies take in and what they produce. This "ecobalance" approach has been developed for some German companies with the advice of Dr Bernd Wagner of the University of Augsburg. One example is Kunert, a German textile manu-facturer: it publishes "ecobalance sheets" weighing its use of electricity, air and mains water against its output of tights, socks and waste. The 1992 report shows the difficulty of cutting what Wagner calls the "fixed ecological consumption levels" of water and energy in line with the 26 per cent decline in the weight of the company's products. A number of German companies, such as the Landes-girokasse of Stuttgart, have also adopted this approach. So has the Danish Steel Works, whose report measures the input of steel scrap, chemicals and energy against the output of pollutants and useful products. A drawback of the approach is, of course, that it does not measure compliance against regulatory requirements.

Few companies have tried to make the leap from measuring quantities of pollutants to attaching cash figures to their environmental impacts. The most famous exception is a Dutch information consultancy, BSO/Origin. Its annual report for 1990 was a pioneering attempt to attach monetary values to the environmental damage done by its operations. Its green accounts totted up the costs of emissions from its energy consumption, pollution from cars and airline flights, dirt from water treatment, incineration and power generated on the company's behalf. The monetary values represented the marginal cost of reducing emissions to the point where the cost equalled the marginal benefits of doing so. Different pollutants required different rules: the cost of treating waste water, for instance, was taken to be that of turning it back into drinking water.

All told, the company's report reckoned that it did environmental damage worth 2.2 million guilders ($1.2 million) in 1990. From this it subtracted "environmental expenditures" such as fuel taxes and water and refuse charges. It virtuously deducted the remaining 2 million guilders of "value lost" from conventional value added. The company has repeated the exercise in three subsequent years: in 1992, it reckoned value extracted at 3.2 million guilders and in 1993 at just under 3.3 million guilders (a reflection of expansion).

Robert Gray, the director of the Centre for Social and Environmental Accounting Research at Dundee University, is critical of BSO's approach: he reckons that it involves adding too many different kinds of environmental costs, measured on different bases.[4] The company's president, Eckhart Wintzen, has a different worry. He is a passionate environmentalist, and would like "ecological book-keeping" to be mandatory for all companies in the developed world: companies would be required to calculate, in cash terms, the "burden a product places on the ecosystem throughout its life-cycle". On this concept of "extracted value", governments would levy an extracted-value tax. The revenue would be used to rebuild the environment. Philips, the Dutch electronics firm that has a 40 per cent stake in BSO, is happy for Wintzen to publish his eye-catching reports, but has been unenthusiastic about his suggestion that the company voluntarily pay its extracted-value tax into a fund to finance good works.

CHOOSING AN AUDIENCE

Just as important as the way environmental reports are constructed may be the way they are used. Many companies have found that the sheer exercise of measuring their activities has been a spur to better environmental performance. The need to publish an account at regular intervals is an important internal discipline.

But if the discipline is to work well, companies need to be clear about their audience. A survey of some hundred large companies found that the key target audience for most American and European companies was not environmental lobbyists or even green consumers, but their own employees. Customers were the most important group for Japanese companies; shareholders were second-most important in the eyes of Americans; and Europeans gave particular weight to trade customers and the media. The survey's authors noted that, given the cost of producing a report, "a surprisingly small number of report makers have carried out much research on the needs of various user groups." One rare exception was BP Chemicals, which held a forum to try to get feedback from those who might be interested in the report; another was Dow Europe, which asked its employees how they felt about its report.[5]

If environmental reports are to be useful to shareholders, they need to give more information on the links between environmental policy and corporate performance. One such area is that of environmental liabilities, which European companies are rarely obliged to give information about: most therefore say nothing (British Coal and Thorn EMI are honourable exceptions). American companies usually say only what they are obliged to say. Britain's Chartered Association of Certified Accountants holds an annual competition for the best environmental reports. Roger Adams, who runs the competition, wishes that more companies would provide environmental information relevant to their financial performance, such as estimates of the amount of capital spending that will be required to keep pace with future regulatory requirements.

Another area where information would be useful to both companies and their shareholders is the efficiency with which environmental standards are met. Baxter, an Illinois health-care firm, quantifies environmental costs (such as pollution control and cleaning up contamination) and savings (such as reductions in packaging and waste), and compares one against the other. Its environmental costs came to $29.4 million in 1992, the latest year for which figures are available. That was 0.3 per cent of sales, compared with an industry average (estimated by a survey) of 2 per cent. Given the rising cost of environmental regulations, this sort of measurement is valuable.

Unless companies think clearly about the purpose of environmental reports, they may become disillusioned with the exercise. A number seem to have been disappointed by the lack of response to their first reports. Unlike annual reports, pored over by market analysts and financial journalists, environmental reports seem less likely to attract attention. Indeed, one Canadian chemical company which distributed its environmental report to its shareholders found that, while some liked it, others wanted to know what all this environmental spending would mean for earnings per share. That response made it wonder whether to produce another one.

WRITING A COOKBOOK

Several bodies have developed guidelines for environmental reports. The earliest set was put together by the Coalition for Environmentally Responsible Economies (CERES). This American group of environmentalists and virtuous institutional investors (such as university pension funds) drew up the so-called CERES Principles after the *Exxon Valdez* disaster of 1989, and campaigned to persuade companies to sign up to them. The principles commit companies to conducting a detailed environmental audit and publishing the findings. Their tough rules alarmed corporate lawyers, and even though 3000 companies were contacted, only about 50 had signed up as of mid-1994. Early in 1994 CERES enjoyed a coup: General Motors said it would sign. Meanwhile, a group of nine large American companies decided to put together their own, blander set of rules in the form of the Public Environmental Reporting Initiative (PERI). By the start of 1994, several (but not all) of the promoters of the PERI principles had published environmental reports based on its guidelines.

The most detailed toolkit was assembled by the United Nations Environment Programme, working with SustainAbility, a British environmental consultancy. In a report issued in 1994 ("Company Environmental Reporting") it set out 50 "reporting ingredients", starting with statements of commitment from top management and of environmental policy, and running through indicators of inputs and outputs to environmental liabilities. Of the 50 ingredients, 20 were defined as "core elements".

One problem with this mass of guidelines (others are on the way from the World Industry Council for the Environment) is that individual industries face enormously different environmental problems. Guidelines that readily fit a car manufacturer may not be appropriate for a hotel chain – unless they are too vague to be really useful. This is a particular difficulty for environmentally sensitive industries, and the most sensitive of all is chemicals. The European chemical industry council has therefore issued its own guidelines, giving more detail about emissions to quantify than most tool kits offer. By 1995 CEFIC expected that every one of its 45 members would have produced at least one environmental report.

ENVIRONMENTAL INVESTMENT

The final step in the greening of corporate behavior, say environmentalists, should be to persuade investors to steer their money into companies on the basis of their environmental performance. Environmental performance has been added to the list of factors, such as bad employment practices and weapons manufacture, used by "ethical investors". Ethical mutual funds, many of them in the United States, have benefited from the growth of public-sector pension funds, whose politically conscious trustees want to do well and do good with the money entrusted to them. The practice may become more widespread if the American Department of Labor, which regulates pension funds, has its way: it has suggested that investing in firms with good employment practices might be made a fiduciary duty for trustees.

Some trustees worry that ethical investing tends to produce lower returns than the usual sort (indeed, in July 1994 a fund was launched specially to invest in "nasty" industries – tobacco, alcohol and gambling – on the grounds that there is money to be made in such industries, especially if ethical investors refuse to buy their shares). In fact, studies of the returns on ethical investment have failed to produce evidence that they under- or over-perform the market in the long run.

A more awkward question is whether such funds are better off avoiding environmentally suspect sectors entirely, or investing in companies that are trying hardest to improve their performance. Funds that take the first view have been keen on shares in Ben & Jerry's (an ice-cream maker), Reebok (shoes) and – intermittently – The Body Shop. But if shareholder pressure is to become an effective tool for improving corporate environmentalism, then such an approach excludes the industries that arguably need it most. For ethical investors, the key question may increasingly become whether it is possible to be a lobbying group and a successful shareholder at the same time.

Companies undoubtedly need good environmental information in order to manage well. If they publish some of that information, they may increase public trust, although that can never be a foregone conclusion. But environmentalists are wrong to assume that compulsory environmental auditing will improve the environmental performance of companies, or create pressure in the financial markets on polluters. The best way to encourage better environmental management is to impose severe penalties on companies that pollute. It is the threat of those penalties that forces businesses to take seriously their environmental liabilities, rather than the compulsory publication of environmental information, in which so much can easily be concealed.

Part V

THE
INTERNATIONAL
ENVIRONMENT

Chapter 17

International Agreements

Nature is no respecter of national boundaries. Governments cannot control where the winds blow, the rivers flow or where migrating species walk or fly. Yet when people in one country harm that bit of the environment they assume to be theirs, many others may suffer, too. Green issues therefore increasingly influence countries' relations with each other, and color international trade and aid.

Disputes sometimes arise because neighboring countries share part of the environment: rivers such as the Rhine or the Jordan, or a stretch of water such as the Mediterranean or the Great Lakes. Sometimes, a disagreement is over differing approaches to the care of resources, such as the atmosphere, the oceans and Antarctica, that are shared by the whole planet. Sometimes, the issue is the treatment of assets (such as coral reefs or elephants) that clearly belong to individual countries, but whose future may affect others, in either material or (more often) spiritual and emotional ways.

All such disagreements may be aggravated by the fact that countries at different stages of development have differing environmental preoccupations. That is understandable: rich countries have generally done more to clean up than poor countries. But the result is that disputes about the rights of future generations to enjoy the environment often become entangled with debates about the current distribution of wealth between rich and poor countries. In such arguments, poor countries sense that they have, at long last, a bargaining chip – something that the rich countries want; rich countries know that their only weapons are access to their markets and their international aid flows.

Rather than resort to using trade or aid as weapons, countries have pinned high hopes on the negotiation of environmental agreements, as the best hope for the resolution of international disputes. Indeed, such negotiations have provided a vigorously expanding source of employment for diplomats. But environmental negotiations are unlike most other foreign-policy discussions. Domestic and international interests often overlap; private industry and environmentalists play an active part; discussions are much more open than most other international debates.[1]

Such agreements have been negotiated with increasing frequency. Two multilateral environmental treaties came into force in the United States between 1940 and 1959; ten between 1960 and 1979; 11 in the 1980s alone. The number of signatories has grown, and so has the scope of such treaties: the most recent have been on issues that affect many countries, or indeed the entire planet. At the Earth Summit in 1992, governments signed treaties on climate change and preserving biological diversity; and in 1994, a treaty to combat the spread of deserts. So many agreements, negotiated in such rapid succession, take the world into uncharted territory. The challenge for the years ahead is turn them into policies, reconciling the differences in values that created the need for them in the first place.

MAKING INTERNATIONAL AGREEMENTS WORK

Like all international agreements, those on the environment rely on the willing co-operation of governments to enforce them. The market is unlikely to help. Even in an individual country government needs to ensure that polluters carry the costs they would otherwise dump on their fellow citizens. The market, unfettered, will rarely deliver what is best for the environment. The costs to individuals and companies of polluting or pillaging the environment will be lower than the costs their activities impose on the rest of society. But no world government can compel international polluters to pay. Agreement will therefore work only if acting together brings more benefits than acting alone.

Imagine a group of countries around a polluted lake. One tries to clean the water by itself. It may make heroic efforts but will achieve little. If all the countries clean up the lake, modest steps may achieve much. But if all but one of those lake-side countries reduce the muck they discharge into the water, the exception will still enjoy the improvement in water quality that its neighbors make possible. In general, an individual country can do best by dropping out of a pact, as long as it cannot be excluded from the resulting gains. It can enjoy the rewards of traveling on the global bus as a "free rider". This is the central paradox of international environmental agreements. Even if all countries do better by co-operating than by acting alone, individual countries often have a powerful incentive not to co-operate.

Countries are more likely to hitch a free ride the more the costs of belonging to an international agreement diverge from its benefits; or the longer the gap between the pain and the gain. Treaties often need to resolve conflicting goals and priorities, and the balance of costs and benefits usually varies from one country to another.

The balance is in part a function of the number of countries involved. If only three countries abut that dirty lake, the gains that each enjoys from ending pollution will be larger than if only two of them clean up. But if a dozen countries are involved, the difference made by the participation of one extra country will be small. The costs of participation to each country are the same, but the gains from co-operating are lower.[2]

An interesting example of the way self-interest can bind countries into an agreement is the treaty to conserve the fur seal, whose numbers in the north Pacific became dangerously depleted in the late nineteenth century by "pelagic sealing" – killing at sea. Four countries hunted the seals: the United States and Russia (which together owned all the islands on which the seals breed), and Japan and Canada (which caught the seals at sea, on their way to the breeding grounds). Under a treaty of 1911, Japan and Britain (on behalf of Canada) agreed to stop pelagic sealing. In exchange, they were guaranteed a share of the seals killed by the other two countries on their island breeding-grounds. The arrangement was a success. Having fallen to about 300,000 in 1911, seal numbers recovered to over 2 million by the 1950s.

The 1911 treaty demonstrated the gains from co-operation: by banding together, the four countries secured the future of a valuable species that might otherwise have died out. It included a sensible system of compensation, to win the participation of those countries that would otherwise have lost out. And it highlighted the argument for creating clear rights of management over a natural resource rather than treating it as open to all comers, and thus vulnerable to over-exploitation.

Such neat bargains are not always possible. There are really only two options to make recalcitrant countries adhere to a treaty: to reduce the costs of participation, or to increase the benefits. To reduce the costs of membership, treaties must achieve their goal at the lowest possible cost to all participants. One approach is to set targets that reflect the differing costs to individual countries of meeting them. A well-designed agreement will try to ensure that the largest changes are made by those countries that find them least expensive. One example is the Large Combustion Plants Directive of the European Community, agreed on in 1988, to reduce the output of sulphur dioxide and thus the acidity of the rainfall in Europe. The agreement allowed countries to set different targets, with Britain (Western Europe's largest coal-burning country) establishing one of the lowest.

Another way to reduce the costs of participation is for some governments to bribe others. The countries that gain most from an agreement may reward those for whom the costs are heaviest. The Montreal Protocol includes a fund for such payments. Under the climate treaty, the Global Environment Facility (GEF) will pay developing countries some of the extra costs of policies to slow global warming. Such payments, however, raise practical problems. How, for instance, can the world be sure that it is not paying a country to do something it would have done in any case? And how can a country be rewarded for introducing market-based incentives (higher energy prices, for instance), rather than making a one-off investment (in energy-efficient light bulbs, say)?

The alternative to bribery is bullying. This may simply take the form of international disapproval. Nobody likes being a pariah. Britain eventually agreed to reduce sulphur dioxide output and to stop dumping sewage sludge in the North Sea principally because of the political costs of being dubbed "the dirty man of Europe". Such name calling is encouraged by a peculiarity of international environmental agreements: the involvement of non-governmental organizations. It is hard to imagine anti-nuclear campaigners playing a constructive role in disarmament talks, but green lobbyists are active participants in many environmental negotiations. Since they are adept at mobilizing popular protest, they also play a big part in encouraging governments to keep their promises.

Pillorying apart, the options for punishment are few. That is why trade sanctions are such a tempting weapon. A growing number of agreements (see the next chapter) allow trade sanctions to punish free riders. Such sanctions are worth applying only if the costs of lost trade do not exceed the environmental gains from wider compliance.

PROTECTING WILDLIFE

The protection of wildlife was the original goal of environmental treaties. But the motivation would not now be recognized as environmental. The species that nineteenth-century diplomats negotiated about were those with a commercial value: fish, seals, vicuna and (to name a 1902 European convention) "Birds Useful to Agriculture". Such species tended to cover creatures that existed outside the jurisdiction of one country (whales), or that moved from place to place (migratory birds). Increasingly, treaties are likely to reflect the fact that the ways countries with many animals and plants treat their natural heritage is of concern to people elsewhere. The process of negotiating the convention on biodiversity proved how difficult it was to turn this concern into policy.

Wildlife treaties, like all other international treaties, need to persuade all the relevant countries that they gain more from adhering to the treaty than from cheating or refusing to sign. One of the ways in which past wildlife treaties have achieved this has been to allow some culling or commercial exploitation of the species involved. But limited culling may be difficult to police. The tension between conservation and regulated exploitation, a recurrent theme in wildlife treaties, is admirably analyzed by Simon Lyster, who now works for the WorldWide Fund for Nature.[3] It is usually simpler to insist on a complete ban on the killing of a particular species than to regulate culling or hunting. But a complete ban may be unreasonable if a commercially valuable stock of creatures recovers and is no longer in obvious danger of extinction.

In the case of whales, fishing countries originally banded together to protect stocks from over-exploitation. The whaling industry had a long history of boom and bust as the discovery of new whaling techniques and hunting grounds led to the exhaustion of one population after another. Because whales are caught in the deep oceans, an international treaty is the only way to affect their numbers. The early emphasis of the International Whaling Commission (IWC), set up in 1946, was on the orderly development of the whaling industry.

But the balance has been shifted by the catastrophic decline of many species and the growth in a number of influential countries of increasingly vociferous lobbies against all whaling. Commercial whaling was banned in 1986. As the stocks of some whales recovered, the animal-rights lobby began to argue that whales should not be hunted at all. As a result, the IWC may fragment, as countries with a tradition of whaling follow Norway and decide unilaterally to resume the hunt. It is harder to reach an effective global treaty centered on a minority moral view ("hunting all whales is wrong") than on a pragmatic issue ("whales are in danger of extinction").

A similar tension between those who want a limited cull and those who want the simplicity and moral absolute of a total ban exists in CITES, the Convention on International Trade in Endangered Species. The provisions of CITES have become increasingly controversial because of the debate over the future of the African elephant. The elephant's numbers collapsed between 1981 and 1989, falling from about 1.2 million to just over 600,000.

To stem this massacre, a decision was made in October 1989 to prohibit all trade in products made from elephants. But five southern African states have persistently argued that their elephant populations are stable or rising, and that trade in elephant products is essential to help to pay for their conservation. Behind the argument over the elephant's future lies a difference of view on how to make elephants pay. For some countries, notably Kenya, elephants are a mainstay of the tourist trade, so these countries have a particular interest in preventing ivory poaching. But protecting elephants is extremely expensive. Zimbabwe reckons that it costs $200 a square kilometre per year to protect elephants from illegal hunting. To provide an incentive to protect elephants in countries where tourists do not or cannot come to look at them, it may be essential to find other ways to make money from the beasts.[4]

The 1992 biodiversity treaty is likely to be effective only if it builds on past experience with wildlife treaties and ensures that signatories gain more from co-operation than from cheating. If poor countries are to have an incentive to conserve their wildlife, they must earn a higher return from conservation than from alternative uses. That will be increasingly difficult: almost all of the enormous growth in the world's population will take place in poor countries. The need to produce enough food will encourage the conversion of more land for agriculture. So if countries are to have an incentive to protect habitat, the increasing demand for farmland will need to be matched by an increasing return from conservation.

It would not be difficult to boost conservation spending in developing countries. The proportion of government spending and national wealth devoted to conservation is surprisingly high in some poor countries, but the absolute sums are tiny compared with spending in the richer nations. Estimates for the World Bank's 1992 *World Development Report* suggested that $1–2 billion of extra direct spending a year on conservation could be absorbed in developing countries, although the amount might increase substantially later on. That sum is roughly what the United States spends annually on conservation.

To work, such spending needs to be sustained. It needs to be treated not as foreign aid or one-off benevolence, but as a perpetual commitment. The prospects are discouraging. The African Elephant Conservation Co-ordinating Group, based in Britain, has drawn up conservation plans for elephants in 33 African countries. Their total cost would be $480 million over five years. That sum, small by foreign-aid standards, but large compared with what voluntary bodies can muster, proved hard to raise. The World Wide Fund for Nature, which spends more than $4 million a year on elephant-related projects in Africa, argues that the failure of donors to turn agitation into money is regarded by African states with "bitterness, anger and skepticism". If the developed countries cannot muster the money to conserve the African elephant, what hope for other animals?

FROM THE OZONE LAYER TO GLOBAL WARMING

The relative ease with which the Montreal protocol was agreed, in September 1987, and the success with which its commitment to reduce CFCs has so far been implemented, have helped to convince people that it will not be much harder to tackle global warming in the same way. This view is almost certainly wrong. The passage of the protocol was eased by at least four factors:

1 The discovery in 1984–85 of the thinning of the ozone layer over Antarctica, and a string of subsequent revelations about the rate

of ozone depletion, convinced negotiators that a real problem existed.

2 Ozone depletion is thought likely to increase the number of cases of skin cancer in the next century. Any environmental threat linked to cancer always stands a good chance of attracting political attention.

3 CFCs are produced by a small number of companies, most of which also produce at least one of the chemicals being used as substitutes for CFCs. Because a world ban on CFCs was an ideal way to lock up the market for the substitutes, the main CFC manufacturers have supported the protocol.

4 The existence of substitutes has reduced the costs of change. Where substitutes can be "dropped in" without big changes in technology – as in aerosols – CFCs have been rapidly abandoned. Where no completely satisfactory substitute yet exists, as with air-conditioning in cars, it has been much slower.

As ever, the smaller the extra cost to a country of signing up to an international agreement and the greater the benefit, the more likely it is to do so. With climate change, the extra costs will be much larger.

The 1992 treaty on climate change was an extraordinary achievement, if only because it was negotiated less than a decade after global warming had first been discussed outside laboratories and took 15 months from start to finish. The climate convention goes further than did the Vienna convention, the first agreement on CFCs. Yet the issues raised by global warming will make it harder to turn agreement into action. For instance:

• Not only is the damage inflicted by climate change difficult to predict; it does not seem to have much impact on human health. It may impose economic costs, but over the next half century, the damage may be quite modest.

• All the countries that produce coal and natural gas stand to lose revenue if the treaty reduces world demand for fossil fuel.

• If only developed countries impose restrictions on their use of fossil fuels, energy-intensive industries may flourish in some of the least energy-efficient countries.

The climate convention signed at Rio is a first step. The really difficult decisions lie ahead. One is the targets for reducing carbon dioxide emissions. How these targets are defined is extremely important. The European Union promised to stabilize carbon dioxide output at 1990 levels by 2000; France and Japan said they would stabilize carbon dioxide output per head; half a dozen countries, including Britain and the United States, said they would stabilize their output of all greenhouse gases. All have picked the target that shows them in the best light, and each will want their particular technique to become the norm. Even so, by the spring of 1995 it was clear that few countries would meet their targets.[5]

There will be other debates down the road. For instance, should targets be set in terms of the global-warming potential of all greenhouse gases or just in terms of carbon dioxide? How far should countries be allowed to offset increases in carbon dioxide by planting trees that will absorb carbon dioxide as they grow? The United States and Canada have specifically said that they will stabilize "net", not gross, emissions. That is logical, given that planting trees may be cheaper than some measures to cut the use of fossil fuels. But how to ensure that the trees are replanted when necessary? And how to persuade poor countries that the rich are not merely buying their way out of environmental action?

How targets are shared out will be a constant bone of contention. One option might be to take a target and then to share out rights to that "stock" of the atmosphere in various ways. Perhaps the fairest might be to allocate rights on the basis of population, on the grounds that every person should have an equal right to the carbon-dioxide-absorbing capacity of the atmosphere. On that basis, the developed countries would already have exhausted all their rights and be in deficit. So it might be more practical to share out rights on the basis of income, which would leave every group of countries with some leeway for further emissions, but give the lion's share to the rich.

Clearly, no distribution of targets will be both fair and efficient (in the sense of ensuring that emissions are reduced where it is cheapest to do so). The more targets are set with an eye to fairness, the more important it will be to allow countries to rearrange their obligations, by paying others to undertake them.

Universities around the world have designed even more sophisticated (although not necessarily more practical) schemes for payments, including the creation of internationally tradable permits to emit a certain amount of carbon dioxide. The initial distribution of permits would be just as problematic as sharing out targets; besides, no example of internationally traded pollution permits exists, and the sums that might change hands under a permit trading scheme are improbably large. So are the sums that governments might raise through taxing carbon dioxide at a common rate and paying the proceeds into a compensation fund for those countries that would otherwise be worse off. Another possibility would be a carbon tax which was set at a nationally agreed level but whose revenues stayed in the country that levied them.

However ingeniously a compensation scheme is designed, and however much money passes across the exchanges, some governments will be tempted to cheat. The countries that expect to gain most from preventing climate change will probably flirt with the use of trade sanctions. The Montreal Protocol provides a precedent, in giving signatories the right to ban imports of CFCs from non-signatories. It is hard to imagine most countries banning imports of fossil fuels, let alone imports of products made with them. It is, however, all too easy to imagine governments imposing a rough-and-ready "countervailing carbon tax" on free riders. The danger with such trade measures, as the next chapter argues, is that their cost, in terms of lost welfare, is greater than the gains in welfare that a watertight climate treaty might bring.

Chapter 18

Trade and the Environment

Few issues encapsulate as vividly the clash between growth and greenery as the arguments over trade and the environment. Two sets of values collide, their clash made more politically explosive by the fears of rich Western countries about the rapid expansion of the newly industrializing countries, which seem to threaten jobs and markets in the West as much as they endanger their environments at home. Compromise is essential, but has often been hard to achieve.

The dividing lines in the trade debate are curious. Industry in the rich countries sometimes finds itself in natural alliance with environmentalists to keep "environmentally inferior" products out of the market. Meanwhile some developing countries, led by Malaysia and India, accuse environmentalists of trying to prevent them from enjoying economic growth, and of interfering with their sovereign right to look after their environment as they think best. "Sovereignty", indeed, is a concept much discussed in the trade and environment debate. Developing countries insist on their right to set environmental standards at the level they judge appropriate. Environmentalists make precisely the same argument in their own countries, complaining that trade rules restrict national freedom to set high standards where these are a trade barrier. Both are equally

224

indignant at the idea that national standards should be a matter for international debate.

Some of the heat in the debate is generated by a clash of culture. The moral certainties of the environmentalists conflict head-on with the pragmatic economics of the trade lobby. The cultural clash is visible even in international meetings of government officials. The old national divisions tend to disappear. Instead, trade officials hobnob at one end of the room, while the environmental bureaucrats talk shop at the other. The contrast between trade officials and non-governmental green groups is even more acute. Gary Stanley, a Washington-based environmental lawyer, contrasts the trade lobby, which is "comfortable with closed diplomatic negotiations and has well-articulated views and a desire to quantify issues", with the environmentalists who combine "distrust of governments with less well-articulated views and a dislike of quantifying".[1] Given such a gulf of understanding, the ferocity of the debate is not surprising. With so little common ground – or desire to find it – compromises are difficult to achieve.

Several themes inform the debate. Environmentalists complain that:

- Trade accelerates economic growth. By stimulating growth, freer trade may cause environmental harm, especially if adequate safeguards are in not place.
- Trade liberalization restricts a country's freedom to set its own environmental standards. Agreements on market access may, for instance, make it harder for a country to apply tough rules on food additives or to set up its own ecolabeling scheme if these appear to keep out imports. The most famous debate between environmentalists and free-traders, the tuna–dolphin row, falls under this heading.
- Trade rules give a competitive advantage to countries with low environmental standards. This issue has allied industrialists in developed countries with Western environmentalists.
- Trade rules hamstring international environmental agreements. Without the option of trade restrictions, it may be hard to make

such agreements stick. Otherwise, countries that continue to cause global and cross-border environmental damage will gain a trade advantage over countries that agree not to do so.

It has never been easy to persuade ordinary voters that freer trade is a cause worth defending. Its economic benefits are readily ignored when foreign competition threatens local jobs. But when companies have clamored for protectionism, it has at least been possible for free-traders to castigate them for being self-interested. That line of attack is harder when demands for protectionism come from environmentalists, who argue that the removal of trade barriers is damaging to the environment.

THE ORIGINS OF THE DEBATE

Environmental challenges to free trade began in the United States, as an attack on the North American Free Trade Agreement (NAFTA) which the United States negotiated with Canada and Mexico. In the course of 1992–93, they spilled over into an attack on the General Agreement on Tariffs and Trade (GATT) and the Uruguay Round of trade talks. (GATT was a treaty with a secretariat, and not, as environmentalists sometimes imply, a free-standing international organization like the World Bank.) The Uruguay talks negotiated the liberalization of more areas of trade, and also agreed to set up the World Trade Organization, a permanent body which replaced GATT's temporary structure at the beginning of 1995.

In the United States, the issue caught the attention of huge numbers of people who had never previously taken much interest in trade. Groups such as Public Citizen, founded by that veteran campaigner, Ralph Nader, formed a broad coalition: one anti-GATT diatribe was signed by more than 300 organizations from the International Ladies' Garment Workers Union to the United Methodist Church to the American Cetacean Society. The event that made the issue catch fire was a row over Mexican tuna-fishing.

This managed to combine three explosive elements: poor environmental protection in Mexico; the deaths of dolphins; and a decision from a GATT disputes panel attacking a law passed by the American Congress. It is by far the most widely publicized clash between environmentalists and free-traders: indeed, almost the only time the two lobbies have clashed head-on.

Behind the row was America's Marine Mammal Protection Act (MMPA), which sets complicated rules that other fishing countries must abide by if they want to sell their produce to the United States, the world's largest market for tuna. Because yellow-fin tuna congregate under shoals of dolphins, tuna fishermen round up the dolphins and trap them, along with the tuna, in the same nets. The law insists that imports of tuna will be allowed only if the exporter has a program to stop dolphin slaughter at least as tough as America's, and if the average number of dolphins killed by its fishermen is no more than 1.25 times that of American tuna vessels in the same year.

Easily the largest tuna-fishing fleet in the eastern tropical Pacific is Mexico's. The American government, well aware that the provisions of the MMPA conflicted with the trade rules to which the United States had agreed under the GATT, was reluctant to implement them against Mexico. So the Earth Island Institute, a Californian lobbying group, took the government to court. In February 1992 the administration was compelled to impose an embargo on tuna imports from Mexico, Venezuela and Vanuatu. Mexico complained to the GATT, and a disputes panel upheld the complaint.

The panel's ruling exposed a number of ways in which the GATT's principles set limits on national environmental policies. The key was the GATT's non-discrimination principle: the rule under which imported products must be treated as favorably as identical domestic ones. The way the import is produced, if it has no effect on the product as such, is not an adequate reason to discriminate against it.

To this principle there are two possible exceptions that might have applied in the tuna–dolphin case. Both fall under Article XX of the GATT, which allows a number of exemptions to the principles of the organization, on condition that they do not entail arbitrary discrimination or disguised trade restrictions. The disputes panel dismissed both.

One exemption allows measures to protect animal health or exhaustible natural resources (the word "environment" does not appear in the GATT's articles). But this exemption applies, said the panel, only when such resources lie within a country's own jurisdiction. The dolphins of the eastern tropical Pacific were clearly beyond America's reach. Nor did a second possible exception apply. To do so, the tuna embargo would have to be shown to be aimed primarily at conservation, and to be the only course open to the United States. Neither point held: for one thing, Mexican fishermen could not know the limits to a year's dolphin catch in advance, because it depended on calculating retrospectively 125 per cent of America's catch that year; for another, the United States had not attempted to negotiate a treaty on preserving dolphins. The restriction therefore smacked more of trade protection than dolphin conservation.

The tuna–dolphin dispute was not about a purely environmental issue. Nice as dolphins are, they are not an endangered species. And if the main goal of environmentalists had been to protect dolphins, it would have been wiser (and cheaper) to help Mexican fishermen acquire safer designs of nets, of the sort used by American fishermen. But environment-and-trade clashes often turn out to be of this sort: better solutions can be found, if environmentalists are willing to concentrate on ends rather than means. Trade restraints are rarely the best way to improve environmental protection.

TRADE AND GROWTH

Of the four strands to the trade and environment debate, mentioned at the start of this chapter, the oldest is the tension between economic growth and environmental protection. Environmentalists worry about a number of trade's impacts. To begin with, trade liberalization encourages traffic of all sorts. In countries such as Austria and Switzerland, through which the trucks of Europe thunder, this aspect of freer trade is especially resented. But it is resented in the United States too. During the NAFTA negotiations, environmentalists drew attention to forecasts that road traffic across the Mexican-American border would rise from 1.8 million commercial vehicles in 1990 to 8 million in 2000, with all the dirt and pollution that entails.

Even without the trade-stimulated increase in traffic, environmentalists notice that rapidly growing economies tend to be filthy economies. Southern China is the world's most glaring example of the environmentally degrading effects of rapid industrialization. Not only may growth itself bring pollution; trade may encourage economies to make their money in environmentally harmful ways. South Asian countries chop down their tropical timber not for domestic consumption but to sell abroad (increasingly, to their South Asian neighbors); the black rhino is threatened because of the market that exists for its horn in many parts of Asia; southern Africa's savannah wildlife is threatened by the lure of the beef markets in Europe.

To these complaints, economists reply that trade may bring environmental benefits, because it increases efficiency and therefore reduces the waste of natural resources. They point out that one of the consequences of agricultural protection is to intensify farming methods and increase the amount of fertilizers and pesticides used in protected countries, such as those of Western Europe. They note that, when Malaysia and Indonesia impose trade barriers on the export of tropical timber to boost their domestic wood-processing industries, the effect is to depress timber prices and encourage the wasteful use of logs. In both cases, trade barriers lead directly to the waste of resources and environmental damage.

Trade may also bring benefits by allowing poor countries to import the newest technologies – ones that, usually, incorporate the best anti-pollution controls. Indeed, developing countries have an opportunity to avoid the dirtiest stages of economic development. They can buy technology that will reduce waste and convert natural resources into products efficiently. Besides, argue economists, when countries prosper as a result of freer trade, they can more easily afford environmental protection. So the enriching effects of trade indirectly help to mitigate environmental damage.

Finally, economists admit that trade-fostered growth may sometimes cause environmental damage. But the cure, they say, lies not in trade barriers but in better environmental policies. It is impossible to bully countries into protecting an environment that they do not value.

Trade and Standards

However, trade liberalization restricts a country's freedom to set its own environmental standards in several ways.

In principle, countries are free to set whatever environmental standards they want for products, provided that imports are treated in the same way as domestic goods. Countries can, for instance, insist that new cars are fitted with catalytic converters – provided that this standard is applied to cars made by both domestic and foreign manufacturers. For instance, product standards may not be used as subtle trade barriers. But the line may be a narrow one. It is not clear, for example, what the implications would be of a state-sponsored ecolabeling scheme that gave a label only to domestically produced products, because only they could meet the environmental criteria it set. Such a scheme would probably not meet international rules. This would be especially likely if it appeared to encourage discrimination against imported products on the basis of the way they were produced. Under the rules of international trade, there is no difference between a free-range egg and one laid by a battery hen; or between a piece of wood from a forest that has been sustainably managed and one that has not.

It is this last point that has been the root of the main recent disputes. In 1992 the Austrian parliament passed legislation requiring all products made of tropical wood to carry prominent labels. If timber from temperate forests had also been labeled, the scheme might have been acceptable under international trade rules. As it was, the threat of a complaint by Malaysia to the GATT and of trade sanctions (Malaysia is an important market for Austrian textiles) forced Austria to back down.

Other threatened trade measures of this sort have so far got nowhere. The Dutch talked of banning imports of tropical timber in 1995, and then realized that to do so would breach not just world trade rules but also the single-market provisions of the European Union. The EU itself thought of banning furs from countries that still use leg-hold traps and cosmetics tested on animals; as of early 1995, it was hesitating. The EU had learnt from the tuna–dolphin dispute what an explosive brew can be mixed from trade, the environment and animal rights.

THE ENVIRONMENT AND COMPETITIVENESS

Environmentalists are keen on the polluter-pays principle. It offers a formula for ensuring that polluters carry the true costs of their polluting activities. Several international bodies whose main concern is not environmental – such as the OECD – have accepted the principle. But how, environmentalists ask, is it to be reconciled with freer trade? After all, if one country insists that its domestic polluters pay, it will find that they are undercut by less scrupulous foreigners selling in their markets at home and abroad.

This argument about what is sometimes dubbed "environmental dumping" wins sympathy from industrialists as environmental regulations in the rich countries grow tighter. In the United States, where the costs of environmental policies are expected to rise sharply in the 1990s, legislators have toyed with plans to impose special duties on imports produced under standards that are less strict than those in the United States. One such proposal was introduced into the Senate in 1992. Even if it had passed, it would not have helped companies which grumble that tough environmental standards handicap them in the markets of third world countries.

Will rigorous environmental standards harm the competitiveness of the countries that apply them? Common sense suggests that they may. But it is hard to find firm evidence that differing environmental standards affect trade or where companies locate themselves. An OECD study, published in 1985, found that pollution-control measures in France, The Netherlands and America might have reduced their total exports by between 0.5 and 1 per cent: a tiny amount compared with the many other factors that affect trade flows. As for location, economists generally argue that environmental standards make less difference than other factors, such as labor costs, political stability, transport and access to markets.

Some economists go further, and argue that high standards may bring offsetting trade advantages. James Tobey, at the OECD, is one of those who take what might be called the "Michael Porter" line (see Chapter 15). He accepts that, as environmental standards are tightened, their extra cost may start to rise sharply.[2] But he argues that tougher standards tend to create technological advances that may give a country a competitive advantage. Since standards are more likely to be leveled up internationally than down, manufacturers in other countries may expect their own national standards to rise as well. They may then have an incentive to buy the cleanest technology available.

That argument is less convincing than the line taken by those environmentalists who point out that, if standards do not significantly affect trade or location, that just shows that standards everywhere are still too low. If standards were as high as they ought to be, trade would indeed be affected. For, if polluters paid the true costs of their dirtiness, controls would make up a much larger part of their costs, and international differences would matter more.

The experience of the rich countries has been that environmental standards do indeed tend to converge upwards, not downwards. Moreover, few countries deliberately advertise their low environmental standards in an effort to attract foreign investors. And even countries with low environmental standards tend to apply higher standards to multinationals than to their own (often state-owned) polluters. The evidence of "eco-dumping" is not yet strong.

But the threat will undoubtedly continue to be used whenever a significant increase in environmental standards is under consideration. For the chairman of Bayer, the last straw was the threat of a European energy tax. "We cannot compete successfully against intense global competition . . . while at the same time shouldering the burden of constantly rising levies," he complained. "If the present proposals to tax carbon dioxide emissions and solid waste were implemented it would no longer be economic to manufacture inorganic pigments and organic intermediates in Germany."[3]

As environmental standards rise, they may well have an impact on competitiveness. The real question is whether that impact can be reduced by the use of trade barriers, and if so whether countries are right to impose them. Trade barriers may indeed make a country's industry more willing to accept high environmental standards: not surprisingly, given that their effect will often be to raise industry's profits. Offered captive markets and freedom from foreign competition in exchange, many companies would be willing to accept fierce environmental controls. But trade barriers do not help industry to compete in world markets. And they do nothing for consumers: indeed, by keeping out low-cost goods, trade barriers tend to leave people worse off than they would be otherwise.

The main argument against trade barriers is the risk that they become part of a slide towards protectionism. Post-war prosperity has been built on liberal trade. Many refinements in domestic environmental policies are possible, to reduce their cost and increase their effectiveness, before countries should risk jeopardizing that.

TRADE AND INTERNATIONAL AGREEMENTS

Perhaps the most intractable trade and environment debate is over the use of trade measures to deal with environmental issues that cross borders, and especially to reinforce international environmental agreements. Such agreements may need to use trade restrictions to tackle global and cross-border environmental damage.

Several multilateral environmental agreements – 17 of 127 examined by the GATT secretariat – contain trade provisions. That is not surprising: trade penalties are among the few weapons countries can use against each other when they disagree about something. Controls on trade are central in two treaties: the Basle convention on trade in hazardous waste and the Convention on Trade in Endangered Species (CITES) which bans trade in African elephants and a large number of other animals and species. In both cases, the difficulty has been separating environmentally harmful trade from trade which does no environmental damage.

In the case of the Basle convention, restrictions are placed on hazardous wastes that are sent abroad to have something useful extracted from them. These wastes are by definition the raw material for another process. Large industries, dependent on shipments of scrap metal and waste paper, have been disrupted by Basle's provisions, which were intended to stop hazardous wastes from being dumped in developing countries without the facilities to treat them. In the case of CITES, countries agree to restrict imports of products made from endangered species. International trade is often what gives an endangered species its commercial value. It may therefore seem logical to destroy that trade. The danger is that, in destroying the value of the species, a ban will also destroy one of the most powerful arguments for protecting it. The treaty has found it hard to draw a line between trade in products from endangered creatures that are illegally hunted, and from the same creatures when they are legally ranched or farmed.

An even more difficult case is that of the Montreal Protocol, restricting the use of ozone-depleting CFCs. It bans imports from non-signatories of CFCs and products containing them. More ominously, one clause commits signatories to "determine the feasibility of banning or restricting, from states not party to this protocol, the import of products produced with, but not containing, controlled substances."

All three conventions impose trade provisions on non-signatories more restrictive than those that apply to signatories. They thus break the GATT's rule that no country must treat one trading partner worse than another. Sometimes, such a threat may not be necessary to achieve a treaty's goals: for example, countries could have set national quotas on their consumption of CFCs from any source, rather than threatening to ban CFC imports from non-signatories. But a general problem remains. If international environmental treaties use trade measures as disincentives to free-riding, then those measures will inevitably be selective restrictions on imports. Moreover, such restrictions will generally apply, not to particular categories of products, but to goods produced by processes that the treaty aims to restrict. Both points will conflict with the rules of international trade.

So far, no country has formally complained about its treatment under an international environmental agreement. Clearly, the more countries sign an agreement, the less likely anybody is to grumble about the treatment of non-signatories. Environmental agreements are not intrinsically weaker (or stronger) than international trade agreements: both rely on the voluntary participation of countries which see the gains of co-operation as greater than the costs. But it may simply be impossible to construct effective international environmental agreements without including the threat of trade sanctions – and, occasionally, using them. The important thing will be to keep such threats to a minimum, and ensure that they are used only when all other possibilities for compromise have been exhausted.

CHANGING THE RULES

Compromise is essential if the environment is not to become a fashionable excuse for greater protectionism. But it will be formidably difficult to redraft the rules of international trade to take account of environmental sensitivities. Take the perfectly sensible point made by David Pearce, Britain's best-known environmental economist, who argues that from the point of view of the importing country, it should be irrelevant whether environmental losses arise during production or consumption: both impose some costs on importing countries.[4] This may be most obvious when the loss incurred during production is suffered directly by the importer (as when acid rain drifts across a border or when CFCs damage the ozone layer). But the importer may also suffer when an exporter chops down its rain-forest or wipes out its rhinos.

Unfortunately, as Pearce admits, it would be virtually impossible in practice to allow exceptions for such "production externalities". The reason is clear from the disputes panel ruling in the tuna–dolphin case. Allow one country to discriminate against one production process on environmental grounds and the result is a whale-sized loophole. Where would discrimination stop? Should exemptions be allowed only when the importing country is directly affected by the environmental policies of the exporter – as when the waterways of Texas and California are polluted by fly-by-night Mexican companies across the border? Should they be allowed when the environmental harm occurs on no-man's land: in the deep oceans or in the atmosphere?

Which products should be banned? What happens if the country imposing the sanctions does not import the offending product? For instance, acid rain arises when electricity is generated, but electricity is rarely traded. Would everything whose manufacture involved the use of electricity in an offending country therefore be at risk? That question may sound ludicrous, but it has already arisen with the American CFC tax. The tax, levied on CFCs in America, applies to imports as well – including those that use CFCs in the manufacturing process. This is proving, as an OECD report pointed out, extremely effective in persuading South-East Asian makers of semi-conductor chips to find alternatives to CFCs for cleaning their product.[5] The market for semi-conductor chips is highly price-sensitive and one where protectionism is tempting. Would the American tax meet world-trade standards? Probably not.

One of the results of the Uruguay Round was agreement to set up a body to find ways to reconcile trade and environment issues.

Developing countries have been hesitant about making this concession to environmentalists. But environmentalists, for their part, are worried that the new World Trade Organization (WTO) will make it harder to use trade measures in pursuit of environmental aims. The disputes process has been changed, so that decisions (such as the tuna–dolphin ruling) will have more force; unilateral trade restrictions will be policed; and the burden of proof in a dispute will lie with the defendant – the country that introduces the environmental measure.

Some have suggested the need for a new institution, to give the environment the international clout that the WTO gives to trade issues. Dan Esty, who was special assistant to William Reilly, the head of the EPA, during the tuna–dolphin row, has argued for the creation of a Global Environmental Organization, or GEO, to provide an "institutional counterweight" to the WTO.[6] The intention would be to pull together the haphazard accretion of institutions – UNEP, the Global Environment Facility, the secretariat of the Montreal Protocol and so on – that currently influence global environmental policy.

Such a body would merely institutionalize at an international level the arguments that divide, in every national capital, the trade ministry from the environment ministry. It would not necessarily become easier to draw a line between the two sides. Yet such a line still needs to be drawn. Clearly no government should be allowed to apply general trade sanctions unilaterally to bully another to adopt a particular environmental policy. Clearly countries should be free to use ecolabeling to draw consumers' attention to the way in which a product has been produced, although such labeling should be as non-discriminatory as possible. But clearly, too, it must be possible, in carefully restricted circumstances, for trade measures to be taken under international environmental agreements.

Indeed, the original GATT agreement nearly made this possible. Ian Fletcher of Britain's Department of Trade and Industry points out that Article XX began life as article 45 of the Havana charter which was to have set up the International Trade Organization as the third cornerstone of the reconstructed post-war economy, alongside the World Bank and the IMF.[7] That charter, stillborn when the United States refused to ratify it, contained an additional exception, covering measures "taken in pursuance of any inter-governmental agreement which relates solely to the conservation of fisheries resources, migratory birds or wild animals". The World Trade Organization, the ITO's linear descendant, needs just that sort of power.

Chapter 19

Aid and the Environment

As environmentalists in the rich world have become increasingly concerned about what happens to the environment in other parts of the globe, so too have they become more angry about damage perceived to have been done by international aid. Criticisms made by environmentalists have probably had more effect on the way aid is used than on any other area of international activity. In particular, they have influenced the World Bank, many of whose loans in the past have gone to big capital projects managed by governments. Some international aid projects have become practical tests of the extent to which it is possible to increase human welfare without harming the environment. Indeed, a growing number seek to improve the condition of poor people and their environment at the same time.

Much of the hostility aid arouses among environmentalists results from the way it has been dispensed. In the past, say environmentalists, aid projects have often been capital-intensive, designed to provide jobs for the donor country's engineering firms and gravy for the recipient country's elite. Their disastrous environmental side-effects would have been predictable if anybody had taken the time to consult local people. Instead, projects were planned by a handful of consultants who jetted in for a few weeks, wrote a report and jetted out. Protecting the environment, such critics insist, requires patience and local knowledge. Official aid programs have often been short on both commodities.

The deepest greens go further, and argue that aid is always bad for the environment. Aid involves importing foreign technologies and changing the established order of things – an order, perhaps evolved over centuries, that may be the best way for humans to exploit nature without irreparably harming it. Besides, say these ultra-greens, the goal of aid is economic growth, and growth harms the environment.

But aid also gives the rich world some purchase on the policies of the poor; environmentalists are keen to see that used to foster greenery. As a result, the question for many people in the aid lobby is not whether aid is bad for the environment, but whether the environment is good for aid. With the cold war over, and aid budgets under threat all over the world, one of the few arguments for aid that sways Western donors is the need to protect the environment in developing countries. As a result, aid donors everywhere are scrambling to appear environmentally correct, and hunting for green projects to give money to.

Under Observation

As they do, they keep one eye on the horde of non-governmental organizations, or NGOs, which gather at the point where environ-mental and development issues intersect. Some of these NGOs, especially in developing countries, use their flexibility and knowledge of local life to be helpful conduits for aid money. Others make life difficult (sometimes justifiably) for donors. In Europe, environmental NGOs tend to team up with those lobbying for aid to promote development. In America, there is less co-operation. Green lobbies put the environment first and development, at best, second.

The World Bank is the donor that America's ferociously green

NGOs watch most closely. One of these groups even publishes a newsletter (*Early Warning*), which alerts environmentalists around the world to un-green activities in the multilateral development banks. The World Bank has come under most fire simply because it is easily accessible in Washington DC and has become increasingly open. But all multilateral development institutions are now chivvied by NGOs. Even the African Development Bank, whose location in Abidjan was long a defence against the attentions of environmentalists, was forced in the early 1990s to bow for the first time to their demands. It was obliged to call off a plan to finance a road that ran alongside the Dzanga-Sangha national park in the Central African Republic. The Bank intended the road to support a coffee plantation, but environmentalists worried that it would encourage intrusion into the park.

A beneficial effect of NGO bullying has been to make donors pay more attention to the effects of their activities on the environment. America's Agency for International Development (AID) was one of the earliest agencies to carry out routine environmental impact assessments (EIAs). Legislation subsequently obliged all federal agencies to conduct such assessments.

The multilateral agencies were slow to follow suit. In 1989 the World Bank began to screen projects routinely for environmental effects. Since then, it has become greener in other ways. Its team of resident environmentalists has expanded mightily, from five in the mid-1980s to more than 200 by 1994. It produces an annual environmental report. It decided in 1993 to hold an annual conference on sustainable development to coincide with its annual general meeting, a scene in some previous years of nasty demonstrations by environmentalists. And it created a new vice presidency for environmentally sustainable development, shrewdly giving the job to Ismail Serageldin, an Egyptian economist, expert on Islamic art, old Bank hand and a man of exceptional charm and intellect.

A turning point for the Bank was the publication, in 1992, of an edition of its yearly *World Development Report*, which surveys a development issue of current importance. That year, the report was devoted entirely to the environment, and to the task of reconciling the goals of development and environmental improvement. It steered a narrow line between the skepticism of developing countries, convinced that environmentalism was a Western plot to deprive them of the affluence the rich world had achieved, and the hostility of Western environmentalists, convinced that the Bank was trying to argue that economic growth was environmentally benign. The fact that the report managed, on the whole, to satisfy moderates on both sides was thanks largely to the deft work of the leader of the team, Andrew Steer, who was made director of the Bank's environment department in 1994.

Today, few donors would undertake a project for a road or plantation without an EIA. Performing such assessments has become the bread and butter of a host of environmental consultancies which have sprung up in developed and developing countries. The assessments vary greatly in quality and effectiveness. The project may be little affected: most such assessments are conducted when the project is already under way. And they are often done in a rush, by foreign consultants with little or no local experience. Bill Adams, a geographer at Cambridge University, recounts how consultants were given six weeks to "green" a controversial dam in Ghana; they took their numbers from back-of-the-envelope estimates by a visiting British academic.[1] The locals, however, may not do the job any better. EIAs often bless the developers' plans, however damaging.[2]

However, some of the consultants who prepare EIAs argue that they can substantially alter the sort of project that donors are willing to finance. John Horbury of ERM, a British consulting firm, wrote his doctorate in the early 1980s on the environmental assessments required by AID. The procedure was, he recalls, "such a pain in the neck that officials simply stopped coming forward with schemes which they thought would be hard to get through".[3] Now, he says, the same tendency is becoming apparent at the World Bank.

Sometimes schemes that do environmental harm may still be worthwhile. Today, though, donors (and recipients if they are wise) prepare the ground far more carefully. In southern Africa, an immense project to divert the Orange River northwards has been carried out with barely a squeak from environmentalists. Lesotho tried to meet their concerns early on by producing a "Water Project Environmental Action Plan". Its findings were built into the project, in an effort to ensure that environmental damage was reduced and that local people benefited.

How Aid is Given

The new emphasis on the environment affects the way aid is given. Increasingly, donors want to add environmental benefits to ordinary development schemes. Borrowers see that this is in their interest too. Embellish a run-of-the-mill proposal for a power plant with a scheme to improve air quality, as the Philippines has done, and it is far more likely to win support.

Better still, from a donor's point of view, is a purely environmental scheme: to conserve the rain-forest, say, or reduce air pollution. The money offered for such schemes often far exceeds the supply of projects. In the late 1980s, Madagascar and Mauritius drew up proposals to conserve their rich, but dwindling, natural heritage; aid donors offered more money – 50 per cent more in the case of Madagascar – than the countries had asked for.

One reason why demand exceeds supply is that environmental aid is hard to package in ways familiar to big donors. Government aid agencies and multilateral organizations find it easiest to administer sizable projects, which will eventually show measurable results. Sometimes loan schemes that can be dubbed "environmental" come in nice large lumps, with a clear rate of return. The plan to use the natural gas that Nigeria now flares off is an example. The burning gas pollutes the atmosphere: using it would bring environmental as well as economic gains.

But many environmental projects are small and complicated. It is hard to know when they have succeeded. They do not have a clear beginning and middle – let alone an end. They require different agencies to deal with each other, and their management costs are high in relation to the small amounts of money required. A typical example might be a plan in Costa Rica, where the Danish government's aid agency joined forces with the World Conservation Union (confusingly better known by its acronym, IUCN) to help 200 families earn a living from fisheries, charcoal-burning and boat trips for tourists among the mangrove trees. The families needed a truck, money to build better kilns and a few chainsaws.

Another instance of the complexities of environmental schemes might be one in Burkina Faso. In 1979 two Oxfam workers, Peter Wright and Mathieu Ouedraogo, were trying to keep tropical seed-lings moist in the northern region of Yatenga. To stop water flushing away across the thin soil, they laid stones in rows to form a mini-dyke, or *diguette*, to collect rain-borne leaves and dead grass, enriching the earth and retaining moisture around the saplings' roots. The technique was not new. But when previously applied, it had often been unsuccessful, because the stones had not been laid along the contours of the soil and merely carried rainwater and soil away from the young trees.

Wright and Ouedraogo found an answer: a length of transparent plastic hose, laid along the ground, filled with water and held up at each end against two sticks of the same length made a simple spirit level. Used to establish contour lines, it allowed stones to be laid far more precisely and thus become a far more effective barrier to erosion. Soon hundreds of farmers were clamoring for plastic piping, and sending their women and children to lug stones from miles around and lay them across their fields.

So far, so good. But aid agencies inevitably wanted to build on this success. That has proved infinitely harder. A Dutch project, anxious to help, brought in sophisticated machinery to measure contours. Wright, now working elsewhere, argues that farmers should be given dynamite and carts and left to build their own dykes. That is cheap. But aid agencies have budgets to spend, and experts to employ.

Nor has Ouedraogo, still working in the north, found it easy to find new ways to help the villagers. In 1993 he tried to persuade them to tether their roaming goats, so that young trees could grow unchewed while goat dung piled up in places where it could readily be collected for manure. That sounds eminently sensible. Not to the village women, who found that they had to add to their long list of daily tasks the job of carrying water and fodder which the tethered animals had previously found for themselves.

Such schemes are difficult enough for NGOs to operate, but would be even harder for government aid agencies or development banks to manage. Several donors already steer a growing part of their budget through organizations such as Oxfam or IUCN. That trend will be fostered by the search for ways to put more money into environmental projects. Some old hands in the aid business worry about forcing too much cash into the hands of NGOs. New voluntary bodies are springing up in the aid business and around the developing world at a tremendous rate, sometimes driven by nothing more admirable than the desire to be a conduit for donor grants.

The search for ways to put more money into environmental projects is encouraging another trend: the increasing emphasis on "capacity building". One of the most difficult aspects of environmental policy is the central role required of developing-country governments. Private firms rarely care much about pollution or the loss of countryside and species. Governments have to devise policies, frame regulations, set penalties and monitor enforcement. In many developing countries, governments struggle merely to stay in power; further demands on their limited capacity to govern are a tall order. Even in stable, well-run countries, few institutions exist to run environmental policy.

More cash is therefore being spent on creating institutions to do these jobs. Horbury describes how ERM's work has changed: "In Asia our early work tended to be feasibility studies for waste-disposal schemes or sewerage projects: clearcut, identifiable projects where our value-added was largely technical. Now we are often involved with designing management systems." In Indonesia ERM designed regional pollution-monitoring and control authorities for two provinces, looking at what their scope should be, what staff they might need, what policies they might pursue. The World Bank helped to foot the bill.

PLANNING AND PRIORITIES

Environmental policy, however, is not just a matter of financing projects here and there. Priorities need to be set. Governments need to work out which aspects of the environment most need to be protected, and how.

Developing countries are now expected to put together a bewildering variety of environmental plans. Richard Sandbrook of the International Institute of Environment and Development in London reels them off:

> They have to draw up a national sustainable-development strategy, a biodiversity plan if they have signed the convention on biological diversity, a climate plan if they have signed the global-warming treaty, a forestry-action plan if they have forests, and a National Environmental Action Plan (or NEAP) if they want soft-loan money from the World Bank. The Thatcherite governments of the rich world are bombarding developing countries with demands for plans in order to appear politically correct, and it is clear that chaos abounds.[4]

The biggest controversy surrounds the NEAPs demanded by the World Bank. Some developing countries resent the Bank, as they see it, foisting its own priorities on them. Their environmentalists often express the sort of views articulated by Aban Kabraji, of the IUCN in Pakistan. She feels that the Bank tried to bounce Pakistan into accepting a NEAP, drawn up by a posse of Swedish consultants, when Pakistan had already produced its own national conservation strategy. Again, much of the problem seems to have been the pressure to find bankable projects to finance. The Bank, she feels, was more interested in drawing up a list of projects to circulate to would-be donors than in letting Pakistan explain its own environmental priorities.[5]

Pakistan had the resources to produce such a plan. Most NEAPs are drawn up in Africa, which also has the greatest concentration of applicants for soft loans. There, the problems are different. A study by Francois Fallous and Lee Talbot describes how many governments have been reluctant to involve NGOs for fear of giving them too much power; internal squabbling has rendered some governments impotent; and others have drawn up plans and then ignored them. The impression is of a well-meaning exercise which has given work to consultants but achieved little else.[6]

Again, Burkina Faso provides an example of the practical difficulties. The country's official environmental policy is built around a plan, called *Gestion des terroirs* or "land management", dreamt up under Thomas Sankara, a populist left-wing president who was overthrown in a coup in 1987. His plan has survived him, and been backed by the World Bank. Under it, teams put together by local governments are trained to help villagers draw up their own local plans to make the most of their sparse natural resources. Villagers are supposed to volunteer for specific jobs such as planting trees or making firebreaks. The government, financed by the Bank, provides cash, training and technical help.

In a country with a long tradition of detailed but ineffectual central direction, such a plan represents – in theory – a sharp break with the past. World Bank officials believe that the government has realized it cannot control development from the center; that villagers need to organize themselves, and bureaucrats must stop making decisions for them. But since no two villages will want the same kind of help, the scheme will be expensive to administer and hard to evaluate. Local officials will not find it easy to stop bossing villagers about. The villagers, for their part, may simply take the proffered carts and seeds and go on farming the way they have always done.

STRUCTURAL ADJUSTMENT

The biggest change in World Bank lending during the 1980s had nothing to do with the environment. The decade saw a huge increase (though by the end, some diminution) in structural-adjustment loans, intended to tide a country over a period of economic

reform. The program was a response to the debt crisis in developing
countries in the early 1980s. In the early 1990s, both the Bank and
NGOs were trying to discover the impact on the environment of
structural-adjustment programs, and the macro-economic policies
they entail. The result was to take both into new territory.

Two studies on the subject, in the Philippines and Mexico, show
how complicated it is to distinguish economic cause from environmental effect. But they contradict some of the charges the environmentalists have often made about the harmful environmental
impacts of forcing a country to reduce its foreign debt and put its
domestic finances in order.[7]

Greens have tended to argue, for instance, that countries with
debt troubles would be tempted to increase the rate of extraction
of natural resources to earn hard currency. In the Philippines,
Wilfrido Cruz and Robert Repetto found that this was not so: the
squeeze imposed by stabilization policies and the collapse of world
commodity prices combined to reduce – not increase – the output
of timber, minerals and most other resource-based products. But
the stabilization program did have unexpected environmentally
harmful effects of a different sort. A huge rise in unemployment
and a 20 per cent fall in real wages in the space of two years accelerated migration to hilly regions where the land was marginal and
the environment most fragile.

Another frequent charge is that public-spending cuts reduce
government help for environmental protection. Mexico's experience suggests that cuts may also fall on programs which are environmentally harmful, such as subsidies for pesticides.[8] And a fiscal
squeeze may lead a government to charge more for the use of natural
resources. Côte d'Ivoire was persuaded by the Bank to increase its
charges to commercial loggers, though by too little to have much
effect on logging. Other countries have been persuaded to raise the
price of energy, a policy with potential for both economic and
environmental benefits.

The two studies show how hard it is to ensure that economic
policies do not have environmentally malign side-effects. In Thailand, for instance, an export tax on rice and rubber encouraged a

switch to growing maize and cassava: crops that do more environmental harm than the ones they replaced. But when the export tax was reduced as part of the country's structural adjustment program, the effect was not benign. Commercial rubber plantations began to spread across high slopes, replacing natural forest and causing landslides. Sometimes, aid officials must think, you just can't win.

Global Compensation Programs

Many of the problems involved in giving effective aid to environmental projects have beset the newest international institution in the field: the Global Environment Facility (GEF). This body, managed by the World Bank, was set up at high speed by the rich countries to put money into projects that bring global – not national – environmental gains. It has come up with some innovative ideas – such as creating trust funds that assure countries of a long-term income for environmental protection – but it has also attracted a barrage of criticism.

Some of the initial complaints reflected teething troubles. At the beginning, some national aid officials were worried about the GEF's choice of projects, which was strongly influenced by one of its sponsoring institutions, the United Nations Development Programme. Many projects were pet UNDP schemes. National aid officials continue to worry about the trust-funds concept: the funds may be hard to control and easy prey to corruption. Environmentalists, for their part, complain that the GEF's choice of projects, at least in its early days, was too secretive and that some of its grants were too large for the recipient countries to handle efficiently.

Other criticisms of the GEF reflect an inescapable dilemma. The Fund is obliged to give money only to projects with global benefits. As a result, other projects, with mainly national benefits, are neglected. The result has been to heighten the distinction between the environmental priorities of donors and recipients. Developing

countries want to spend money on projects that will save the lives
of their citizens; donors want environmental aid to be spent on
projects that reflect the concerns of the rich world.

THE AID CONUNDRUM

It is not easy to find ways to give aid that clearly improve the
environment. In developing countries as in rich ones, public money
is usually only a small part of the solution to environmental
problems. Indeed, the solution is more likely to be found in *not*
spending public money: in removing subsidies or insisting that
capital projects (such as dams and roads) are self-financing.

Good environmental policies therefore do not need to be expensive. But they make formidable demands on the quality of government administration. Well-designed regulations, efficient management of public assets such as forests and fisheries, the definition
and enforcement of property rights and the effective punishment
of those who break environmental laws are what really matter. Such
tasks are difficult for all governments, because they often involve
measures that are, at least in the short term, unpopular with powerful groups in society – be they multinationals, loggers or motorists.
They are especially difficult for the poorest countries, whose
governments are often the weakest.

A Checklist for Governments

How ought the wise government to apply the ideas in this book? Here are a few principles to keep in mind.

1. Accept that the state of the environment is essentially government's responsibility. A cleaner environment will not come about entirely as a result of unfettered market forces, any more than streets will be lit or criminals brought to justice.

2. Because environmental issues touch so many other areas of government, effective environmental policy must ultimately be the responsibility of the head of state. In the same way, a company that takes the environment seriously needs to set a clear line of responsibility right up to the chief executive. Governments also need an environment minister with clout and an adequate budget, and machinery to co-ordinate decisions across departmental boundaries.

3. Set performance goals and publish regular progress reports. This is a good task for an independent agency, which can be relied upon not to rig the numbers. Try to compare results with what is being achieved by other countries at a similar level of development.

4. Put the body with responsibility for enforcing environmental policy in strong hands. Give it enough money to employ honest, well-trained staff. Set it clear rules, and publish them. Leave it alone.

5. Set clear priorities for environmental policies. Encourage public debate on which goals matter most and why. Remind the country at every opportunity that some goals need to take precedence. Try to estimate the cost of alternative strategies, and publish the results.

6. Use the market where possible. Environmental taxes will not only raise revenue (which can be recycled to help those on low incomes and to help people live in more environmentally friendly ways). They will also make clear the true costs of environmental policies, and so encourage people to ask how much they are prepared to pay for a cleaner environment.

7. Explore ways to work with industry to improve the environment, by setting standards your best companies can aspire to meet. If they develop useful new technologies, they may gain markets around the world, and the costs to society of meeting high standards will be reduced.

8. Scrap all subsidies that have harmful environmental side-effects, including farm subsidies and tax breaks for mining. Encourage the pricing of environmental assets in ways that reflect their true scarcity, whether they be road space or fresh water.

9. Look for ways to create and enforce private property rights in environmental assets such as fisheries and forests. Provided the terms of ownership are correctly specified, private ownership will usually protect resources more efficiently than state or communal ownership.

10. Remember that, as people grow richer, they care more about a cleaner environment. Excessive concern for the present will create

problems for the future. Given the unexpected nature of environmental change, those problems could even catch up with you before you leave office.

Notes and References

CHAPTER 1

1. World Bank (1993) *World Development Report 1992* World Bank, Washington DC, p 7.
2. World Bank (1993) *World Development Report 1992* World Bank, Washington DC, p 115.
3. World Bank (1984) *Population Change and Economic Development* World Bank, Washington DC, p 51.
4. Clarke, Robin (1991) *Water, the International Crisis* Earthscan Publications, London, p 13.
5. World Bank (1993) *World Development Report 1992* World Bank, Washington DC, p 100.
6. Thomas, David H L, Ayache, Fethi, and Hollis, G Edward (1991) "Use and Non-use Values in the Conservation of Ichkeul National Park, Tunisia" *Environmental Conservation* 18(2) Summer, pp 119–130.

CHAPTER 2

1. (1994) "Exhaust pollution 'killed 160 in four days'" *Independent* 23 June, p 5.
2. Ames, Bruce (1990) "Misconceptions about Environmental Pollution and Cancer" *World Energy Council Journal* December, pp 34–50. See also Ames, BN, Magaw, R, and Gold, LS (1987) "Ranking Possible Environmental Hazards" *Science* 236, pp 271–280.
3. Regulatory Program of the United States Government, April 1991–March 1992, Office of Management and Budget, Table 2, p 12.

4. van Houghton, George, and Cropper, Maureen (1994) "When is a Life too Costly to Save? The Evidence from Environmental Regulations" *Resources*, Winter (published by Resources for the Future).

5. Study by Chauncey Starr, cited in Reilly, William K (1994) *Risky Business: Life, Death, Pollution and the Global Environment* Institute for International Studies, Stanford.

6. Portney, Paul (1994) "The Contingent Valuation Debate: Why Economists Should Care" *Journal of Economic Perspectives* 8(4), pp 3–17. This issue also contains other articles on the strengths and weaknesses of contingent valuation.

7. "On Contingent Valuation Measurement of Nonuse Values" in Hausman, J (Ed) (1993) *Contingent Valuation: a Critical Assessment* North Holland Press, Amsterdam.

8. Brenton, Tony (1994) *The Greening of Machiavelli* Earthscan Publications, London, p 254.

9. Cline, William (1992) *The Economics of Global Warming* Institute for International Economics, Washington DC.

CHAPTER 3

1. Brenton, Tony (1994) *The Greening of Machiavelli* Earthscan Publications, London, p 20.

2. Cline, (1992) (see note 9, Chapter 2).

3. Maddox, Bronwen (1994) "Campaigners All at Sea" *Financial Times* 12 November.

4. Parkin, Sara (1989) *Green Parties: an International Guide* Heretic Books, London, p 25.

5. For the best account, see Brenton, 1994 (see note 1 above).

CHAPTER 4

1. Portney, Paul (Ed) (1990) *Public Policies for Environmental Protection* Resources for the Future, Washington DC. Much of what follows is taken from this excellent book.

2. Haigh, Nigel (1987) *EEC Environmental Policy and Britain* (second edition) Longman, London.

3. Haigh, Nigel, and Irwin, Frances (Eds) (1990) *Integrated Pollution Control in Europe and North America* Conservation Foundation, Washington DC; Institute for European Environmental Policy, London.

4. Royal Commission on Environmental Pollution (1976) *Air Pollution Control: an Integrated Approach* (fifth report, CMND 6371) HMSO, London, para 265.
5. (1990) *The Economist* 17 February.
6. Helm, Dieter (1993) "Reforming Environmental Regulation in the UK" *Oxford Review of Economic Policy* 9(4), p 3.
7. Portney, Paul (1982) "How *Not* to Create a Job" *AEI Journal on Government and Society* November–December, p 36.

CHAPTER 5

1. OECD (1989) *The Application of Economic Instruments for Environmental Protection* OECD, Paris.
2. Barde, Jean-Philippe, and Opschoor, Johanes Baptist (1994) "From Stick to Carrot in the Environment" *OECD Observer* 186, p 23.
3. (1988) "Project 88: Harnessing Market Forces to Protect our Environment", a Public Policy Study sponsored by Senators Timothy E Worth and John Heins, Washington DC. A second study was sponsored by the senators in May 1991.
4. Pederson, William F Jr (1994) "The Limits of Market-based Approaches to Environmental Protection" *Environmental Law Reporter* April.

CHAPTER 6

1. World Bank (1993) *World Development Report 1992* World Bank, Washington DC, p 149.
2. See note 1, p 100.
3. See note 1, p 101.
4. Pulles, Tinus, and de Leu, Leo (1994) Study cited in *Global Environmental Change Report* August, p 8.
5. Brenton, Tony (1994) *The Greening of Machiavelli* Earthscan Publications, London.
6. OECD (1989) *Agricultural and Environmental Policies: Opportunities for Integration* OECD, Paris, pp 34–35.
7. Reynolds, Russ, et al (1993) *Impacts on the Environment of Reduced Agricultural Subsidies: a Case Study of New Zealand* Ministry of Agriculture, New Zealand.

8. Repetto, Robert (1985) *Paying the Price: Pesticide Subsidies in Developing Countries* World Resources Institute, Washington DC.

CHAPTER 7

1. Haigh, Nigel (1987) *EEC Environmental Policy and Britain* (second edition) Longman, London.
2. Bate, Roger (1993) "Coase's Lighthouse" *Economic Affairs* June.
3. I am grateful to James Cameron of FIELD for this point.
4. Macrory, Richard (1994) *Loaded Guns and Monkeys – Responsible Environmental Law* Environmental Law Society inaugural lecture, Imperial College Centre for Environmental Technology, London.
5. Acton, Jon Paul, and Dixon, Lloyd S (1992) "Superfund and Transaction Costs" RAND, Santa Monica, California.
6. For a fuller discussion, see O'Riordan, Tim, and Cameron, James (1994) *Interpreting the Precautionary Principle* Cameron May/Earthscan Publications, London.

CHAPTER 8

1. Meyer, Carrie (forthcoming) "The Greening of National Accounts: The Role of Ideas in a Theory of Institutional Chance" *The Review of Income and Wealth*. Meyer, Carrie (1993) *Environmental and Natural Resources Accounting: Where to Begin* World Resources Institute, Washington DC, gives an excellent overview of the issues in this chapter.
2. Repetto, Robert, et al (1989) *Wasting Assets: Natural Resources in the National Income Accounts and Accounts Overdue: Natural Resource Depletion in Costa Rica* World Resources Institute, Washington DC.
3. Bartelmus, Peter, Lutz, Ernest, and Schweinfest, Stefan (1992) "Integrated Environmental Accounting: A Case Study for Papua New Guinea" Environmental Working Paper 54, World Bank, Washington DC.
4. Congressional Budget Office (1994) *Greening the National Accounts* March.
5. Harrison, Anne (1993) "National Assets and National Accounting" in Lutz, Ernst (Ed) *Towards Improved Accounting for the Environment* World Bank, Washington DC.

6. Keuning, Steven J (1992) National Accounts and the Environment Occasional Paper NA 053, Central Bureau of Statistics, The Netherlands.

CHAPTER 9

1. (1994) "IPCC Prepares Special Report for Berlin Conference" *Climate Change Bulletin*, United Nations, issue 5, fourth quarter.
2. Houghton, JT, Jenkins, GT, and Ephraums, JJ (Eds) (1990) *Climate Change: the IPCC Scientific Assessment* Cambridge University Press, Cambridge.
3. Cline, William R (1992) *The Economics of Global Warming* Institute for International Economics, Washington DC, pp 34–5.
4. See note 3 above, pp 47–8.
5. US Congress Office of Technology Assessment (1994) *Climate Treaties and Models: Issues in the International Management of Climate Change* US Government Printing Office, Washington DC.
6. See note 3 above, p 191.
7. See note 3 above.
8. OECD (1992) "The Economic Costs of Reducing CO_2 Emissions" *Economic Studies*, OECD, Paris, pp 112 and 116.

CHAPTER 10

1. Ross, Marc H, and Steinmeyer, Daniel (1990) "Energy for Industry" *Scientific American* September, p 47.
2. US Congress, Office of Technology Assessment (1990) "Energy Use and the US Economy" OTA-BP-E-57, US Government Printing Office, Washington DC.
3. Lovins, Amory (personal communication).
4. Schipper, Lee (1991) "Energy Savings in the US and other Wealthy Countries: Can the Momentum be Maintained?" in Tester, J, Jefferson, W, Wood, David O, and Ferrari, Nancy *Energy and the Environment in the 21st Century* MIT Press, Cambridge Mass. p 476.
5. Ayres, Robert (1991) "Energy Conservation in the Industrial Sector", in Tester, J et al, see note 4, p 363.
6. Cavanagh, Ralf quoted in "Cool It: a survey of energy and the environment" *The Economist* 31 August 1991.

7. Willrick, Mason quoted in "Cool It: a survey of energy and the environment" *The Economist* 31 August 1991.
8. Joskow, Paul L, and Marron, Donald B (1993) "What Does Utility-subsidised Energy Efficiency Really Cost?" *Science* 16 April, p 281.
9. Ruff, Larry "Environmental Protection through Energy Conservation: A 'Free Lunch' at Last?" in Tester, J et al, see note 4, pp 810–11.

CHAPTER 11

1. MacKerron, Gordon (1992) "Nuclear Costs: Why Do they Keep Rising?" *Energy Policy* July, pp 641–53.
2. Marshall, Walter quoted in "Nuclear Power: losing its chances" *The Economist* 21 November 1992.
3. See note 2 above.
4. IAEA unpublished internal report.
5. International Energy Agency (1994) *Energy Policies of IEA Countries* IEA, Paris.

CHAPTER 12

1. Rathje, William, and Murphy, Cullen (1992) *Rubbish: the Archeology of Garbage* HarperCollins, New York.
2. Maxwell, Bret (1989) "The Solid Waste Disposal Market" First Analysis Corporation, Chicago, p 19.
3. (1992) *Waste Age*, Washington DC, May, pp 18–28.
4. Fischer, Fred (1989) "United Kingdom Waste Industry" First Analysis Corporation, Chicago, p 3.
5. Wiseman, A Clark (1990) *US Wastepaper Recycling Policies: Issues and Effects* Resources for the Future, Washington DC.
6. Fullerton, Don, and Kinnaman, Thomas C (1994) "Household Demand for Garbage and Recycling Collection with the Start of a Price per Bag" Working Paper, Carnegie Mellon University.
7. Coopers & Lybrand (1993) *Landfill Costs and Prices: Correcting Possible Market Distortions* HMSO, London.
8. Brown, Bill quoted in "All that remains: a survey of waste and the environment" *The Economist* 29 May 1993.
9. ERM (1992) "Economic Instruments and the Recovery of Resources from Waste" a study by Environmental Resources Ltd. HMSO, London.

CHAPTER 13

1. Wilson, EO (1992) *The Diversity of Life* Harvard University Press, Cambridge, Mass.
2. Solow, Andrew, Polasky, Stephen, and Broadus, James (1993) "On the Measurement of Biological Diversity" *Journal of Environmental Economics and Management* 24, pp 60–8.
3. Weitzman, ML (1993) "What to Preserve? An Application of Diversity Theory to Crane Conservation" *Quarterly Journal of Economics*, February.
4. Swanson, Timothy "The Economics of Extinction Revisited and Revised" CSERGE Discussion Paper 92-00, and "The Economics of Biodiversity Convention" CSERGE Discussion Paper GEC 92-08, London.
5. Browder, John quoted in "Forest Sceptics" *The Economist* 26 May 1990.
6. Easterbrook, Greg (1995) *A Moment on Earth* Viking Penguin, New York, pp 211–28.
7. Hudson, Wendy (Ed) (1993) *Building Economic Incentives into the Endangered Species Act* Defenders of Wildlife, Washington DC, October.

CHAPTER 14

1. Schmidheiny, Stephan, with the Business Council for Sustainable Development *Changing Course* (1992) MIT Press, Cambridge, Mass.
2. Elkington, J, and Hailes, J (1988) *The Green Consumer Guide* Gollancz, London; published in the US in 1990 as *The Green Consumer: You Can Buy Products that Don't Cost the Earth*, Viking Penguin, New York.
3. McDonald's: see "Management Brief: Food for Thought" *The Economist* 29 August 1992.
4. Whitehead, Bradley: see "Management Brief: Food for Thought" *The Economist* 29 August 1992.
5. See note 4 above.
6. Some of these arguments are put in Portney, Paul (1993) *Product Life-Cycle Analysis: a Public Policy Perspective*.
7. Whiting, Bill quoted in "Goody two-shoes" *The Economist* 2 November 1991.

Chapter 15

1. Walley, Noah, and Whitehead, Bradley (1994) "It"s Not Easy Being Green" *Harvard Business Review* May–June.
2. Porter, Michael (1991) "America"s Green Strategy" *Scientific American* April.
3. Catalytic converters have been mandatory in the US since 1975; in Britain since 1993.
4. Brown, Bill quoted in "All that remains: a survey of waste and the environment" *The Economist* 29 May 1993.
5. Oates, Wallace, Palmer, Karen, and Portney, Paul (forthcoming) "Environmental Regulation and International Competitiveness: Thinking about the Porter Hypothesis" *Journal of Economic Perspectives*.
6. Walley and Whitehead, 1994 (see note 1 above).
7. Gore, Al (1992) *Earth in Balance: Forging a New Common Purpose*, Earthscan Publications, London (cited in Walley and Whitehead, see note 1).
8. Walley and Whitehead, 1994 (see note 1 above).

Chapter 16

1. McLean, Ron quoted in "How green is my company?" *The Economist* 10 March 1990.
2. (1994) Company Environmental Reporting UNEP/SustainAbility, p 23.
3. See note 1 above.
4. Gray, Robert quoted in "How green is my balance sheet?" *The Economist* 3 September 1994.
5. Deloitte Touche Tohmatsu International, IISD, SustainAbility (1993) *Coming Clean*.

Chapter 17

1. For the best recent analysis from a diplomat's viewpoint, see Brenton, Tony (1994) *The Greening of Machiavelli* Earthscan Publications, London, p 20.
2. This analysis has mainly been developed by Scott Barrett of the London Business School.
3. Lyster, Simon (1985) *International Wildlife Law* Grotius Publications, Cambridge.

4. Barbier, EB, Burgess, JC, Swanson, TM, and Pearce, DW (1990) *Elephants, Economics and Ivory* Earthscan Publications, London.
5. (1995) "EU Unlikely to Meet CO_2 Target" in *Global Environmental Change Report* VII (4), February. This report is an excellent source of information on international agreements.

CHAPTER 18

1. Stanley, Gary see "Trade and the environment: the greening of protectionism" *The Economist* 27 February 1993.
2. Tobey, James (1993) "The Impact of Domestic Environmental Policies on International Trade" in *Environmental Policies and Industrial Competitiveness*, OECD, Paris.
3. Cable, Vincent (1994) "The Impact of Environmental Policy on Trade" Royal Institute of International Affairs (mimeo).
4. Pearce, David (1993) "Can GATT Survive the Environmental Challenge?" in Bergesen, HO et al (Eds) *Green Globe Yearbook*, Oxford University Press, Oxford, pp 55–64.
5. O'Connor, David C (1991) "Policy and Entrepreneurial Responses to the Montreal Protocol: Some Evidence from the Dynamic Asian Economies" OECD Development Centre Technical Paper 51, Paris.
6. Esty, Daniel C (1994) *Greening the GATT* Institute for International Economics, Washington DC.
7. Fletcher, Ian quoted in "Sharing: a suvey of the global environment" *The Economist* 30 May 1992.

CHAPTER 19

1. Adams, Bill quoted in "Aid and the environment: the greening of giving" *The Economist* 25 December 1993, and see Adams, WM (1992) *Wasting the Rain* Earthscan Publications, London, for a blistering attack on such consultants.
2. Horbury, John quoted in *The Economist* 25 December 1993 (see note 1).
3. Ibid.
4. Sandbrook, Richard quoted in *The Economist* 25 December 1993 (see note 1).
5. Kabraji, Aban quoted in *The Economist* 25 December 1993 (see note 1).

6. Falloux, Francois, and Talbot, Lee M (1993) *Crisis and Opportunity: Environment and Development in Africa* Earthscan Publications, London.

7. Reed, David (1992) *Structural Adjustment and the Environment* Earthscan Publications, London; Cruz, Wilfredo, and Repetto, Robert (1992) *The Environmental Effects of Structural Adjustment Programmes: the Philippines Case* World Resources Institute, Washington DC.

8. London Environmental Economics Centre (1992) "Case Study for Mexico" in Reed (see note 7 above).

Index

265